Lost in the Echo

Lost in the Echo

The Story of Linkin Park

Matt Karpe

WHITE OWL
AN IMPRINT OF PEN & SWORD BOOKS LTD.
YORKSHIRE – PHILADELPHIA

First published in Great Britain in 2026 by
White Owl
An imprint of Pen & Sword Books Limited
Yorkshire – Philadelphia

ISBN 978 1 03613 395 5

A CIP catalogue record for this book is
available from the British Library.

Typeset by Mac Style
Printed in the UK by CPI Group (UK) Ltd, Croydon, CR0 4YY.

The Publisher's authorised representative in the EU for product safety is Authorised Rep Compliance Ltd., Ground Floor, 71 Lower Baggot Street, Dublin D02 P593, Ireland.
www.arccompliance.com

For a complete list of Pen & Sword titles please contact:

PEN & SWORD BOOKS LIMITED
47 Church Street, Barnsley, South Yorkshire, S70 2AS, England
E-mail: enquiries@pen-and-sword.co.uk
Website: www.pen-and-sword.co.uk
or
PEN AND SWORD BOOKS
1950 Lawrence Road, Havertown, PA 19083, USA
E-mail: uspen-and-sword@casematepublishers.com
Website: www.penandswordbooks.com

Contents

Introduction

On 5 September 2024, it seemed the entire rock community were either sat in front of their computers, phones, or TVs, waiting in suspense for the clock on the screen to countdown to zero. There had been a nervous anticipation for a while, since a previous countdown had slowly dissipated over a number of days, only for the clock to restart, to the annoyance of millions of Linkin Park fans around the world. Depending on where you lived, that Thursday morning, afternoon, or evening would soon feel like you were witnessing a momentous occasion, not necessarily on par to when the Beatles broke America after appearing on *The Ed Sullivan Show* in 1964, when Jimi Hendrix headlined Woodstock in 1969, or when Queen's twenty-four-minute performance stole the show at Live Aid 1985. To a generation who grew up with Linkin Park, though, this felt like a really big deal.

Not many outside the band's inner circle, or the lucky members of the Linkin Park Underground fan club who managed to get a ticket, knew quite what to expect ahead of the event, but as soon as the stream went live and the lights went out, the ominous hum of a typically electronic intro gathered pace and Linkin Park entered the 25,000 square feet Stage 30, inside Warner Bros. Studios in Burbank, California. But this wasn't quite the Linkin Park people had grown to love since their groundbreaking mainstream inception in late-2000. How could it be? For one, the rock world had been in a collective mourning and emotions were still raw from the tragic and untimely passing of Chester Bennington some seven years prior. Rock music has created, and will forever create, such 'remember where you were' moments, and 20 July 2017 is another of those dates that left many of us stunned, heartbroken, and for a while inconsolable. Like the deaths of Hendrix, Jim Morrison, Freddie Mercury, or Kurt Cobain, Chester's hit hard, and how Linkin Park could go on without him was a question that for seven years, no one had an answer to.

As Mike Shinoda, Dave Farrell and Joe Hahn took to the stage for their long-awaited public reunion, they also brought along Colin Brittain, to replace the band's original force behind the drumkit, Rob Bourdon. Also joining them was Alex Feder, Linkin Park's new touring guitarist. Launching straight into a brand new song titled 'The Emptiness Machine', an intense and hard-rocking number which instantly revealed some of those key elements of the band's revered sound, for many this was an intriguing way to begin proceedings, perhaps a little surprising even, but most certainly it was exciting. And when Emily Armstrong joined the fray on the second verse, the long-running rumour of Linkin Park seeking a female vocalist to help carry on the band's legacy proved to be more than just prospective hearsay.

The fully-fledged concert that this new era of Linkin Park performed that day paid homage to their illustrious career, and to Chester. A hint of sadness still loomed in the air, but the smiles on each of the band member's faces showed they were at least able to enjoy doing again what they had always done best. The guitars, bass and drums were all on point, Mike rapped and sang as well as ever, and Emily showed off her vocal dexterity that fans of her previous band, Dead Sara, were already well accustomed to.

During the show, 'The Emptiness Machine' was made available for immediate streaming, and a brand new album titled *From Zero* was announced, its name partly referencing Linkin Park's early incarnation under their Xero guise, and to symbolise their second coming. That Linkin Park had reformed, brought in a new singer and drummer, began rehearsing together, writing together, and recording a whole album together, in a day and age where the media usually gets wind of almost everything going on in the entertainment industry, it appeared the band had pulled off one of the biggest coups in living memory.

Linkin Park's return was never likely to fail. Sure, there were a number of detractors early on who couldn't envisage the band continuing on without Chester's iconic voice and endearing personality, his talent a major reason why the sextet became so successful in the first place. However, the overriding positivity that surrounded *From Zero* upon its release on 15 November 2024 more than justified Linkin Park's decision to dust off the cobwebs and come back reinvigorated. Time heals, after all.

Today, a whole new legion of fans has joined the original soldiers (the nickname given to the band's diehard supporters) in following everything Linkin Park. Live shows in huge stadiums are continually selling out in a matter of hours, and the new material that has been released has birthed even more hits to add to an already weighty honour roll. The band are as big as ever, arguably as good as ever, and the euphoria surrounding them makes it feel like it's the early Noughties all over again.

This is just the latest chapter in Linkin Park's remarkable history, which began way back when…

Fig. 1

Beginning at Xero

The Whisky a Go Go has long been the musical pulse of the Sunset Strip, and is steeped in rock and roll folklore. Since first opening its doors on 16 January 1964, the former commercial real estate and banking property, turned Parisian-themed discothèque, turned live music club, has continually welcomed a who's who of iconic artists.

Filling a void left by many LA acts who uprooted to bigger and more opulent venues in the ever-expanding Las Vegas, the Whisky was soon hosting everyone from Jimi Hendrix and the Velvet Underground to the hottest exports that the UK had to offer, such as Led Zeppelin and The Who. In establishing itself as the heartbeat of American pop and rock, the Whisky also pledged diversity and inclusivity by becoming one of the first venues to breach the racial divide, booking Otis Redding, The Temptations, and other R&B acts to perform a different but equally emotive type of music.

Not unlike any other club experiencing their fair share of struggles at one point or another, the Whisky twice closed down – in 1974 and 1982 – but each time it reopened, the Whisky a Go Go, located at 8901 Sunset Boulevard, helped spearhead the latest musical phenomenon of the time. In the mid-70s it was the punk rock explosion, before the hair metal craze followed a decade later. And then there was the grunge and nu metal movements of the '90s, both of which were supported and promoted by the Whisky and the neighbouring clubs during those formative years.

From early on, the Whisky played host to artist showcases, where every act who took to the small but hallowed stage dreamed of following in the footsteps of The Doors, Frank Zappa or Mötley Crüe by securing a lucrative recording contract based on strong live performances. On 10 December 1998, five days after Death had slayed on their *Sound of Perseverance* tour, and four days before the burgeoning hip hop star Eminem freestyled his captivated audience into a sweaty submission, six dudes known locally as Xero 818 strolled into the Whisky a Go Go for their most important show yet.

Mike Shinoda, Mark Wakefield, Brad Delson, Dave Farrell, Joseph Hahn and Rob Bourdon had grown to be a relatively tight unit since coming together as one in 1997. They regularly rehearsed and recorded but they had only sporadically played live shows, and the timing of the public showcase wasn't filling the band's management with a great deal of confidence. Jeff Blue had fought Xero's corner from the moment Brad walked into his office at Zomba Music Group and confidently handed the vice president of A&R a four-track demo tape that he and his bandmates had recently recorded. Although majoring in Communication Studies at UCLA, Brad's focus somewhat shifted after he attended a talk that Blue was giving at the prestigious Los Angeles university. Blue had successfully guided the early careers of Korn, who at the time was one of America's hottest metal bands, the up-and-coming rap metal troupe Limp Bizkit, and he was now presiding over a young but talented R&B singer by the name of Macy Gray. During his talk, Blue offered one lucky student an internship to help build Gray's career and promote other artists on Zomba's roster, and Brad got the job. But Brad was quick to boost the standing of his own band, who he told his new boss were better than Limp Bizkit, but who were struggling to attract any record label interest. Brad realised that having an ally such as Jeff Blue could go a long way in helping Xero take the next step forward.

Ahead of the public showcase at the Whisky, Blue, along with Danny Hayes and Scott Harrington, whom Blue had assigned to represent Xero as entertainment attorneys, shared their reservations on the band going through with their planned performance. In attendance were thirty-plus high profile industry scouts from virtually every major record label imaginable, who between them had discovered or overseen the careers of everyone from Madonna and Whitney Houston, to Bruce Springsteen, Red Hot Chili Peppers and the Notorious B.I.G. In a pre-cursor to how the evening might pan out, the one person who had displayed any significant interest in Xero, Geffen's David Simone, was unable to attend the showcase, and the band's backs already looked to be against the wall. Fearing that a less than perfect performance would all but burn every bridge with prospective labels, Blue implored Xero to pack up their gear and go home. But Xero was made up of six young, confident, and talented musicians who believed in their innovative brand of rap rock, even if others didn't.

Xero's first ever show had taken place at the Whisky some thirteen months prior, on 14 November 1997. In being able to open for local metal maniacs System of a Down, and the headlining SX-10, who were fronted by Cypress Hill's Sen Dog, Xero had to pay to play. Their fee came from selling tickets to friends, family and anyone else they could attract to the concert, but as with most debut performances, theirs was hardly a profound moment in the annals of time. By the end of the third song in their set, almost all the A&R scouts in attendance had vacated the floor, underwhelmed by what they were witnessing. For Jeff Blue, though, who was already accustomed to the band's demo tape, he'd seen enough in their disjointed show to offer Xero a development deal. He recognised talent when he saw it and his credentials spoke for themselves, now all he had to do was convince others that Xero was a band worth taking a gamble on.

Xero 818 – the numerical addition to the band's name stemmed from the area code of their San Fernando Valley base – were fifteen minutes late to the stage on what was the biggest night of their lives so far. When they did begin playing, Brad had to bring a halt to proceedings so he could retune his guitar, and the showcase appeared to already be turning into a farce. The band's thirty-minute set consisted of the four tracks from their demo tape, and early iterations of others that would later become huge anthems in their own right. But all hope seemed to be lost when at the end of their set, Xero 818 was greeted with an almost empty floor. Only Blue, Hayes, Harrington and friends of the band remained, and the alleged $150 that Brad had paid the sound engineer to make Xero sound good had seemingly been for nothing. In less than two days, seven labels sent official rejections, while executives from Geffen and Virgin were given their marching orders for what their bosses presumably felt was poor judgement in showing any type of interest in a band like Xero. The majority of criticism centred around Mark, the lead singer and traditionally the focal point of any band. He suffered greatly from anxiety, which in turn led to him experiencing crippling stage fright, and when much of the feedback from the showcase focused on his offkey vocals, it left Xero with a tough decision to make.

Their live performances and stage presence may have required a lot of work, but musically there was something intriguing about the band. They weren't attempting to rehash the styles and trends of the past, nor the present for that matter. Instead, their bold vision found them fusing rap, rock and electronics into a hybrid approach that sounded unlike anything else coming out of Los Angeles at the time. In recent years, only a small handful of acts had been able to meld rock and rap with such fervent prowess and earn success in doing so. Rage Against the Machine's rise attested as much to Zack de la Rocha's anti-authoritarian lyrical content as it did to his venomous rapping over funk-tinged instrumentation, but in the process the LA quartet had set a high bar for others to try and reach. With a little help from Jeff Blue, Limp Bizkit was tipped for big things when they rose out of Jacksonville, Florida, with their 1997 debut album *Three Dollar Bill, Y'all*. Although clearly influenced by Rage Against the Machine, Limp Bizkit's aggressive and expletive-filled brand of rap metal appeared less profound lyrically, and more built on attitude and arrogance, but with the arrival of the nu metal movement, the band and their enigmatic frontman Fred Durst, had made the first step towards global domination.

The idea that two disparate genres like rock and rap could join forces as one was for a long time considered an unimaginable prospect. That was until Run-D.M.C. and Aerosmith shattered the glass ceiling with their outlandish collaboration in 1986. 'Walk This Way' had originally featured on Aerosmith's 1975 album *Toys in the Attic*, and the choice cut helped the Boston-based hard rockers make their mainstream breakthrough. Just a decade later, though, Aerosmith's fortunes were on the decline as drug addictions and internal strife marred the band's creativity. At a time when the increased prosperity and profitability of an incessant hair metal movement became quite the immovable object, any rock artist outside of that flamboyant realm, such as Aerosmith, was no longer being so heavily supported or promoted by their record label.

Two thirds of Run-D.M.C. didn't even know who Aerosmith was when their producer, Rick Rubin, suggested they record a cover of 'Walk This Way' for inclusion on their third LP, *Raising Hell*. The hip hop trio had been freestyling over the song's looped intro for some time during live performances, and to incorporate rock into their music wasn't necessarily alien to them by then, having recorded some rap rock tracks of their own on their previous album, the rather appropriately titled *King of Rock*. But bringing in Steven Tyler and Joe Perry to play a feature role on a song the duo had written eleven years before, and releasing it as a single, gave a good indication of whether both worlds could coexist, and if indeed there was a gap in the market for such a fusion to make an impact.

Some saw Aerosmith's involvement as a desperate ploy to reaffirm their weakening foundations in 1986, but the collaboration paid dividends for everyone involved. *Raising Hell* – one of Mike Shinoda's favourite albums, and one that made him want to become a rapper – made the top three of the Billboard 200 and hit number 1 on the Top R&B/Hip Hop Albums chart. 'Walk This Way' was later released as a single after Run-D.M.C. was shocked to learn the song was getting strong exposure on both urban and rock radio stations, and it became the first song by a hip hop group to grace the top five of the coveted Hot 100. The accompanying music video, with its powerful symbolism of two contrasting acts performing either side of a wall, only for Tyler to break down the implied barrier that had for so long stifled any potential association between rap and rock artists, was a big hit on the popular *MTV* network, which played a big part in the song's commercial performance. *Raising Hell* has long been considered the album that ushered in the golden age of hip hop, while Aerosmith experienced a much needed revival of their own thanks to the 'Walk This Way' remix when their 1987 album *Permanent Vacation* went multi-platinum. By the mid-90s, and with a newfound ability for writing infectious stadium-sized ballads, Aerosmith resurgence saw them becoming one of the biggest rock acts on the planet.

Five years on from 'Walk This Way', a 15-year-old Michael Kenji Shinoda is attending his first concert with his father, Muto, acting as chaperone. Mike likes heavy metal music, but he lives and breathes hip hop, and on 19 October 1991 he gets the best of both worlds when he witnesses Anthrax and Public Enemy co-headlining the 16,000 capacity Irvine Meadows Amphitheatre in Orange County. The show's crowning moment comes at the very end of the night when, during the final throes of Anthrax's pulsating set, Public Enemy join the thrash metal juggernauts onstage to duet on a raucous rendition of 'Bring the Noise'. The song remains one of the highlights of Public Enemy's seminal 1988 album *It Takes a Nation of Millions to Hold Us*

Back, having previously gained significant exposure through its inclusion on the *Less Than Zero* movie soundtrack seven months prior. 'Bring the Noise' is a gripping diatribe that placed the hip hop world on notice. Within its effortless flows and augmented lyrics, Chuck D and Flavor Flav lead the argument that hip hop deserves to be genre as equally respected as rock. Its statement was later justified by Public Enemy's crossover appeal with fans of heavier music, thanks in no small part to Anthrax's role in supporting hip hop's rise out of the underground. Vocalist Joey Belladonna and lead guitarist Dan Spitz had previously collaborated with the Brooklyn mob Untouchable Force Organization, on the 1987 single 'Lethal', while rhythm axeman Scott Ian regularly sported Public Enemy t-shirts during live performances. That the two acts could potentially come together on a record was still somewhat inconceivable in the early '90s, but when Anthrax unveiled their *Attack of the Killer B's* B-sides and rarities collection in June 1991, the second track was none other than a cover of 'Bring the Noise'. Anthrax had been playing the song in their live sets since 1989, so producing a studio recording wasn't that much of a hardship. Sampling the original vocals over an onslaught of chugging riffs and a machine gun rhythm section, the cover was never going to light up the mainstream charts quite like 'Walk This Way' had, but it did fare well in the UK by reaching 14 on the singles chart. More than anything, though, the song had worked wonders in bringing the heavy metal and hip-hop communities together like never before.

The intense performance of 'Bring the Noise' by two acts intent on out-slaying one another on that Irvine Meadows stage lit a fire in the belly of an inspired Mike Shinoda. Born on 11 February 1977 in the Panorama City area of Los Angeles, and later raised in Agoura Hills, Mike, a third generation Japanese American, was a creative type who wasn't one for resting on his laurels. From a young age he undertook classical piano lessons for almost a decade, before moving on to the keyboard, where he began writing his own video-game inspired music. When hip hop fever took over, Mike taught himself how to rap and freestyle, imitating the techniques of others in order to generate an identity of his own. Using samples he'd also created, Mike then started producing his own rap demos.

Bradford Philip Delson, a native of Agoura, was born in the unincorporated region on 1 December 1977. Developing a close friendship with Mike during their time at Agoura High School, Brad had an early jazz upbringing which included learning and playing the trumpet in his elementary school orchestra. Everything changed when he first picked up an electric guitar, and for five years Brad took lessons that steered him towards becoming a skilled but concealed kind of player. An avid fan of heavy metal, with Metallica being a particular favourite band, it was Brad who introduced Mike to music that was a little more extreme to what he'd been used to. Brad enjoyed Metallica's sophisticated songwriting and their overly long tracks that were comprised of multiple contrasting sections, and while he could shred with the best of them, Brad preferred his playing to be more reserved in comparison to how his heroes would often express themselves. To him it wasn't about showing off with fancy solos and lavish licks, and for a long time he was against the idea of playing guitar leads altogether.

Brad's first foray into playing in an actual band came in 1995. The not-so affluently named The Pricks performed a raw burst of rap metal that also possessed an abundance of punk rock attitude, and that was about as much substance as the band desired. Playing to solely frat party crowds, The Pricks recorded a demo cassette at some point and enlisted the support of a local promoter by the name of Mike Giangreco, but like so many high school bands, attention spans soon waivered and The Pricks' fledgling career petered out before it ever began.

Also part of The Pricks was Mark Wakefield, who was a little older than those he would soon join forces with, but who also dreamed of being part of a successful rock band. Born on 31 May 1974, Mark met Dave Garrett while studying art at the California State University Long Beach (CSULB), and with The Pricks dead in the water, the two began jamming together before deciding to form a band they would name Relative Degree. Mark called upon Brad to handle guitar duties, and Garrett, who was a promising bass player, had just the drummer in mind to complete the line-up. The shy and reserved Robert Gregory Bourdon was born in Calabasas on 20 January 1979, and he'd been playing the drums since the age of 8. Inspired by the music of Aerosmith after meeting the band's drummer Joey Kramer backstage at one of their concerts, and Faith No More, who rose to fame with their own rap metal hit 'Epic' in 1990, Rob played in a cover band called No Clue in sixth grade, before his parents made him join the Calabasas High School

Jazz Band four years later. Although Rob only stuck it out for two months, in that time his playing had caught the attention of Garrett, who invited Rob to join his alternative rock band, Karma. Rob's groove and rhythm-based playing style had come from listening to funk acts like Sly and the Family Stone, and James Brown, and although Karma disbanded within six months, he and Garrett were soon reacquainted upon the official formation of Relative Degree, whose musical style expressed a mix of funk, rap and ska punk.

Instead of plotting their way towards obtaining a record deal, Mark, Brad, Dave and Rob set an entirely different goal for themselves. All they wanted to do was play one show at the Roxy Theatre. Just a stone's throw from the Whisky a Go Go, the Roxy opened on 20 September 1973, where for the first three nights Neil Young performed with his band Crazy Horse (then known as the Santa Monica Flyers). Bruce Springsteen, Bob Marley, Ramones and many other iconic acts would grace the stage of the equally intimate Roxy over the years, and Relative Degree was intent on adding their name to a distinguished list of past performers. For a whole year the band enthusiastically rehearsed three or four days a week, by repeatedly running through the twelve or so songs they had written. Ahead of the long-awaited show, which was booked for 17 May 1996, Rob brought in a couple of his friends from his brief stint in his high school jazz band to play the ska elements of the songs in the live environment.

Mike was one of Relative Degree's biggest supporters, and being friends with Brad and Mark, he would regularly hang out and watch the band practice. On occasion, Mike would even provide samples for some of the songs. Upon the demise of Relative Degree, which came a short time after the band had accomplished their goal of playing the Roxy, Mike and Mark started writing music together. With Mike's influences including Public Enemy, Run-D.M.C., A Tribe Called Quest and the Notorious B.I.G., and Mark leaning towards guitar-heavy acts like Rage Against the Machine, Red Hot Chili Peppers and local acts such as System of a Down and Deftones, the idea of fusing rock and rap with a prominent electronic edge felt fresh and exciting to the duo.

Together, they wrote and recorded an early four-track demo tape, and a copy of it was sent to Paul Pontius, who was working for Immortal Records and orchestrating the careers of Korn, and the funk-inspired rap metal band Incubus. The demo had been recorded in Mike's bedroom-turned makeshift studio, and by now he'd become quite the producer despite the lack of equipment at his disposal. Using a second-hand mixing board and a Tascam Porta 07 to record the songs straight to tape, the limitations of the four-track recorder meant that Mike had to use a drum machine to supply the beats that he had created himself. Mike also used an Akai 5900 sampler to reel off the electronic elements that gave the songs greater depth, and Xero a wholly unique identity in comparison to the other rap rock acts who were coming up around the same time. Impressed by how professional the demo sounded, which he presumed had been made in a proper recording studio, Pontius called Mike three days after receiving the tape to find out more about this promising new band going by the name Xero. Hearing that the songs were the work of just two collegegoers, Pontius advised Mike to make Xero a full band and begin playing live shows to build on the strong foundations already in place. Mike took Pontius' feedback on board and, wanting a guitar player whose capabilities were more advanced than his and Mark's, Mike called upon his friend Brad to join Xero's expanding line-up.

There are two known versions of the Xero demo tape. The first features a shopping cart on its black and white cover, and the second presents a drawing of a baby with a blue surround. Both tapes revealed a writing credit for Brad on the opening track 'Rhinestone', and also for Joseph Hahn. A second generation Korean American born in Dallas, Texas, on 15 March 1977, Joe moved to Glendale, California, when he was 8 years old. First trained in the violin before learning the guitar, it was in high school where Joe's infatuation with hip hop found him becoming a full-time DJ. Highly skilled in twisting sounds and manipulating beats, Joe started out with drum machines and turntables to make his own demos, and as computers became more advanced throughout the '90s, he would acclimatise himself with the latest software packages to further develop his sounds and techniques, having never wanted to be known simply as a scratch DJ.

Upon graduating Herbert Hoover High School, Joe enrolled in the Art Center College of Design in Pasadena, where he studied illustration and met fellow student Mike Shinoda. The two bonded over their passions for art and hip hop, before Joe moved on within a year and began work as a character design and storyboarding illustrator for TV shows and movies including *The X-Files*, *Species*, and *Outer Limits*. The history surrounding Xero's full-band formation is at times a little thin, but at some point it seems Joe recorded with Mike and Mark on 'Rhinestone', the initiation song that friends and unsuspecting record label scouts would hear upon playing the demo tape for the first time. In 1997, Joe and Mike's paths would cross again when the DJ accepted an invitation to officially join Xero.

Within the early moments of 'Rhinestone' and the ensuing 'Reading My Eyes', 'Fuse', and 'Stick N Move', there is more than enough to suggest that Xero were a rather competent rap rock act who offered something a little different to the likes of Rage Against the Machine, Limp Bizkit and others, who were coming up in the LA area. The combination of Mike's constructive and powerful bars and Mark's cleaner deliveries, which did at times hint of a singer lacking confidence, signified an unusual two-pronged vocal lead. Other than in the cases of Run-D.M.C. and Aerosmith, Anthrax and Public Enemy, or the various combatants on the critically acclaimed *Judgement Night* movie soundtrack released in 1993, no singular band was using two vocalists in the rap rock game. Musically littered with corrosive riffs, and juxtaposed with ambient and earnest melodies, Xero also possessed the ability of throwing in pop hooks that implied they might have a commercial edge, should such an audience ever find their way towards the band.

David Michael Farrell, or 'Phoenix' as he became more commonly known, was born in Plymouth, Massachusetts, on 8 February 1977. By the age of 5, he and his family had relocated to Mission Viejo in Orange County, and as a keen musician he began learning the violin. He'd initially wanted to follow in his brother's footsteps in getting to grips with the cello, but his brother was three years older, and a first-grade Dave was too small to play such a large instrument. During eight years of classical training, he would eventually try out the cello, as well as the viola, while maintaining his violin playing. Not long after beginning high school, Dave's mother showed him the basics of the guitar, which became his instrument of choice, and in 1995 he joined the ska punk band Tasty Snax, first as a guitar player, before switching to the bass when the position desperately needed filling. It was during his time in the band that he was assigned his 'Phoenix' nickname, which reportedly stemmed from the Ben Stiller movie *Mystery Men*, and after a girl in Dave's high school had told him his original name was 'boring'. It was a nickname that would stick with him for his entire career.

Signing to the Orange County label Screaming Giant, Tasty Snax received some decent exposure when their one and only music video for 'Run Joseph Run', the title track from the band's 1998 debut album, was aired on TV screens in *Vans* clothing stores all over the US. At times wedged between the latest promos from Green Day, No Doubt and the Beastie Boys, the catchy and rather summery song didn't sound out of place alongside those of artists with a much higher standing. At the same time, Dave was studying philosophy at UCLA, where his roommate was one Brad Delson, and as Xero continued to make small progressions, Dave regularly got to hear what the band was working on. He was also aware they were in search of a bass player, and when Brad invited Dave to join the band, he accepted, while also remaining committed to Tasty Snax.

Rob had also come on board by now; having taken the disbandment of Relative Degree hard, he'd turned to drink and drugs to mask depression. When Mike phoned Rob and asked if he would be interested in hearing some music he and Mark had been writing, Rob liked it and jumped at the opportunity to take up a new drumming gig, which meant Xero finally had its completed line-up.

It's easy to look back now and say that Linkin Park were destined to succeed, despite the endless struggles they encountered in getting the band fully off the ground. With their combined talents, it was surely only a matter of when, not if, the stars would align for them. Unfortunately, though, Paul Pontius' interest in Xero had long subsided since he'd first received a copy of that early demo tape, but the constructive criticism and advice he'd passed on to Mike had served the band well. Very soon they would have Jeff Blue fighting their corner, to support and mentor them from the ground up. At first, some of the band members questioned whether Blue was the right man to guide them forward, but in October 1998, some nine months after they were first offered a development deal, Xero finally accepted it and they signed with Zomba Music.

Who Can Rock a Rhyme Like This?

In the aftermath of the ill-fated public showcase at the Whisky, Xero parted company with Mark. While he'd played an integral role in the band's initial formation and the music they had already written and recorded, it became abundantly clear that Mark's vocal inefficiencies, which were marred by his severe anxiety when performing live, were a key reason why Xero was stuck in such a rut. It would be unfair to place the blame solely at Mark's door, though, because the music the band was presenting to potential record label suitors also proved to be a sticking point. Xero was undeniably a rap rock band, even though they didn't share the anti-political stance of Rage Against the Machine, nor the party funk exploits of the Red Hot Chili Peppers, who in their early days also liked to incorporate rap into their music. Xero was also far removed from the false bravado that Limp Bizkit was emitting on their debut album, but even so, Xero continued to be measured against such acts. Being so heavily reliant on the use of electronics and having two vocalists leading their charge instantly separated them from the rest of the crop, and while their vision seemed to be laid out for everyone to see, record labels just couldn't get their heads around what Xero was all about.

Mark was far more comfortable being behind the scenes, and during his time in Xero, he'd picked up a bit of industry knowhow. And by frequenting the local rock scene and forming relationships with other up-and-coming bands like System of a Down, Mark's new career path saw him enter into artist management, where upon joining the Velvet Hammer Music and Management Group, he began working with Taproot, a heavy four-piece out of Ann Arbor, Michigan, who, early on, were playing their own brand of abrasive rap metal.

Not long after Mark's departure, Dave also chose to leave Xero. In building on the attention they had received from the title track's music video, Tasty

Snax were set to embark on their first national tour in support of their *Run Joseph Run* album, and the opportunity to travel across America for a year wasn't something that Dave could pass up. Ultimately, the bassist was honouring his prior commitment to Tasty Snax, who at the time had more to offer him than Xero could.

For a few months Xero moved forward, with Mike taking the reins as the sole vocalist and bringing his friends onstage to sing with him during live shows. But having often written songs and lyrics from the perspective of a dual vocal partnership, the search was soon on to find Mark's official replacement. Xero didn't know it at the time, but the answer to their prayers was some 400 miles Southwest of Los Angeles, in Phoenix, Arizona.

* * *

Chester Bennington was somewhat of a local celebrity in Phoenix. For almost four years he'd fronted the grunge-influenced band Grey Daze, and the talented ensemble had built up a dedicated following from playing the local area and often opening for bigger acts whose tours rolled through the city, and nearby Tempe. Grey Daze was formed in 1993 by drummer Sean Dowdell, and bassist Jonathan Krause. Chester had recently vocalled in Dowdell's comedically named Sean Dowdell and His Friends?, a band as equally flippant but who still had a decent fanbase from performing in and around Phoenix for almost eighteen months. Taking what he'd learned in his first band, Chester joined Grey Daze, as did guitarist Jason Barnes.

To the uninitiated, Chester was just another rock singer whose powerful live performance and unyielding stage presence commanded everyone's attention. He was shy, diminutive, and rather nerdy looking, but the stage was his sanctuary and no matter how big or small his platform, it was where Chester felt most alive. Seeking strength from his vulnerability, for a small amount of time on any given night that Grey Daze had a show, Chester could lay his demons to rest, and in doing so he revealed himself to be a natural born performer.

Born on 20 March 1976, Chester Charles Bennington experienced an often horrific childhood. A victim of sexual abuse that began when he was just 7 years old and continued until the age of 13, Chester also had to witness the deterioration of his parent's relationship, to the point that Susan and Lee eventually filed for divorce. In what was still a fairly uncommon move in the late '80s, Lee was granted custody of Chester and his three siblings Renee, Tobi and Brian. A police detective who worked in sexual crimes, but who unfortunately had no knowledge of his own son being a victim of such, Lee regularly pulled double shifts and he was rarely at home. Renee, Tobi and Brian were all at an age where they were able to seek their own independence and get their own places, or at least spend most of their time out and about with friends, which left Chester to grow accustomed to the feelings of abandonment and loneliness. It's quite understandable that with the cards he'd been dealt, Chester was left feeling extremely angry and pissed off with the world, but he was at least able to find a degree of solace in drawing, and writing poetry expressed in lyric form. By the age of 11, he'd also found another alternative to coping with his parents' divorce and his ongoing abuse, suffered at the hands of an older male friend who had also been abused when younger. Chester became a prolific drug user who dabbled in cocaine, and smoking weed and meth. In high school he suffered from bullying, and his intake of drugs would soon extend to LSD and opium.

Through everything, Chester remained a music buff, and from a very young age he would tell anyone and everyone that he was going to be a singer one day. Things finally began to fall into place during his sophomore year at Greenway High School, on the Northside of Phoenix. It was a time for new beginnings, where the rockers, the jocks, and the nerds tended to come together as one. Chester was instantly drawn to those who donned a grunge dress sense and listened to Nirvana, Pearl Jam and Alice In Chains, and who were influenced to form rock bands in their parents' garages. And everyone was drawn to Chester in return. With his new friends he could finally be himself, and he was often joking around and never taking himself or anything else too seriously, except for music. Chester gained some self-confidence from joining a musical theatre group, where he learned how to naturally express himself, and as part of a stage production that was taken across America he was given his first experiences of performing in front of large audiences. It led him to wanting to be a full-time performer. His vast musical palette ranged from Jane's Addiction and Pearl Jam, to the darker aspects of The Cure and Depeche Mode. He loved the industrial tendencies of Ministry and how the band played around with multiple vocal effects, and he became absorbed by the poetic lyricism of The Doors' Jim Morrison. Another favourite of Chester's was Stone Temple Pilots, and he dreamed of being their lead singer.

In October 1994, Grey Daze released their debut album *Wake Me*. To say that Chester Bennington put the world on notice would be a lie, as physical CDs of the album were only distributed to local record stores, and a couple of songs were given minor airplay on Phoenix-based radio stations. But across its twelve-track, forty-five-minute running time, *Wake Me* unveiled a singer who was still testing his vocal abilities and their limitations, yet the grit and emotion he was consistently expelling urged listeners to sit up and take notice. After just one playthrough of 'What's in the Eye', or the stunning 'Morei Sky', it was evident that Chester's lyrics captured his most vulnerable moments. Thanks to Grey Daze, he'd finally found a way to release some of his inner torment, and with the power of his lyrics being and reinforced by the explosive musicianship of Barnes, Dowdell and Krause, Chester now had a solid support scheme and a band of brothers who understood the traumas he'd experienced as a youngster, and allowed him to vent his feelings of anger, desperation, and even shame, through music.

Grey Daze eventually drew the attention of Real Records, an independent label based in Los Angeles, who had seen the band regularly opening for established acts such as No Doubt, Suicidal Tendencies, and Type O Negative. Upon the release of their second album *…No Sun Today* in 1997, Grey Daze reached their peak. 'B12', and a cover of Dramarama's 'Anything, Anything' gained moderate rotation on local radio, while four years of hard work had steered the band into the position of selling out the 2,000 capacity Electric Ballroom in Tempe as a headline act. It seemed that everything was now in place for Grey Daze to rid themselves of the confines of Arizona and finally take their music across America and, in the hope that bigger offers might soon come their way, the band hired Scott Harrington as their entertainment attorney. A small tour of Southern California followed at the beginning of 1998, in which some of the dates acted as showcases for major label executives, but no one offered Grey Daze a deal. As time went on, frustration grew within the band due to their inability to get signed, and after a disastrous show at their regular haunt of The Big Fish Pub in Tempe,

Chester decided to leave the band later in 1998. Nothing would come of the working relationship with Scott Harrington either, not for Grey Daze anyway, but he remained friends with Chester and he would send demos to the singer from time to time. For well over a year, Chester hunted for a new project that he could get on board with. He hung around the local rock scene and recording studios, but there was nothing suitable for his pulsating voice. In the meantime, he worked menial jobs to pay his mortgage and to support his wife Samantha, who Chester had married on 31 October 1996, and during his fruitless search in finding a new band, Chester gave himself six more months before he'd have to call time on his music career for good. Then, as his countdown fast approached, Chester received a phone call from Jeff Blue.

Scott Harrington's partner at his *Manatt, Phelps & Phillips* law firm was Danny Hayes, and when the latter mentioned he had a band in Los Angeles who was searching for a new singer, Harrington immediately recommended Chester Bennington. Chester's name was passed on to Jeff Blue, and while he was in Texas attending the annual South by Southwest conference, he phoned Chester and attempted to sell this exciting young rap rock crew by the name of Xero. It's likely that Blue's passionate pitch went a long way in peaking Chester's interest, and while he wasn't overly struck on hip hop, he accepted Blue's offer of being sent over a demo tape to check out the vibe of Xero, and so Chester could add his vocals over a couple of the tracks. Upon hearing the demo, which is believed to have featured the tracks 'Esaul', 'Pictureboard', and an updated version of 'Rhinestone', Chester was impressed with the unusual style of music the band was making, and especially the electronic nuances that were so heavily integrated into the songs. He wasn't so keen on the vocals, though. On the second side of the tape were the instrumental tracks, and Chester made a conscious effort to specifically build on and improve the melodies in the choruses. Going above and beyond in wanting to make his audition tape sound as good as could be, the singer enlisted the services of three friends from the Phoenix scene to learn the instrumentals and play them live in a studio, and instead of attending his own party to celebrate his 23rd birthday, Chester entered a practice space known locally as The Base, with Jay and John Kereny, and Barton Applewhite. The three musicians had more recently been playing together in a band called Size 5, while Barton had also been part of the popular Kongo Shock, a ska troupe who stood alone in Phoenix in playing such a style of music. Kongo Shock released two albums, *Dick Triple Flip* in 1995, and *Ride the Bus* in 1997, and when the band went in search of a new singer in 1998, Chester Bennington answered the initial call. Exclusively for this book, Barton reflects on how Chester came to briefly join Kongo Shock, and the recording of the Xero audition tape:

I met Chester just by proxy of the local music scene. I didn't get a lot of personal time with him until one of the shows Kongo Shock had where he was helping doing the sound, and we became a little tighter with him then. At this point I had not heard much Grey Daze as our genres were fairly different, so we didn't play any shows together, we just had practice rooms in the same complex. I didn't really know the prowess of Chester's vocal skills until he auditioned for our band, but if you would've told me to pick somebody in our local scene in the '90s that would've made it to the level he did, I probably wouldn't have picked him. That is not a slight on Chester at all, it's just sometimes you get surprised by a serious talent like that.

Kongo Shock was a pretty successful local band. We had done quite a bit of touring the previous few years, and it was our primary source of income. Our lead vocalist had left the band to move back to Canada, so we auditioned some vocalists and Chester came along. He was our guy for sure. He was somewhat of a friend of ours and as far as I know, he was pretty excited to try out and he'd looked up to our band. At that point he had dreadlocks and was really into reggae, and we were a ska band that did some reggae flavoured stuff as well. During the audition, he was really leaning into the reggae vocal stylings, and we explained to him that it really wasn't our vibe, but still we wholeheartedly wanted him in our band. I believe we had a couple of rehearsals with him after that, and we had a barbecue with him and Samantha at their place, but due to internal reasons, Kongo Shock decided to disband before we ever got it back off the ground.

The Xero audition thing happened really quick. At this point I was in a band called Size 5. The drummer and guitar player were brothers, and they were closer to Chester than I was. They had a local band named Lemon Krayola that had been in Phoenix for many years, who were also in the same practice complex as all of us. Apparently, Chester had reached out to Jay (Kereny) and told him he had an audition for this band in LA that had label interest, or maybe even had a deal lined up. He headed over to our practice studio with a video camera on a tripod and hummed us a few bars of a song idea he had with some lyrics he'd written. We whipped up the song in probably ten minutes or so and took a few passes as it, Chester singing in front of the camera with us in the background, and the rest is history.

The tape had Chester's stamp all over it. His vocals were fiery, and the distorted rasp he had moulded during his time in Grey Daze was now providing a soluble kinship with Mike's fearless rapping. When Jeff Blue heard a tiny snippet over the phone of what Chester had concocted, he promptly made arrangements for Xero's prospective new singer to be in Los Angeles as soon as Zomba's offices opened their doors on the Monday morning.

Xero had previously put out a vacancy in the *Music Connection* magazine, and for three days they sat through the auditions of other hopeful singers, even though they'd already welcomed Chester into the fold by this time. While generally unknown outside of Arizona, in Chester Xero felt like they had a seasoned musician among their ranks, one who had a few years of recording and live experience under his belt, and who could help them go to the next level. More importantly, the chemistry between Chester and the band was instant, and the early rehearsals only enhanced the feeling that their union was a match made in heaven.

* * *

To signify Xero entering into a new and exciting era, the band transformed into Hybrid Theory. The new name was suggested by Joe, to perfectly demonstrate their penchant for fusing different styles together, and they spent much of their time in their HiFi Hollywood rehearsal space at 6330 Hollywood Boulevard. Having culled all previous music they'd been working on before Chester joined the band, a new batch of songs were written that explored new territory. Mike and Brad continued to create the core of the music, which brought seemingly distant elements together, while Chester leaned into his traumatic childhood and innate sadness to provide a darker edge to the lyrics, and deeper emotion to the vocals. The new songs featured a strong emphasis on each member's individual strengths, while the collective input meant that for the first time, writing credits were more regularly shared between them.

While Xero was hunting for a new singer, the bass position that Dave had vacated proved just as difficult to fill. Andrew Lanoie was the first to come in to temporarily fill the position, before Kyle Christner embraced the gig on a full-time basis. He'd already been playing live shows with the band when he began recording bass parts for an upcoming EP, and while Kyle's involvement in the evolution of Linkin Park remains a minor footnote, his name became a little more known when, in November 2023, he filed a lawsuit against the band. To celebrate the twentieth anniversary of the *Hybrid Theory* album, a deluxe boxset was released and for the first time, the preceding EP was made officially available on all streaming platforms. For one reason or another, Kyle was never credited on the original tracks, and his later lawsuit found him seeking royalties for the songs he'd played on. In April 2024 he reached an 'amicable resolution' with his former bandmates, for what was cited as 'valuable contributions at a pivotal time in 1999'.

The *Hybrid Theory EP* indeed remains a vital part of Linkin Park's glorious history, and on the back of the Xero demo tape, it provides further evidence of the band's fastidious approach to songwriting. While the playing styles and melody structures are rather uncomplicated, they are in contrast to the depths that each song treads sonically and emotionally. As layered as the EP is, it does possess the sound of a band still finding its feet, and it can be forgiven for feeling a little disjointed when you consider Hybrid Theory's youthfulness. The EP is also distinctive, though, and organic, and filled with the same kind of intrigue that would soon be surrounding the band on a much larger scale.

Of the six official tracks, only three maintain an early exploration of the band's rap rock sound. Instead, Hybrid Theory, and especially Mike, chose to invest just as much time on the hip hop side of proceedings. The boombox bounce of 'Step Up', and the robotic pulse of 'High Voltage', which was influenced by the Beastie Boys' 1998 hit 'Intergalactic', finds Mike paying homage to some of his greatest inspirations while he continues to forge his own path as a highly skilled MC, boasting intricate rhyming capabilities via an elaborate lexicon. Juxtaposed with Mike's rapping are the unrefined and tortured vocals of Chester, which had greatly developed from his time in Grey Daze, even if his gritty snarl remains shrouded in the aesthetics of grunge, and sets up the heavier songs on the EP to be far more obscure in comparison to pretty much all of his future work. The murky and rather unsettling vibe extends to the music, where the brash guitars and grinding bass only fuels the tension, while the ominous mood of Joe's electronics supply a doomed ambience. The hooks on which Chester leads, such as 'And One', which is believed to be the first song Hybrid Theory wrote upon the singer's arrival, aren't so instantly catchy as those that would come a short time later, but the Middle Eastern intro of 'Carousel', and the car alarm sample that dictates the rasping 'Part of Me' do enough to persuade early listeners that this exciting new band had strong potential, and were capable of writing a hit song with a little bit of experience under their belt.

The EP was largely recorded in Mike's apartment studio, before a week or so was spent in an LA studio with Andrew 'Mudrock' Murdoch. Murdoch was becoming a much sought-after record producer in the ever-expanding nu metal scene at the time, having worked with Powerman 5000 on their 1996 debut LP *The Blood-Splat Rating System*, and Godsmack's eponymous self-titled first album in August 1998. Murdoch co-produced the EP alongside Mike, who by now was already well-accustomed to the recording and mixing processes, but who was unafraid to seek professional guidance if it helped make the songs better. The EP was, after all, the band's latest ace in their pack as they continued in their quest of acquiring a record deal.

Just 1,500 copies were pressed on CD and distributed via Hybrid Theory's own Mix Media label. Some were sent out to record labels and sold to friends and early fans of the band, and the rest were simply given away. At a time when artists were beginning to realise the benefits of building an internet presence, Hybrid Theory were innovative in their attempts at getting themselves noticed by a wider audience. Instead of just relying on people paying for a physical copy of their new CD, the band uploaded the tracks to MP3.com, where they could be downloaded for free. At the time, and coinciding with the rise of nu metal, came a boom in internet piracy. Napster had started it all in June 1999, but within two years the file-sharing site would already cease its operations after lawsuits were filed against founders Shawn Fanning and Sean Parker, by Metallica, Dr. Dre, and a number of major record companies. As bad as illegal downloading was for the entertainment industry, and in this instance the music sector, up and coming artists had less to lose, and they could perceive the benefits in allowing people free access to their art, especially as they were starting out and required a listenership to build a fanbase. Hybrid Theory was quick to act on this alternative outlet for their music, and each member of the band would spend time in internet chatrooms, music forums, and even other bands' websites, spreading the word of a hot new rap rock act coming out of Los Angeles, and providing links to where people could find out more about them. From there, they started up their own street team, which offered direct contact with fans through phone calls and handwritten letters, as well as printing their own T-shirts, stickers, and other promotional items they would spend hours each day personally packaging up and shipping out at their local post office. Such a DIY aesthetic immediately began to pay dividends for the band, and the positive reaction they received to their music gave them the ammunition they required in choosing to focus on the band full-time. A career playing music together was beginning to look possible for Hybrid Theory, and their big break was just around the corner.

Fig. 3

Unleashing a Monster

After playing over forty showcases to almost every major label imaginable, Hybrid Theory finally secured a record deal with Warner Bros. in August 1999. In truth, there hadn't been many potential suitors in that time, just some minor interest shown but soon rebuffed because of the reservations surrounding Mark's vocals and Hybrid Theory's unusual sound. The biggest opportunity that had arisen since Chester's arrival was with Gary Kurfirst's Radioactive Records/MCA, whose own interest was soon eradicated when the singer accidentally spat in the face of the label's boss during one particular burst of vocal enthusiasm in the middle of a live show.

Instead, Hybrid Theory entered Warner through the back door, thanks in no small part to Jeff Blue, who for some time had been headhunted by the label. Their offer of him becoming vice president of A&R was ultimately accepted on one condition: that Blue brought Hybrid Theory with him. On 9 August 1999, the band played their 44th and final showcase at S.I.R. Rehearsal Studios on Sunset Boulevard, for Warner's head of A&R, Joe McEwen. In McEwen, Blue had at long last found someone who was intrigued by Hybrid Theory's sound, who was impressed by their early demo, and who was appreciative of the talents of the musicians and their forward thinking in wanting to distance themselves from the rap rock norm. In a full circle moment, the band Blue had believed in from the very beginning was now the first he would be working with in his new job, signing Hybrid Theory to a development deal which allowed the band to purchase new instruments and recording equipment, and have access to better studios. They were also assigned a manager, Rob McDermott, who'd impressively helped steer the industrial/nu metal act Static-X (also signed to Warner) to mainstream success with their debut album *Wisconsin Death Trip* earlier in 1999. In Rob, Hybrid Theory now had a hungry and innovative manager who could help guide them, who was personable, and who could provide his own ideas in building the band towards realising their artistic vision. No one could have foreseen the Agoura Hills outfit's meteoric rise throughout the course of 2001, when their faces were plastered on the covers of the biggest music magazines as their debut album sold in its droves, and their songs lit up the radio airwaves and climbed the most prestigious charts across the globe. But none of that had come easy, and they found out early on that Hybrid Theory was wrong to think that their days of grinding for every ounce of prosperity would be over upon signing with Warner Bros. Records.

The initial order of business was to begin work on their first full-length album, and like they had when Chester first joined the band, all the songs they were working on around the time of the self-titled EP were scrapped. Mike and Brad continued to lay down the foundations of the new music, before Mike and Chester got together to work on the lyrics. The rest of band were invited to write their own parts, before they came together as one to evaluate what they had and how the pieces could fit into a song. The problems the band experienced often surrounded the very record label who had signed them to their illustrious roster. In order to secure the services of Jeff Blue, Warner had little choice in taking on Hybrid Theory too. Other than Joe McEwen, there weren't many supporters of the band among the label's ranks, and they didn't hide the fact that it would take a lot for them to be won over by their latest signees. The band's backs were firmly against the wall from the outset, and the demos of their new material were heavily analysed and critiqued to death. The tension only increased when initial searches for a producer proved fruitless, until they finally managed to nab Don Gilmore. Don had engineered Pearl Jam's mega-selling debut album *Ten* in 1991, and more recently he'd been rooted firmly in working with alternative rock bands. He'd also openly admitted to not understanding the dynamics of hip hop, which of course was a vital part of Hybrid Theory's signature sound. Don was a perfectionist in his chosen field, he knew what made a great record and what didn't, and if it meant the results of the material would benefit from it, he had no hesitation in getting his clients to repeatedly rewrite or rerecord, time and time again.

Don respected Hybrid Theory for trying to do something unique, and he'd never heard a singer like Chester Bennington before. Although he didn't think the band were amazing, he knew there was something about them that was unlike anything else coming out at the time. The producer's penchant for perfectionism was always going to irk a set of young musicians who until now had a linear vision of wanting to do things their own way, and it didn't take them long to realise the pitfalls in having to bow to record label demands. Mike and Chester were constantly asked to rewrite song lyrics, the instrumentation was reworked on multiple occasions, and the stresses and strains of that first professional recording process would cast itself across the entire album. In the end it would all be worth it, even if at times the band may have considered giving up on their dream and returning to Agoura, or Arizona, but Don Gilmore's dictator-like mentality would reap the desired results for everyone involved. 'With those guys, when I'd ask for these things and I'd push them to do better, they would,' said Don in an interview with Billboard in 2017. 'They would maybe get frustrated and angry, but the results were insane.'

More than anywhere else, the tumultuous effects of those recording sessions can be heard on 'One Step Closer', the explosive and confrontational debut single that was released ahead of the full-length album, on 29 August 2000. To the wider public, this was to be their introduction to an up-and-coming band by the name of Linkin Park. To avoid any confusion with the rising Welsh electronic/house group Hybrid, who were loosely tied to Warner Records and were considered to be the next Massive Attack or Underworld, Linkin Park was born after an in-house 'pick a new band name' session. Each member curated a list of potential names before they would collectively agree on the best contender, and when the initial attraction of Plear, Probing Lagers and Platinum Lotus Foundation subsided, it was Chester's 'Lincoln Park' that won out. On 24 May 2000, the band registered the linkinpark. com web domain, the change in spelling arising because the original form was already taken. Unbeknownst to the band at the time, many of the big cities in the US had a park or community that went by the name of Lincoln Park, including Chicago, Seattle and Santa Monica. Regardless, the new name change and how it was spelt possessed its own charm with Linkin Park's growing fan base later in the year, to the point that no matter where they were performing, the band were mistakenly believed to be a rising local act. Compared to Hybrid Theory, the name change had created a different kind of ambiguity, which no longer defined nor hinted at the style of music they was creating.

As rap rock began to take over the airwaves with Limp Bizkit, Hed PE, P.O.D., and Papa Roach causing a major stir, 'One Step Closer' posed a different kind of question. Its succinct two-and-a-half minute running time didn't allow any part of the song to rest on its laurels, and from Brad's antagonistic opening riff to the first bout of full band instrumentation, or Joe's emphatic turntable scratches and the bounce of the rhythm section, Linkin Park had come out all guns blazing. And then came Chester's powerful lead vocal, which emitted his anger at Don's actions in the studio that drove the frontman to the verge of musical paralysis. While various members of the band's management had pushed for another choice of lead single, Linkin Park saw 'One Step Closer' as the song that revealed their true mission statement, from its abrasive power and hip-hop undercurrent, to the strong demonstration of Mike and Chester bouncing off one another on that now iconic chorus. And then there is the bridge of all bridges, with Chester's 'Shut up when I'm talking to you!' salvo retorted through a shuddering scream and delivered with breakneck precision. The song is heavy but it's also hooky, and it did just enough to qualify itself for mainstream radio, even if in reality it probably had no reason to be recognised as being so accessible. 'One Step Closer' made people sit up and take notice of Linkin Park, and even though the song's main charge is influenced by a hard taskmaster record producer, kids all over the world were able relate to the song's lyrics of frustration, desperation, and anger in a different way. Upon Linkin Park's debut, teenagers and young adults all over had a new band that they could call their own, and 'One Step Closer' was just a small taste of what was to come.

*   *   *

Linkin Park recycled the 'Hybrid Theory' name for the title of their debut album. Like it had served the band beforehand, it was now used to encapsulate the plethora of styles that are spread across the twelve-song track listing. Recorded at NRG Recording Studios in North Hollywood between March and June 2000, it wasn't just the issues surrounding 'One Step Closer' that caused the sessions to regularly hit an impasse. While demos were sent to

Warner to document the band's progress, questions began to be raised by some as to whether Linkin Park needed a rapper after all. In a sinister plot, which Mike has spoken about in subsequent interviews, Chester was approached about becoming the face and voice of the band; the sole singer, and the star of the show. For any rapping parts, the label's idea was to bring in outside musicians, with one option reportedly on the table being a reggae singer by the name of Matt Lyons to vocal on 'In the End', if you can imagine. Their plan for Mike was to relegate him to keyboard duties, or even worse – kick him out completely. But Chester refused to buckle. He himself was still acclimatising to being in the band, as somewhat of an outsider among a gang of close friends. But the bond he'd formed with them all and with Mike in particular, was stronger and far more important to him than corporate superstardom. Chester knew the band had talent, and the songs on the *Hybrid Theory EP* had shown that in parts, and as long as everyone stuck together and continued doing things *their* way, they had a shot at making it big. Chester rebuffed Warner's offer and so Mike remained in the band. It was his band, after all, and without Mike, the machine was never going to function like it had up until now. In a further twist, Mike was asked to alter his rapping style to imitate that of Limp Bizkit's swaggering frontman Fred Durst, which served as the final straw for Linkin Park who decided to cut all communication with their Warner contacts unless it was to specifically discuss the music they was working on.

In 2005, Mike's Fort Minor hip hop side-project released its debut album *The Rising Tied*. On the album is the short, sharp, and to-the-point track 'Get Me Gone', which offers a small insight into the fraught situation he found himself in five years earlier. In the song, he also alludes to Warner wanting to present Joe as wearing a cowboy hat and lab coat, and going under the stage name 'The Doctor'. It's perhaps ironic that less than two decades prior, Matt 'Dr. Fink' Fink was sporting a not too dissimilar gimmick when playing the keyboards and synthesisers in Prince's band The Revolution, who also happened to be signed to Warner at the time. In 'Get Me Gone', Mike's triumphant line of 'But my band had my back so we did the tracks/ put out the album and the talk went flat' emphasises Linkin Park's intention of sticking together at all costs. They may have been employees of Warner, but in no way did it mean the label owned the identity of the band, nor their integrity.

The recording of *Hybrid Theory* was completed by the end of May, and the album was mixed the following month. Don Gilmore, and Warner's David Kahne both attempted to mix some of the songs, but Linkin Park wasn't impressed with the results of either man's efforts. Instead, the band turned to Andy Wallace, who boasted a huge list of high profile credits that included mixing Slayer's *Reign in Blood*, Nirvana's *Nevermind*, Rage Against the Machine's self-titled debut, and more recently albums by nu metal luminaries such as Soulfly, Limp Bizkit, Sevendust, and Disturbed. Linkin Park joined Wallace at Soundtrack Studios in New York City, and they was confident that his sonically influential presence and ability to capture aggressive but also intricately melodic music could help shape *Hybrid Theory* into the album the band had envisaged. After three attempts, Wallace concluded mixing in late-June.

Next, Linkin Park was sent out on their first bout of intense touring. Their initiation began at the State Theatre in St Petersburg, Florida on 22 July, as support to the up-and-coming nu metal act The Union Underground. The Texas quartet was signed to Columbia Records and had just released their major label debut *...An Education in Rebellion*, and the fifteen-date trek allowed Linkin Park the chance to play to some of their biggest crowds thus far. At the time, they were still largely unknown, but it didn't take long for them to start winning people over, and the band's momentum continued during the Ridin' High Tour with the hip hop group Kottonmouth Kings, which Linkin Park joined on 11 September as 'very special guests'. The tour marked the return of Dave, who had now finished up with The Snax. Dave's return spelled the end for Scott Koziol, who was the latest bass player to fill Linkin Park's most troublesome position. After Kyle Christner had departed, various musicians auditioned before the band enlisted the services of Seattle-born Ian Hornbeck. Though Ian was only ever considered a stand-in he was still tasked with helping continue the writing and recording of *Hybrid Theory*, in which he earned credits on three of the album's tracks. Unfortunately for Ian, his continuous issues with drugs prevented him from ever being considered as an official member of the band, which is when Scott Koziol's talents were presented via a musician referral service. First,

Scott received an introductory phone call from Rob, before the drummer sent out a CD for the prospective new bassist to absorb the style of music he would be expected to play, and to learn the music ahead of auditioning. After multiple try outs and full-band rehearsals, Scott came in to help finish recording *Hybrid Theory*, and with the Union Underground tour fast approaching, take up the position of the band's touring bassist.

By the time Linkin Park settled into the Kottonmouth Kings tour, 'One Step Closer' was already gaining radio traction. The music video equally ascended and took over the likes of *MTV*, *TRL* and in the UK, *Kerrang!*. Filmed in an abandoned subway tunnel below Bunker Hill on 8 and 9 September, the 'escapist action movie video' was based on a concept thought up by Joe, and directed by former porn shooter Gregory Dark. Given free rein by Warner to do what they wanted but without an overly large budget, the dark and vivid but rather plotless promo features a full band performance (including the outgoing Scott Koziol), face-painted monks carrying out martial arts exercises, and Chester screaming the song's intense bridge while hanging upside down from the tunnel's roof. The rock world had been given its first taste of Linkin Park, and although 'One Step Closer' had less of an emphasis on the band's hip hop element at least vocally, the sight of this energetic and powerful band with a two-pronged vocal assault affirmed their intention of wanting to knock the rap rock trend off its axis from the very beginning.

Linkin Park now had a song in their setlist that people were growing familiar with, and one they could sing along and mosh to. The buzz that was soon surrounding the band helped enhance their live performances, and as they grew more cohesive as a unit, so did Mike and Chester as a vocal combination. The duo bounced off one another to the point that even between songs, they would goof around and make jokes, or finish off one another's sentences. But when they launched into the next song it was back to business, with an effortless rap flow here and a piercing scream there; the two of them still a long way from being seasoned pros, but the sense of a growing brotherhood was being translated onto excited concertgoers night after night. The hype around Linkin Park was becoming more real by the day.

The release of *Hybrid Theory* was initially planned for the first quarter of 2001, but with the rapid rise of 'One Step Closer' and the overwhelming response to Linkin Park's performances on the Union Underground tour, Warner saw the benefit in striking while the iron was hot. After rushing to finalise the album's track listing and running order, and designing its cover art and the packaging, *Hybrid Theory* was unleashed on the US market on 24 October 2000, long before its worldwide unveiling at the end of January 2001. For Linkin Park, it was imperative that the cover art was just as creative and eye-catching as the music it was promoting, and with Joe and Mike having backgrounds in artistic design, the duo took a particular interest in how they wanted the cover to look. In seeking some outside assistance, they called upon Frank Maddocks, who at the time was building an impressive portfolio that would later secure him a job with Warner as an art director. Earlier in 2000, Maddocks had designed the cover of Deftones' sprawling third opus, *White Pony*. Unlike the genre-bending ingenuity of the music, however, Maddocks nominated for effective simplicity, where a plain grey background (or white, red or blue, depending on which issue of the album you came across) was only interrupted by the small silhouette of a galloping white pony in the bottom right corner. Maddocks met with Joe and Mike to go over their ideas for *Hybrid Theory*, some of which were inspired by the elusive underground UK street artist, Banksy. Taking Mike's stencilled drawing of a soldier carrying a flagpole, Maddocks added to it a pair of detailed dragonfly wings, which for further effect were dripping with wet ink. The juxtaposition of the two pieces was intentional, the downbeat and faceless soldier referenced Linkin Park's heavier musical elements, while the fragile wings portrayed their softer side, and their melodic nuances. The captivating art also included tiny excerpts of song lyrics, and the band's sprawling logo, made up of a stencilled font containing backwards N's, which appeared to be in tribute to Nine Inch Nails, who Linkin Park had previously cited as a major influence on their sound.

With only one single to test the waters, the hype surrounding *Hybrid Theory* wasn't quite on the scale of that for Limp Bizkit, Papa Roach or Slipknot, for example. Not yet anyway. A week before *Hybrid Theory*'s release, Limp Bizkit returned with their third album, the incomprehensibly titled *Chocolate Starfish and the Hot Dog Flavored Water*. The band's previous LP, *Significant Other*, had cruised to the top of the Billboard 200 in June 1999, having sold almost 650,000 copies in its first week. Just sixteen months later, *Chocolate*

Starfish… usurped its predecessor by shifting over a million, which was a then-record for first-week sales of a rock album. In stark contrast, the opening week numbers for *Hybrid Theory* sat around 50,000, but for Linkin Park this could be considered a success, and a sense of validation that after years of struggling to be heard, understood and given a fair shake, the tides were finally turning. Limp Bizkit may have been the leaders in the rap rock game in that moment, but Linkin Park's arrival proposed some new candidates who were making a play towards stealing their mantle.

As well as they had fared in opening for The Union Underground and Kottonmouth Kings, the following Kings of the Game and Master Bay Tours were the ones to propel Linkin Park even higher up the ladder. Importantly, the band was now on bills with fellow rap rock acts, meaning their music had more of a chance of appealing to crowds of whom the majority were made up of teenagers and early-twenty somethings, the band's key target audience. Fifteen dates alongside Project 86, Hed PE, and the headlining P.O.D., who were out promoting their newly platinum-certified *Fundamental Elements of Southtown* album, took up most of November, before Linkin Park joined Papa Roach for a December run. The Vacaville, California four-piece were experiencing their own breakout year in 2000, which began in March with the release of their powerful debut single 'Last Resort'. The song's exploration of suicide awareness was raw and emotive, but it also signified the arrival of a host of new rap rock acts who, like Papa Roach, were choosing to tackle deeper and darker subject matters in their music.

By the time Linkin Park were opening for Papa Roach, 'One Step Closer' was still their only song being played on the radio, but *Hybrid Theory* had already earned gold certification in the US. On 10 January 2001, the album went platinum, and from then on, an estimated 100,000 copies were being sold in America each week, to the point that *Hybrid Theory* became the biggest-selling album of 2001, eclipsing artists such as Destiny's Child, Jennifer Lopez, Alicia Keys and Michael Jackson.

In total, four singles were released from *Hybrid Theory*, and each one played its part in maintaining the album's mainstream prosperity. For a band who had built themselves up as a rap rock outfit, each single (and the other album tracks) contained distinct elements that separated Linkin Park from the rest of the crowd. They literally sounded like no one else, and anyone who came out after them were ultimately deemed imposters. After 'One Step Closer' came 'Crawling', which was released in February 2001. The song is dominated by Chester's intense vocal prowess, and his lyrics find him revisiting his past issues with addiction, and the lack of self-confidence that came with it. 'Crawling' is the polar opposite of 'One Step Closer', where for starters, the sauntering tempo in the verses is comforted by Chester's delicate vocal. Over a haunting keyboard riff which is reminiscent of Depeche Mode, another of Chester's early inspirations, and a stuttering beat, the quiet-loud dynamic finds the verses building towards a soaring chorus, which makes its impact through Chester's emotionally potent scream-singing. The heavier guitar work may have been built around a simple riff, but the melody incorporated in the hook does enough to emit the song's reflective triumph in overcoming the odds.

The wider reaction to 'Crawling' upon its release ensured its hit potential, and the song reached 79 on the Hot 100, while also securing top five placings on the Mainstream and Modern Rock charts. In the UK, the second single reached 16, which was eight places higher than had been achieved by 'One Step Closer'. Allaying any fears of being tagged as one trick ponies, 'Crawling' shows an emotionally deeper side of Linkin Park, while also putting Chester's wide-ranging vocal talents front and centre. How he orchestrates his voice in his now fully furnished style is a million miles from his work-in-progress status during his time in Grey Daze, and when 'Crawling' won the Best Hard Rock Performance Grammy in 2002, even the rest of the band put its success down to Chester's dynamic range, and the emotional arc in his writing.

Due to a desire to quickly follow up single releases in Europe, 'Papercut' was released in June 2001. It was no accident that the song was chosen to open *Hybrid Theory*, having been considered by the band to offer the perfect representation of everything Linkin Park was about. Exploding into action with a Timbaland-inspired hip-hop bounce, Brad's pulsing riff, and Joe's swirling electronics, the emphatic intro leads into many people's first experience of a Mike Shinoda rapping masterclass. While the lyrics detail the ill-effects of anxiety and paranoia, the song's breathless pace and arena-sized chorus justifies both its place as the album opener, and as a dead cert for a single. With no US release, the UK was always going to be the primary audience for 'Papercut', and the song proved popular enough to peak at a highly respectable 14 in the country's singles chart.

* * *

2001 was an understandably chaotic year for Linkin Park, whose stock continued to rise as *Hybrid Theory* kept selling in its millions. The band spent most of the year on the road, where after a handful of dates in Europe in early January as part of a mini promotional campaign, they embarked on their first American headline tour. The Street Soldiers Tour, in which Alien Ant Farm and Taproot were the support acts, included performances in such venues as The Fillmore in San Francisco, the House of Blues in Chicago, and New York's Roseland Ballroom, as Linkin Park began to attract audiences in their thousands. Through March, the band reacquainted themselves with Taproot, who were now managed by Mark Wakefield, to support Deftones on the Back to School Tour. At this point, Taproot were promoting their debut album *Gift*, which was released in June 2000 through Atlantic Records, Linkin Park continued to put the world on notice by rifling through the majority of songs on *Hybrid Theory*, and Deftones presented their captivating live show via a soundtrack of cuts from their majestic *White Pony* album, and the previous but equally stellar *Around the Fur*. The tour ran riot across Europe before culminating on 25 March at the Manchester Apollo, and while they were in the UK, Linkin Park visited BBC Studios in London, to record performances of 'Crawling', 'Papercut', and 'In the End' for *Top of the Pops*. To give an indication of the company Linkin Park was now keeping, the performances were spread across three separate episodes of the popular weekly TV show, which aired in April, June and October, and were bookended by the current cream of the pop crop. It meant that anyone tuning in to watch three minutes of blistering nu metal were also made to endure the latest hits from Janet Jackson, Robbie Williams, Shaggy, Mis-Teeq and Britney Spears. For Linkin Park to be mentioned in the same breath as those artists was a small price to pay for writing such commercially successful rock songs.

Airmiles continued to be racked up with a US-to-Europe tour between 14 April and 4 June, before the band visited Australia, New Zealand and

Japan for the first time. Another return to Europe then found Linkin Park playing the Rock IM Park festival in Germany alongside Guns N' Roses, Radiohead, Limp Bizkit, Tool and Slipknot. The festival season was now in full swing, and the hottest ticket in America was Ozzfest. The brainchild of Ozzy and Sharon Osbourne and now in its fifth year, Ozzfest was *the* bill to be on for many of the rising nu metal acts. The American leg of the tour ran for thirty-one dates, and because of Linkin Park's increasing notoriety, the band was given a coveted main stage slot. Early on they found it hard to win over hostile crowds, many of whom were there for Black Sabbath, the headline attraction and one of the most popular heavy metal bands of all time. Despite its immeasurable ascent, there was still a lot of nu metal detractors out there who considered the movement a blot on the heavy metal history books. Acts like Korn and Limp Bizkit were blamed for taking heavy music out of the underground and into the mainstream, and the anarchic events of Woodstock '99, which was largely triggered by nu metal's angst-ridden demographic, had forever left a sour taste in the mouth. The music itself was deemed less technical than rock and metal should be, and largely void of guitar solos, and the looks of the bands, many of whom sported adidas tracksuits, baggy jeans, spiked hairstyles and piercings, likened nu metal to some kind of freakshow. That the movement was closely tied to hip hop didn't go down well with staunch metalheads either, and while multiple nu metal acts cited the likes of Metallica, Pantera and Slayer as major influences, rarely did their music support such claims. While millions of disenchanted youths embraced the nu metal movement, there was a whole army of others who simply wanted nothing to do with it, and whenever they could, they made their feelings loud and clear.

Crazy Town was another rap rock band who had risen out of Los Angeles in 1999. Their debut album *The Gift of Game* had been propelled to platinum status by one song and one song only, 'Butterfly', which sampled a Red Hot Chili Peppers guitar lick and had an overly hip-hop vibe that was filtered with a pop rock stomp. On the day *Hybrid Theory* was released, 'Butterfly' soared to the top of the Hot 100, and the song had such massive crossover appeal that it also entered the dance and pop charts. With their rise came accusations that Crazy Town was a manufactured band, something which Linkin Park would also face a short time later. In some ways it was easy to see why, with both band's youthful good looks and choreographed stances scattered across magazine covers and billboards, and their promo photos likening them to the latest boyband being pushed down people's throats. Furthermore, and in Linkin Park's case, as heavy and angry an album as *Hybrid Theory* was, it contained none of the petulant swearing that littered a lot of the nu metal albums that were coming out, and their rather clean cut persona only fuelled the speculation that the band may not have been as authentic as they seemed. Upon joining the Ozzfest line-up, Sharon Osbourne had even gone as far as to say that Crazy Town and Linkin Park were there 'for the girls', which only increased the speculation of both bands being some kind of industry plants.

That Crazy Town were part of the main stage festivities on Ozzfest was, with hindsight, a poorly calculated ploy, and the band was booed and bottled into submission from the very first show. The mood wasn't any better when Linkin Park came onstage next. The band screamed, they riffed hard, but they too rapped, and their electronic Massive Attack intro didn't do them any favours either. The disastrous beginning meant they spent the rest of those early sets trying to seek a level playing field, but they simply didn't have enough time to win their audiences over. Their fortunes would change, however, a week or so into the tour, when they came out fighting with a new intro. It wasn't often Linkin Park bowed to peer pressure, but thanks to Joe, the band was now hitting the stage to the breathless instrumentation of Slayer's 'Raining Blood', which pumped up the crowd from the get-go. Very soon, people were reacting to scorching performances of 'One Step Closer', 'Papercut', and 'Crawling', with positivity and an appreciation for what Linkin Park was trying to accomplish. 'It changed the whole tour,' said Mike when looking back on those early Ozzfest shows in an interview with *Noisey* in 2018. 'All we needed to do was extend an olive brand and say, "we get you".' The Black Sabbath worshippers may not have left Ozzfest to rush out and pick up a copy of *Hybrid Theory*, but at least by the end of the tour, Linkin Park had won over a fair share of their critics.

* * *

When listening to it in its entirety, *Hybrid Theory* feels like a greatest hits collection. There is no filler whatsoever. Succeeding the opening double-pronged assault of 'Papercut' and 'One Step Closer' comes the rather unheralded 'With You', which features guest credits for the instrumental hip hop duo The Dust Brothers. Comprised of Michael 'E.Z. Mike' Simpson and John 'King Gizmo' King, The Dust Brothers had provided samples and beats for various hip hop artists throughout the '80s and '90s, as well as producing Beastie Boys' classic sophomore album *Paul's Boutique* in 1989. More recently, they had collaborated with Korn on 'Kick the P.A.', for inclusion on the *Spawn* movie soundtrack, and they produced Hanson's pop smash 'MMMBop' in 1997. When The Dust Brothers were approached by Linkin Park to produce 'With You', they instead sent over some samples for the band to reassemble and build the song from, and it became another perfect amalgamation of rap and rock, which of all the songs on *Hybrid Theory* is the one most in-keeping with that whole nu metal vibe. Containing a standout vocal back and forth in which Mike and Chester detail the decline of a relationship, while Joe's eerie electronics and dizzying scratches face off against Brad's heavy guitars and some low-end bass. 'With You' may not have been given the same spotlight as the two songs that came before it, but it continues the album's early momentum with understated aplomb, before being rounded off by another soaring chorus that is saturated in electronic gloom.

Next, 'Points of Authority' finds Linkin Park utilising the digital technology at their fingertips. Mike's abilities of operating in a recording studio had long been known, and in using his experience of making mashups in his teens, he delved into Pro Tools like a kid in a candy store. 'He almost plays some of the recording technology like an instrument,' said Brad when speaking about Mike in 2021, having written a basic guitar line for 'Points of Authority' that Mike cut up and rearranged into a different sequence. The song further emphasises the importance of hip hop to Linkin Park's sound, with its boombox drumbeat and a glitch effect to Mike's rap vocal which was shaped by The Roots' lead MC, Black Thought. The song's rousing chorus, which is led by Chester's war cry of 'You like to think you're never wrong', wasn't written until Linkin Park entered the studio with Don Gilmore, but its results came from the band wanting something that was melodic, but that also leaned on the heavier side.

After 'Crawling' comes 'Runaway', which is the first of a handful of songs that may have sounded familiar to those who had followed Linkin Park from their Xero and Hybrid Theory days. 'Runaway' emerged out of the ruins of 'Stick N Move', with only the guitar chords and some drum grooves remaining intact from its original appearance on the Xero demo tape. It was brave of the band to delve back into their past, where such songs had long ago been written off by label execs, but on the flipside their relative obscurity had given Linkin Park the opportunity to go back and improve on the tracks and give them a new lease of life. 'Runaway' reveals a band who are still attempting to master song structures, but its hugely melodic and catchy chorus proved a hit with radio stations who began playing the song even though it was never released or even considered as a potential single.

Titled 'Sad', and then 'SuperXero' in its demo stages, 'By Myself' is the result of a conscious effort by the band to write a song with softer verses, and have a chorus full of 'the nastiest, loudest sounds', as Mike described it. Recording early versions of the track kept many a Glendale neighbour up at night as Mike and Chester worked on them, where through thin walls, Chester's repeated takes of devilish screaming would run late into the night. But neither he nor Mike could hear their neighbours' aggravated bangs and cries because they were wearing headphones, fully caught up in the moment as the duo created musical fire. The final recording is just as punishing in its heavier moments, where its corrosive overtones were inspired by the abrasiveness of Ministry and Nine Inch Nails, and therefore makes 'By Myself' the menacing outlier of the album.

'A Place for My Head' matured from 'Esaul', a song that was written by Mike and Mark as far back as 1996, and was partially inspired by Mark's love of the up-and-coming Deftones. 'Esaul' is also one of the tracks that Chester sang on his audition tape, and while constantly evolving over time, it never lost any of its intensity. 'A Place for My Head' successfully treads the gap between genres, and like the other tracks Linkin Park had salvaged from the past, it was given a lyrical overhaul by a set of musicians who were constantly developing into better writers, and who were willing to tackle themes that gripped millions of angst-ridden teens. The verses are highly creative, from the pounding percussion and raw electronics that reveal a hip hop undercurrent, to Mike's venomous rapping surrounding family feuds. In the live environment, the hardcore-infused number quickly became a popular set closer, thanks in no small part to its furious bridge built around another otherworldly procession of Chester's screams, and a potent chorus refrain.

Of those early Xero tracks, 'Rhinestone' had earned the most attention from being included on a Zomba Music CD sampler in 1998, and in an episode of the 1999 TV series *The Crow: Stairway to Heaven*. As of October 2000, the now 'Forgotten' offered another fine example of Linkin Park's modern rap rock formula. Again, the original had been stripped down to its core and only its prominent verse melody and hook remained, and in the *Hybrid Theory* sleeve notes, Mark rightfully receives credits on 'Runaway', 'A Place for My Head', and 'Forgotten', even if each of those songs had greatly benefited from their years of rejection and renovation.

'A Cure for the Itch', although the penultimate track, provides a tiny break in the album's breathless flow by bringing Joe's DJ talents to the forefront. The interlude of sorts leans into trip-hop territory, which began with Mike coming up with a beat and some strings, before Joe did the rest, the scratching and stuttering samples he provides both experimental and methodical. It's easy to sometimes forego his contributions on other songs by getting lost in the waves of the heavy guitars, rhythm sections or vocals, but 'Cure for the Itch', unlike the shortened 'Technique' on the previous EP, gives Joe the platform to take the lead and really show the world what he could do with his decks.

With keyboard hooks and guitar harmonies influenced by Depeche Mode, the closing 'Pushing Me Away' gives *Hybrid Theory* the big time finale it deserves. Wanting another melodic rock song similar to that of 'Crawling', but never once thinking of it as an emulation, Linkin Park cut out the hip hop and go full-on arena rock with this ballad of sorts. As 'Papercut' began the record, 'Pushing Me Away' ends it with the same unremitting energy, where Chester's assertive vocals carry the song's theme of being unable to walk away from a frayed relationship. With one of the strongest choruses on the entire album, made up of soaring melodies and possessing such strong singalong capabilities, 'Pushing Me Away' brings *Hybrid Theory* to quite the pulsating climax.

* * *

Without 'In the End', *Hybrid Theory* would still have been considered an incredible debut album. But with it, *Hybrid Theory* became an instant classic. Today, when that piano melody kicks in on the radio, even those who don't consider themselves a fan of Linkin Park immediately recognise the song that is playing, such is the universal notoriety of 'In the End', and the legacy it has pathed for itself.

It took quite some time for Linkin Park to perfect the song, but even in its initial stages there was a sense that the band had a potential smash hit on their hands. 'The moment I played that demo for the other guys, they knew that song was special,' Mike told *Kerrang!* in 2020. The demo in question was created in one night after Mike holed himself up in the band's Hollywood rehearsal space, as he attempted to write a song that could take Linkin Park to the next level. Of course, he had no idea that 'One Step Closer' and 'Crawling' would do so well on the charts and give the band a platform to build from, but at that moment, if any song was going to stand a chance of excelling in the mainstream environment, 'In the End' was it.

The song that cements Linkin Park's blending of styles, where the rap verses perfectly transition into the biggest of pop-tinged choruses, as subtle electronics and that memorable piano melody continually lurk underneath. Even more, the song is as powerful lyrically as it is musically, and the emotional weight of the track would go on to play an integral part in millions of teenagers' lives in that early part of the new millennium. *Hybrid Theory* covers such a wide array of uncomfortable topics, from family breakdowns and feelings of alienation, to inner turmoil and a longing to find one's own identity. But the most gut-wrenching moment of the entire record comes in that first chorus line of 'I tried so hard and got so far, but in the end, it doesn't even matter'. The dejection and frustration in Chester's revelatory confession is just as painful to hear today, but like the band themselves, it is honest, and courageous. The early inspiration for the lyrics came from Mike reminiscing on everything he and his bandmates had gone through to get to this point, and 'In the End' was a kind of happy ending. But for Chester, the words resonated for different reasons, as he thought back to the toils of his past. Like Linkin Park had done for each of their songs, they added a degree of ambiguity to the lyrics that meant the listener could embrace them in their own way, to find solace, or to relate them to what was going on in their own lives. Even so early on, Linkin Park possessed an ornate ability in being able to connect with their fans, which formed a togetherness and an understanding that helped make people realise it was okay to not be okay. It's part of why *Hybrid Theory* is such a special album, where even in its complexity and challenging the standard sounds of music, the contrast of destructive anger with controlled melodies, along with an intimate outpouring of emotion, didn't only provide catharsis for the people writing it, but for the millions who were listening to it too.

For much of the writing and recording sessions, 'In the End' was set to go under the name of 'Untitled', until the R&B singer D'Angelo released his hit single 'Untitled (How Does It Feel)' in January 2000. Because of the prominence of those three little words in the chorus, 'In the End' seemed like the only natural choice for the song's new moniker. A heap of demos that are available online today show just how far 'In the End' was worked on to get it over the finish line. Frequent lyric changes were made on the advice of management who, upon hearing the early versions of the track, were left questioning Mike's position within the band. Despite the changes that were made though, the main piano piece, guitar harmonics, beats and melodies all remained from Mike's first demo, and they form the song's stunning spine and pave the way for Chester and Mike to focus on the song's soul-destroying monologue. In hindsight, quite how Warner didn't consider 'In the End' as a potential single from the outset feels like another spectacular own goal on their part. Its heavy rap influence was the main reason why the label discarded it so quickly and chose to lead with the rock-orientated duo of 'One Step Closer' and 'Crawling', but in September 2001, 'In the End' was sent to radio ahead of a single release in October, just as Linkin Park was preparing to join the Family Values Tour.

Masterminded by Korn and debuting in 1998, Family Values was intended to become an annual event that ran across America for approximately six weeks. The first two years brought rock and hip hop together like very few travelling festivals had done before, where in '98, Ice Cube joined Korn, Limp Bizkit, Orgy, Incubus and Rammstein, and '99 saw Mobb Deep, Run-D.M.C., Method Man and Redman sharing the stage with Staind, Filter and the year's headline act, Limp Bizkit. Because of the competition from the Anger Management and Summer Sanitarium tours in 2000, Family Values took the year off, but it returned in 2001 with a rock-heavy line-up where Spike 1000, Deadsy, Staind and Static-X were each tasked with warming up the crowds, before Linkin Park embraced the role of direct support to the headlining Stone Temple Pilots. Family Values was a good tour to be on for Linkin Park, but for Chester it was a really big deal. He was a huge Stone Temple Pilots fan and in his younger years he'd dreamed of fronting the band, and on regular nights of the tour he would join the grunge icons onstage to perform their fan favourite track, 'Dead & Bloated', from their mega-selling *Core* album. Each performance created a special moment for Chester, but it wouldn't be the last time he'd get to share the stage with the band.

As Family Values rolled on, 'In the End' continued to climb up the charts in the US. On the back of the success of the previous singles, the song's music video was given a huge budget, and a large proportion of the funds went on incorporating the latest CGI. The fantasy-like video also contains band performances filmed during regular stops on Ozzfest, and considering Warner had shown very little interest in promoting 'In the End' early on, they were now putting a lot of investment into making the final single from *Hybrid Theory* its biggest hit. Both video and song were heavily rotated on every major TV channel and radio station, rock-orientated or otherwise, and slowly but surely 'In the End' was propelling its creators into uncharted territory.

'I think it's a perfectly beautiful song,' said Brad, when discussing the legacy of 'In the End' with *Kerrang!* twenty years on. 'It's honest, the emotional sentiment is just so visceral and compelling.' Though lyrically downbeat, it was a rare feat in 2000 that any band, let alone upstarts like Linkin Park, could relay such a deeply personal message in a song where its music sounded so uplifting. In a sea of nu metal dirge, 'In the End' sparkled in its rich invention. It's understandable why Linkin Park had been thrown into the nu metal category on the back of 'One Step Closer', but with 'In the End' the band was spreading its wings and swinging for the fences. They were doing everything they could to stand out from an overindulgent crowd of rap rock wannabes, while at the same time driving the sub-genre to its commercial peak. With *Hybrid Theory*, and 'In the End', Linkin Park was single-handedly changing the landscape of heavy music forever.

Fig. 4

Reinterpretations

In April 2002, the multinational alternative rock outfit Cyclefly released their second album, *Crave*. *Crave* was the follow-up to 1999's *Generation Sap*, which was lauded by music critics, some of whom had tipped Cyclefly to be 'The next big thing' in rock. As intriguing as the multiple layers and textures within their music, Cyclefly made the gallant attempt of breaking America before they even had laid any solid foundations in Europe. *Generation Sap* was recorded at the legendary Sound City Studios in Van Nuys with producer Sylvia Massy, who had worked with an esteemed list of artists including Prince, Tool and the Red Hot Chili Peppers.

During their unfortunately short existence (the band split up in 2003), Cyclefly secured lucrative tour support slots with Tool, Live, Bush, Iggy Pop and Linkin Park. Cyclefly's connection to Linkin Park dates back to the summer of 1999, when one of their explosive live performances heralded a new fan. Chester enjoyed the band's energetic stage presence, Declan O'Shea's mercurial vocal style, and the sophistication of the songs being projected onto the crowd inside the LA club Pretty Ugly, on a warm 30 June evening. This was before Linkin Park had even taken off as a band, but from that night on, Chester and Cyclefly became good friends, and they regularly hung out at various LA haunts for food and drink, and at times even to jam together.

When Cyclefly released the punchy 'No Stress' as the lead single from *Crave* in March 2002, the promo sleeve revealed a massive sign of approval from a musician whose name was now carrying far more weight behind it. The message running across the top of the sleeve read, 'Cyclefly is one of my favourite bands and their new record is one of the best I've heard in a long time. If you don't like it, you suck! – Linkin Park's Chester Bennington'. When *Crave* arrived a few weeks later, the album's second track 'Karma Killer' revealed a surprising guest spot from Chester, in which his throaty snarl backs up Declan O'Shea's mesmeric lead. The song rocks hard, and is just one of the highlights on a record flooded with memorable moments. In some ways, the collaboration with Chester earned Cyclefly an element of credibility from those who were less familiar with the band, but from other corners, the Ireland-based rockers were harshly chastised for appearing to have cashed in on Linkin Park's recent success. Either way, 'Karma Killer' has stood the test of time, and the song creates a tiny snapshot of the friendship that had grown between both parties since their very first introduction.

For this book, Cyclefly's guitarist and primary songwriter, Ciaran O'Shea, looks back on his friendship with Chester, the legacy of 'Karma Killer', and supporting Linkin Park in Europe in September 2001:

The first time we met Chester was when he came to see us play at the Pretty Ugly club, the one Taime Downe from Faster Pussycat was running. After the show we hung out with Chester, and he later came to see us when we were supporting Live at the Mayan Theatre. The first time we met him was just after he'd auditioned for a band that turned out to be Hybrid Theory, and we became just really good friends, and he was a fan of our band. We hung out a lot. He would come down to the studio, we would jam together, we would go for food. He was just a really nice and wonderful person.

When Hybrid Theory started making music, I would hear all the demos for the EP, and then also for the album, about six months before it came out. We were already recording *Crave* at that time, and we would swap demos with Chester. We would send him what we were working on and vice versa, and then he sent me the board mixes for *Hybrid Theory* while we were in Parkage Studios in Sussex with our producer Colin Richardson. We listened to them, and we were stunned. The music was amazing.

The nu metal movement had been coming on for a while. As a band, we were more on the Kyuss, Queens of the Stone Age, stoner rock end of things with what we were listening to, and Jane's Addiction. But going into our second album, we were really into Deftones and Korn. When we were on the cycle of *Generation Sap*, I think Incubus had just broken through with 'Pardon Me', and it was all over the radio. 'Break Stuff' had come out too, and the scene needed a shake up because in America especially there were so many bands imitating each other, and all of that was kind of killing the scene a bit. We were in a scene in the UK where we were friends with Pulkas and Pitchshifter, and One Minute Silence, so looking back I'm sure we felt one of those scenes was going to go. There was a really strong underground scene in the UK, but the American scene just took over once the Slipknot's came along, and then Linkin Park. They were a little late to the game, but they just so happened to do so much better than everyone else. Like when Nirvana killed grunge, and I think Sepultura killed thrash metal, Linkin Park just finished nu metal because they were very hard to top.

'Karma Killer' was written and demoed in May 2000, and then when we were in Larrabee Studios in Hollywood mixing the *Crave* album, Chester said he would come in and do a vocal. He came in one afternoon and recorded his parts in a matter of hours, and that was the same week Linkin Park were due to perform 'One Step Closer' on the *Late Night with Conan O'Brien* show. A little later, Cyclefly lost our longtime managers, and when 9/11 happened, the music industry changed completely. 'Karma Killer' had been remixed by Bill Appleby at Ocean Way in Los Angeles, and we all really loved the mix that was intended to be released, but it was ultimately nixed to be a single. We had discussed going out to the States to do a video with Linkin Park, but the label wasn't behind us at all on it. Universal never worked it, and the dominoes for Cyclefly had certainly begun falling at that point. Once we went to Universal, they didn't know what to do with us because we felt we were more like an old rock or punk band in the vein of Jane's Addiction or whatever, but the label didn't have a clue what we were, and they couldn't really sell us.

We supported Linkin Park for two shows of their European tour in September 2001. The first was at the Palladium in Cologne, Germany, and the second was at the Heineken Music Hall in Amsterdam, Netherlands. We just got a call, and I don't know if someone else was supposed to be playing, but we were asked to jump on the tour maybe a week before it kicked off. I think Lostprophets opened, then it was us, Puddle of Mudd, and then Linkin Park. When we played 'Karma Killer', Chester came onstage to perform the song with us both nights. It just spontaneously happened if I remember correctly. Chester was watching the show, and he just picked up a mic and walked out onto the stage and the response was incredible. The venues went nuts. On both nights it was fantastic. We'd done a lot of tours with big crowds prior to that. We had done Tool dates, Live and Bush dates in America, Reading Festival and Woodstock '99, but those two shows were really good shows, and Linkin Park was fucking fantastic. I cannot say that enough. They were so young and still learning, but they were the most professional band I have ever seen or come across.

They were just an incredible bunch, and they had an incredible formula. Mike was an incredible band leader, and Chester was just the best singer I've ever heard. I kind of had that feeling the first time we jammed together, before any Linkin Park singles were even released. You just knew it. He just had that ability to project, he was a very hard worker, and he was very focused on what he was doing. I can't really stress how good a band Linkin Park was. What a nice bunch of people.

In 2001, Linkin Park played over 160 shows worldwide, but the end of the *Hybrid Theory* tour cycle was finally coming into view. Much of the time the band had spent on the road was filmed for their first DVD, *Frat Party at the Pankake Festival*, which dropped on 20 November 2001. The fly-on-the-wall documentary serves as a generally light-hearted affair and gives an insight into the young men behind the music. It captures the laughs and the pranks, but it also catches the moments of struggle, fatigue and contemplation of how getting to where they wanted to be was always going to come at some kind of cost. The DVD also features Linkin Park's early music videos, as well as bonus content and 'hidden eggs' which unlock further features, and in no time at all, the allure that surrounded Linkin Park helped *Frat Party at the Pankake Festival* ship over 100,000 units in the US.

The tour that brought the curtain down on the *Hybrid Theory* cycle was Linkin Park's first as an arena headliner. Having taken the blueprint of Family Values in bringing rock and hip hop together as one, Projekt Revolution was far more driven in spreading its mission statement. The entire tour was of Linkin Park's own doing, and they were keen to give the event a community feel by inviting members of the LPU to meet up at shows and form new friendships. Projekt Revolution ran across America from 29 January to 24 February, and joining the headliners was the mashup pioneer DJ Z-Trip, the rising nu metal band Adema, and the rap crew Cypress Hill. Regular dates also welcomed DJ battles, where the winner was given the opportunity to perform on the tour's final stop in Las Vegas. The inaugural Projekt Revolution proved to be a big success, and it was the latest thing Linkin Park had touched that turned into gold. Like Korn had planned Family Values to be, the first Projekt Revolution wouldn't be the last, and as Linkin Park grew bigger, their very own festival-like event would become an annual thing moving forward.

It seemed almost poetic that three days after the culmination of Projekt Revolution, Linkin Park was at the Staples Center in Los Angeles for their first Grammy Awards. In total, the band received three nominations at the 44th annual ceremony, but they came up short to Alicia Keys in the Best New Artist category, while U2's *All That You Can't Leave Behind* pipped *Hybrid Theory* to win Best Rock Album. They did, however, scoop the Best Hard Rock Performance gong for 'Crawling', which overcame killer cuts from Alien Ant Farm, P.O.D., Rage Against the Machine and Saliva. It was a cornerstone moment for Linkin Park, and just a matter of weeks later, 'In the End' rose to its peak position of 2 on the Hot 100. The anthem was only prevented from making it to the top spot by Jennifer Lopez's 'Ain't It Funny', but still, 'In the End' had secured Linkin Park their first bona fide megahit. It was the icing on the cake for the band who, after two long years of blood, sweat and tears, and with a few lows but many highs, had gone from being an unknown and unfancied rap rock band being written off as just another flash-in-the-pan nu metal act, to one of the leading forces in modern rock.

* * *

In comparison to their frantic touring schedule in the year prior, Linkin Park wrapped up their live performances for 2002 as early as 4 March. Playing a benefit concert for the paediatric hospice TrinityKids at the House of Blues in West Hollywood was significant for being the last time the band's setlist would comprise almost solely of *Hybrid Theory* songs, after which it was expected they would disappear from the limelight to recharge their batteries, and then get to work on their next album. That wasn't to be the case, however.

Before his guest spot on 'Karma Killer' arrived on Cyclefly's *Crave* album, Chester made an appearance on Jonathan Davis' *Queen of the Damned* soundtrack, which was released in the February. A sequel of sorts to the 1994 movie *Interview with the Vampire*, *Queen of the Damned* follows the rock and roll exploits of the vampire Lestat, and in Davis' first assignment outside of Korn, the frontman wrote and provided vocals for five tracks that Lestat's band perform in the film. But, because the soundtrack was released through Warner Bros. Records, Davis' contract with Sony meant his voice was unable to appear on audio distributed by a rival label, so the tracks were shared out between singers who in one way or another were affiliated with Warner. Chester was one of them, and he sang on the moody 'System', where his vocal flits between a harmonic verse lead and a guttural chorus burst, over music that is shrouded in gothic nuances. 'System' doesn't possess one of Chester's more memorable performances, but as the company Linkin Park was keeping became all the more distinguished, opportunities to collaborate with other artists were beginning to become a more regular occurrence for the band.

The same thing applied to Joe and Mike, and their hip hop street cred led to the duo working with the New York DJ collective The X-Ecutioners. Written and produced by Mike for inclusion on The X-Ecutioners' second album *Built from Scratch*, 'It's Goin' Down' contains samples of the *Hybrid Theory EP* track 'Step Up', and the unreleased demo 'Dedicated'. Fused with Mike's signature rapping, some vibrant Linkin Park-esque guitar flurries, and littered with an exuberant concoction of turntable technicalities from both Joe and The X-Ecutioners, 'It's Goin' Down' hints at what a potential solo career might sound like for Mike; something that sat in the rap rock genre, but was more directly rooted in hip hop.

The single crept inside the Hot 100 at 85, but in the UK it fared much better, reaching number 7. The music video features all of Linkin Park, in which Dave, Joe, Mike and Rob perform the instrumental, and Brad and Chester make cameo appearances later on. In the aftermath of its single release in March, 'It's Goin' Down' was frequently mistaken for a new Linkin Park song, however the track and the *Built from Scratch* album signalled a major breakthrough for The X-Ecutioners, who had spent many years grafting for their big moment since their early incarnation as X-Men in 1989. There is no doubt that Linkin Park's involvement on the track and in the video went a long way in helping The X-Ecutioners achieve their advancement into the mainstream, such was the Agoura six's increasing global appeal at this time.

*   *   *

Behind the scenes, Linkin Park had been working on ideas for their follow-up album to *Hybrid Theory*. During Ozzfest the band made use of a mini studio that had been built into the back of their tour bus to amass a wealth of riffs, samples, and beats. At the same time though, and attesting to his persistent drive in always wanting to create, Mike was pursuing another venture in wanting to remix a handful of *Hybrid Theory* songs.

Mike's vision was to strip the songs of their rock sensibilities and steer them deeper into hip hop territory, while also shrouding them in a smorgasbord of electronics and reworking their structures to separate them from their previous iterations. He also went in search of collaborators by sending out stems of music for others to rearrange and apply their own stamp to. As either performers or producers, there were friends from the rock scene that Linkin Park had immersed themselves in for the past eighteen months. There were artists who at one point or another had influenced Mike, and then there were underground artists that Mike was listening to, who were yet to become household names. The project, which began small and quickly snowballed, wasn't about teaming up with the biggest names in music, it was all about artistic integrity and wanting the songs to shine in their alternative forms. To rework songs that were more or less already perfect was dangerous, and risked undoing all the hard work Linkin Park had put in to get to this stage, but Mike knew how to bring his vision to fruition without threatening his band's reputation.

Perhaps he'd learned what not to do from Limp Bizkit, whose own attempt at a remix album, *New Old Songs*, had been released in late 2001. Or maybe it had served as inspiration for him to follow suit; either way, Mike wanted to steer clear of big name producers, unlike Limp Bizkit, who cashed in on their standing as one of rock's biggest acts to bring in Timbaland, P. Diddy, The Neptunes and William Orbit to remix songs from the band's three studio albums. Each track was flushed of its anthemic heaviness and renavigated into hip hop, but they had been done without the authenticity that such an endeavour required. Following up the mega-selling *Chocolate Starfish and the Hot Dog Flavored Water* with *New Old Songs* was as intrepid as *Reanimation* doing likewise with *Hybrid Theory*, but the underwhelming response to *New Old Songs* was a red flag to which Mike had to pay attention, and avoid the same mistakes that had befallen his nu metal brethren. But Mike knew how to make all the pieces fit, and how to navigate the producers and guest artists by going as far as to adapt to their work schedules, while tirelessly overseeing the entire project from beginning to end.

What could have been two or three remixes put out as B-sides or just thrown online as free downloads, turned into an hour-plus kaleidoscopic journey that seamlessly interwove hip hop, electronica and rock, and was presented as one innovative package. *Reanimation* transcended experimentation through the utilisation of soundscapes that were far more advanced than what Linkin Park's artistic boundaries should have afforded them at such an early stage of their career, but as the band had already shown on more than one occasion, they were a different breed who enjoyed exploring unfamiliar enclaves to which virtually none of their nu metal contemporaries would have dared, or even considered, going.

Each reimagining was a step into the unknown. They were often extended from their original forms, with new parts made up of atmospheric instrumentation, and intros that set the scene for all that was to follow. There were new verses complete with new lyrics, and occasionally alternative stanzas reused from earlier demos, and to create perfect symmetry, the song titles were also 'remixed'. 'Pts.OF.Athrty' arrived a good four months before *Reanimation*, and whether or not Linkin Park had planned to release further singles, this was the one and only to be taken from the album. During the *Hybrid Theory* cycle, the band had pushed for 'Points of Authority' to be a single, but Jeff Blue was reportedly behind the decision to eliminate the song from contention. Fast forward to mid-2002 and the band had now cut ties with Blue. They were undoubtedly appreciative of his efforts in getting them signed, and for helping steer the band towards the success they had already experienced, but the relationship between both parties had long since become untenable, and during a reshuffle within Warner's hierarchy, Blue moved on and took a job with Interscope Records.

Remixed by Jay Gordon, whose own band Orgy relied heavily on electronic textures in their music, 'Pts.OF.Athrty' is a strong first indication of exactly what Linkin Park had set out to achieve with *Reanimation*. The remix breathed new life into the track, its dystopian voyage full of swarming electronics and glitched vocal effects creating further depth, while still maintaining the core of what made 'Points of Authority' a fan favourite in the first place. Released on 20 March, and alongside a fully futuristic CGI music video that presented a battle to the death between robots and an alien race, 'Pts.OF.Athrty' picked up major rotation across radio and TV. Remixes had rarely been commercially viable, but the single still reached a high of 9 in the UK. In America, however, the only chart on which the song placed was Modern Rock Tracks, at 29, which suggested *Reanimation* was more than likely going to cater for Linkin Park's hardcore fanbase, rather than luring in new listeners.

Elsewhere on the album, 'Enth E End' is given a hip hop makeover by KutMasta Kurt, who looped the piano melody and erased the entire rhythm section in favour of a boom bap beat to attribute to its street vibe. While 'Wth>You' doesn't veer too far from the original cut, its crowning moment (and a highlight of the entire album) comes in Aceyalone from Haiku D'Etat's impressive rap verse, which leads perfectly into Chester's compelling bridge and final chorus. Jonathan Davis' involvement on '1 Stp Klor' adds a gloomy progression to an already dark electro jaunt, and his vocal trade-off with Chester that comes later in the track felt like a combination that everyone in nu metal had been dying to hear at the time. Also making appearances from the rock world are Deftones' guitarist Stephen Carpenter, whose abrasive riffing on 'By_Myslf' bolsters the heaviness of the original. Taproot's Stephen Richards incorporates his snarled vocal to the industrially charged 'P5hng Me A*wy', while Aaron Lewis from Staind features on an absorbing take of 'Krwlng', where the eerie stringed intro supplies the track's otherworldly ambience.

The Alchemist and Jurassic 5's Chali 2na ('Frgt/10'), Styles of Beyond's Cheapshot and Jubacca ('Ppr=Kut'), and The X-Ecutioners ('X-Ecutioner Style') are among those who help give *Reanimation* its prominent hip hop edge by creating interesting twists and turns on how each song could sound in an alternative field. Also given the remix treatment are a couple of tracks that weren't on *Hybrid Theory*. 'High Voltage' is the first, which featured on the earlier EP and was remixed by Evidence and Pharoahe Monch and showcased as 'H! VLTG3'. The other is one of the most intriguing tracks on the whole of *Reanimation*, a reworking of 'My December'. As 'One Step Closer' gathered momentum through the summer of 2000, Linkin Park found themselves on the radar of the LA radio station KROQ-FM, who invited the band to join their Almost Acoustic Christmas show. To coincide with the annual event, DJ's Kevin & Bean also put together compilation albums that were sold exclusively in the LA area, where the proceeds were shared out to local charities. Released on 28 November 2000 and entitled *The Real Slim Santa*, that year's album featured festive rock numbers from Blink-182, Orgy, U2, Weezer, and Linkin Park. 'My December' was written specifically for the album, by Mike while he was on the road with the band in early-October, and in two days 'My December' had been recorded and mixed at The Loft in Nashville.

Driven by a keyboard melody not unlike that of 'In the End', 'My December' is a sparse but haunting track. The spine-tingling electronic jousts and minimalistic percussion forges its ponderous mood, which is in line with Mike's lyrics that were inspired by being on the road and away from loved ones. Chester's delicate vocal offers a stunning contrast to those heavier deliveries across *Hybrid Theory*, where his tone and harmonies more than match the emotional angle that runs through the song. 'My December' was a B-side on the UK issue of 'One Step Closer', which came out in January 2001, and as a bonus track on the Japanese edition of *Hybrid Theory*, before a remix by Mickey Petralia found its way onto *Reanimation* over a year later. When approaching artists in the album's initial stages, Mike reached out to the Icelandic singer Björk, but she was only interested in collaborating on a full song. Instead, Kelli Alli from the British electronic group Sneaker Pimps supplies backing vocals on 'My<Dsmbr', and her voice, which isn't too dissimilar to Björk's, floats nicely behind Chester's spine-tingling lead. Musically, the track's blossoming synths and jagged electronics give off an '80s new wave vibe, and the sombre tone of the authentic keyboard piece is now replaced by Petralia's dry riff. 'My<Dsmbr' holds onto its reflective nous, but its sanguine makeover is one of the album's go-to moments and perfectly encapsulates Mike's thought process as he began to shape *Reanimation*.

Released on 30 July, *Reanimation* went straight to number 2 on the Billboard 200. Even though it was a remix album, its chart placing emphasised just how in demand Linkin Park were, and while it may have been chiefly created by Mike, and with only minimal roles undertaken by the rest of the band, *Reanimation* was still a Linkin Park album and people all over embraced the record as if it was a new studio release. Having sold over 4 million copies, *Reanimation* has gone on to become one of the best-selling remix albums of all time, and once again, Linkin Park's risk of wanting to push the boundaries of genre had paid off in the most unsuspecting of ways.

Fig. 5

Close to Something Real

When Linkin Park returned with a brand new single in February 2003, the furore surrounding them, the song, and a long-awaited new album had reached fever pitch. The success of *Reanimation* could easily have led to some questioning whether the band was already turning their backs on the rap rock sound that helped turn them into superstars, but any concerns were quickly extinguished within those opening few seconds of 'Somewhere I Belong'.

The song feels like a natural progression from where *Hybrid Theory* left off, with all the Linkin Park fundamentals remaining firmly in place. There are those swooning electronics, rap verses that lead into a big radio chorus, and an emotionally charged bridge. But what became more apparent early on was a change in the band's lyrical mindset. Across *Meteora*, there are still mutterings of abject consternation, but there is also a confidence about Linkin Park and an optimism that had stemmed from the experiences and opportunities the band had grasped over recent times. After years of singing about pain, paranoia and relationship struggles, Chester's triumphant chorus line of 'I Wanna find something I've wanted all along, somewhere I belong' in the album's lead single appears to find Linkin Park approaching some light at the end of the tunnel.

Meteora is equally as short and succinct as *Hybrid Theory*, in fact its standard running time is a whole minute less than its predecessor. Once again, there was no room for any filler. The album's overall sound is a continuation of that which had engrossed so many millions of listeners on *Hybrid Theory*, but the experimentation is much more advanced this time around. The samples are more inventive and evoke different moods. There are string sections, the use of Japanese flutes, and there is even a song that is so far removed from the realm of rock that radio listeners could have been forgiven for thinking it was coming from an entirely different band altogether.

By 2003, the cracks in nu metal's once impenetrable armour were starting to show. Limp Bizkit had lost their charismatic guitar player Wes Borland, and their popularity was already waning before they released the critically underwhelming *Results May Vary* in the second half of the year. Korn's spotlight was also somewhat diminishing, and the mixed reaction to their 2002 album *Untouchables*, which cost a reported $4 million to make and was leaked online two months before its release, served as the first nail in the band's commercial coffin. Other acts such as Deftones, Incubus and even Papa Roach, who all had platinum records to their name and were once paraded as potential nu metal flagbearers, were now conscientiously distancing themselves from the scene they had been immediately thrown into, and as 2003 moved forward, there was a new breed coming through who would steer rock and metal in a completely different direction. Post-grunge, metalcore and the New Wave of American Heavy Metal were all primed to lead this new charge, and major record labels earmarked the likes of Nickelback, 3 Doors Down and Seether, Killswitch Engage and Lamb of God as artists they should be looking to invest in. At the same time, emo and pop punk was emerging out of the underground to offer an exciting but capricious alternative to chugging riffs and meaty growls, where bands such as Alexisonfire, Good Charlotte, My Chemical Romance, Taking Back Sunday, Thrice, Thursday and The Used were all given platforms to bring their emotionally volatile music into the mainstream.

The landscape of rock and metal was indeed undergoing its latest transformation, and *Meteora* would serve as one of nu metal's final throes. Linkin Park hadn't envisaged it as such, but then again they had long been opposed to the nu metal tag for as long as it had been cast around their necks. The band had a clear focus in what they wanted to achieve with their sophomore album, while in the process further expanding their soundscapes as they continually developed into better musicians. It would have been easy for them to create a re-hash of *Hybrid Theory*, but that was never on the cards. Sure, there are songs on *Meteora* that would not have felt out of place on the first record, but as a complete package, *Meteora* presented the next step in Linkin Park's refinement. The band was obsessed with making each song better than the last, to the point where the only pressure they felt came from within. 'You can't control the commercial success of a record, so there's no point in investing energy in that,' said Brad in an interview with *MTV* in 2003. 'But the quality of your record is entirely up to you, and you can't blame anyone else if you write crappy songs.'

To the outside world, topping *Hybrid Theory* was going to be a next to impossible task. It may have been Linkin Park's debut album, but somehow they had contrived to create a bona fide classic at the very first attempt, but such was their confidence in their own ability, they knew they could emulate it with *Meteora*. Once all the ideas from the tour bus recordings were revisited, the band had around eighty different song concepts. Those concepts were then whittled down to just fifteen and taken into NRG Studios, where Linkin Park chose to once again work with Don Gilmore. If the *Hybrid Theory* sessions had taught them anything, it was that the results would be worth the pain. In striving for perfection, each member had to up their game ahead of recording, which began just a matter of weeks after the completion of *Reanimation* in April 2002. In the build-up, Rob dedicated up to ten hours a day practising the drums, while Brad stepped out of his own comfort zone to experiment with various guitar tones for the first time. As for Dave, who wasn't in the band when Linkin Park worked with Don on *Hybrid Theory*, *Meteora* was to be his true initiation with the producer, and being a talented bass player in his own right, Don's nurturing would at times cause Dave to re-evaluate his own skill levels after being repeatedly pushed to the limits of what he could do with the bass guitar. Mike and Joe diligently worked on new beats and samples, after exploring new approaches in how to create them, while Chester searched within himself for lyrical inspirations, and how to channel the results with what was quickly becoming recognised as one of the biggest voices in the rock genre.

Each song was tracked in the specific order of drums, guitars, bass, scratches/electronics, vocals, which made for a focused recording process, but that isn't to say the sessions weren't without their complications. Unlike during the *Hybrid Theory* sessions, Linkin Park no longer had to deal with any record label or management conflict. The band had earned the full trust of Warner, but Don was still there to play chief antagonist by having Mike and Chester rewrite lyrics or song parts, as well as getting the others to rerecord their pieces until they captured the perfect take. Some of the biggest issues surrounded 'Somewhere I Belong', which was the first song to be written for *Meteora,* but the last to be finished. Its chorus, which would become one of Linkin Park's most famous, endured endless rewrites along the way, and the hook that stuck was, incredibly, Mike and Chester's fortieth attempt. Even then, 'Somewhere I Belong' may never have seen the light of day because, during the final week of the band deciding on the songs that would form the album's official track listing, Chester fell ill. Linkin Park had a big problem, because they knew 'Somewhere I Belong' was a great song and one that was good enough to be the lead single, but Chester was yet to record his final vocal and now he was unable to because his voice was shot. Time was against the band, and they were faced with either culling the song completely, or waiting for Chester to get better. The latter would have forced the release of the album to be delayed not just by weeks, but months. That wasn't an option, so during their time at Soundtrack in December 2002, where Linkin Park reacquainted themselves with Andy Wallace to mix the record, a fully fit Chester returned to the vocal booth to record his final parts. It was an unconventional way of doing things, but the band had already proved their penchant for going against tradition on more than one occasion, and with 'Somewhere I Belong' finally ready to be mixed, disaster was averted at the eleventh hour.

The intro of 'Somewhere I Belong' provides another example of Mike's experimental nous. Easily mistaken by some to be a keyboard riff, the opening part had actually begun as a chord progression Chester had played on an acoustic guitar, before Mike dipped into Pro Tools and cut it into four parts and then reversed them. The song's general structure is similar to that of 'In the End' and therefore serves as a kind of companion piece, but where the smash hit single had thrived under the weight of its emotional torment, 'Somewhere I Belong', with no less intensity, stands out through the resilient message that Mike and Chester's lyrics were projecting.

The album's title was inspired by a rock formation of the same name, located in Thessaly, north-western Greece. Surrounded by stunning panoramic scenery and with a complex of Eastern Orthodox monasteries built on top of it, 'Meteora' was a name that grabbed Linkin Park's attention as soon as they came across it because it sounded huge, and they felt it attested to their second album being greater than the sum of its parts, as well as believing it outweighed what they had accomplished on *Hybrid Theory. Meteora* is a journey of moods and atmospheres, where each song is an exploratory chapter marked by a wider array of sounds, themes and motivations. And each song intentionally blends into the next, where from the moment you press play and until the final beat of the closing track, Linkin Park's sophomore album faithfully unmasks its immaculate construction without taking a single pause of breath.

Following the thirteen-second intro of 'Foreword', which captures Mike's brutal baseball bat assault on an old CD player and burner, 'Don't Stay' lights the touchpaper with its heavy and grinding guitars. The song is the first in which Brad tunes to Drop B, having toyed with a number of variations (including what Mike called a 'Spanish or reggae-style sound') before developing the progression that sparks 'Don't Stay', and *Meteora*, into life. It's the ideal opener, and one that is a little rawer in the mix compared to anything on *Hybrid Theory*, but no less scratch-filled and saturated with angry bursts. Although there are moments of positivity that emanate throughout, there is clearly still a great deal of pent-up frustration bubbling under Chester's surface, where he dials in on his inability to trust, on needing to distance himself from those who are bringing him down, and on his journey of personal and physical recovery. Whether it's the fraught chorus line of 'Just give me myself back and don't stay', or 'The very worst part of you is me' during the vocally emphatic 'Lying from You', or 'Giving up a part of me, I've let myself become you' on the anthemic hook of 'Figure.09', Chester's ability to draw in his audience with emotionally captivating lines remained a key point in Linkin Park sustaining that empathetic connection with their already devout fan base.

If *Hybrid Theory* had put the world on notice of Chester's vocal integrity, *Meteora* cemented him as one of the finest singers in the game by 2003. His resounding performance on 'Lying from You', a stinging rock number with a mechanical beat and pulsing electronic swathes, is one that is impossible for anyone else to replicate, as the singer uses his entire arsenal to match the song's vitriolic rhythm section. 'Hit the Floor' feels like the album's 'By Myself', with its moody hip hop-led verses and beat making way for a scathing chorus. Perhaps some of the band's more unsavoury experiences of the music industry tell here, as Chester's indignant screamed hook attacks those who are more than happy to step on others in their quest to get to the top. Rob's extreme persistence towards practising the drums plays a significant role in him producing one of his finest ever performances on the mellow ballad 'Easier to Run'. He was never the type to use flashy fills, but his rhythms and patterns are often more complex than he is given credit for. His driving grooves have long proved essential in distinguishing the impact of a song, and throughout Linkin Park's discography you can hear Rob's drumming is centred on creating the relevant atmosphere, which constantly builds the dynamic range that would ultimately cascade throughout an album's entire musical landscape. His impressive performance on 'Easier to Run' was recorded in just a few takes, where, with subtle nuances, he underlines his prowess behind a drumkit and, when required, his trusted powerhouse grooves. 'Easier to Run' is an overly melodic number that brings a sense of melancholic calm to an otherwise fast-paced first half of *Meteora*, but as time passed the band fell out of love with the song; being slower than any track they had previously written, its pop rock pomp was later considered by Mike to be 'melodramatic'.

Next, Linkin Park incorporate some live strings into the pulsating 'Faint', which summons a new outlet for the band to unleash their uncompromising aggression. The combination of violins, violas and cellos, which were arranged by Canadian composer (and father of the singer songwriter Beck) David Campbell, create a piercingly theatrical melody that builds the song into a marauding rocker full of agitated guitars and robust breakbeats. From the off, 'Faint' was a guaranteed pit-pleaser, its 2:42 running time taking no prisoners as Mike spouts sharp rap verses and Chester goes for the jugular on those equally relentless chorus refrains. Of the many discordant breakdowns and bridges the band would write over the years, 'Faint' is one of the highlights, and Chester's madcap war cry of 'Hear me out now, you're gonna listen to me like it or not' offers the weight and resonance that ultimately drove the song towards instant fan favourite status.

The heavily underrated 'Figure.09', which preserved its demo title, carries one of the album's strongest choruses, and in its intro has a conga-like drumbeat that came from Joe tapping distortion pedals on his turntable needle and vinyl. 'From the Inside' stems from Dave wanting to write a song in a 6/8 time signature, as all the band's previous tracks had followed the same 4/4 pattern, and the stirring verses supply the best evidence yet of

Linkin Park combining disparate rhythms in a way they had never previously entertained. With its strong hip hop insistence, 'Nobody's Listening' lets the beats and samples act as the song's backbone. The guitars are muted here, and the intriguing addition of a Japanese flute loop initially consigns 'Nobody's Listening' to the role of album outcast, until Mike and Chester's resounding vocal arrangement brings the song marginally back into line and justifies its inclusion on the final track listing.

As the *Hybrid Theory* singles did, each one from *Meteora* seems to intentionally explore contrasting styles. 'Somewhere I Belong' is the stadium-sized anthem that sits firmly within Linkin Park's rap rock stronghold, while 'Faint' acts as the vehement roof-raiser in which the band goes harder and faster than ever before. Both songs were immensely popular on radio and TV, but for one reason or another neither became the crossover hit they perhaps deserved to be. 'Somewhere I Belong' reached 32 on the Hot 100, and 'Faint' stalled out at 48, the positions a far cry from what 'In the End' had previously achieved. Whether *Meteora* was considered as good as, or even better than, *Hybrid Theory* was irrelevant, because the album itself was always going to fly off the shelves upon its 25 March release. *Hybrid Theory* encountered a slow rise that took well over a year, four singles, and countless tours to reach its pinnacle, however *Meteora* launched straight out the gate with first week sales in America going well over 800,000. Its prosperity wasn't so much down to 'Somewhere I Belong' being an incredible lead single, but more down to the band that was releasing the album. Rock still had a comparable grip on the mainstream charts in the early months of 2003, and it wasn't a great surprise when *Meteora* debuted at the top of the Billboard 200. In the twelve weeks preceding its release, Evanescence, AFI, Kid Rock and Zwan had all sat in the top five at one time or another. For some of those acts, the chart placings opened new doors and opportunities, after spending years trying to get to such a point, but none of those acts were called Linkin Park, and by 2003, Linkin Park could do no wrong. In all likelihood, the band could have followed up *Hybrid Theory* with a pop punk album or maybe even a death metal album, and it still would have gone to number 1, such was their crossover appeal.

As of mid-2025, *Meteora* stands at eight times platinum in the US (physical sales and streams combined), which is still some way off the twelve times platinum *Hybrid Theory*, and where the debut album was aided by the belated single release of 'In the End', the legacy of *Meteora* was paved with its third single, 'Numb'. The song's arrangement isn't anything out of the ordinary, in fact 'Numb' was conceived only a week before Linkin Park was due to enter NRG Studios and begin recording. Its straightforward rock approach is supplemented by that now instantly recognisable and haunting keyboard hook, but it's Chester's remarkable vocal that elevates 'Numb' from being just a prodigious album closer, to a certified classic. 'Numb' correlates to 'In the End' in its pained, beaten-down-by-life subject matter, where the lyrics explore conformity and the losing of one's personal passion. Most impressively, it is *how* Chester portrays those feelings, by once again demonstrating his extensive vocal range to accentuate every beleaguered line. Such stories have been told by many a singer over the years, but Chester was better than most at displaying the kind of emotions that could strike the listener to the core of their very being. And having a band behind him who could reinforce the words he was passionately singing with absorbing melodies, and music akin to the emotional depth of the story being told; that was the true skill that throughout their career, separated Linkin Park from the rest of the crowd.

As with 'In the End', 'Numb' was also a slow burner in climbing the Hot 100. Released on 8 September, the song followed in the footsteps of 'Somewhere I Belong' and 'Faint' in topping the Modern Rock Tracks chart, where it stayed for twelve consecutive weeks. 'Numb' also went to the top of Mainstream Rock Tracks for three weeks, before in the first week of March 2004, it reached a high of 11 on the Hot 100. The lasting impact of the song is so much more than its chart positions though, where in the years since its release it has been used in movies, in video games, and it still trends on social media from time to time today. It has also been covered more times than anyone realises, by artists across genres including rock, pop, hip hop, and even classical. Each artist who has covered 'Numb' has tried to incorporate their own imprint, and while some have achieved pretty admirable results, no one has ever been able to replicate Chester's tortured confessional, where the line of 'I've become so numb, I can't feel you there' carries the same excruciating affinity as it did some twenty-plus years ago. Every time you hear it still feels like the first time.

Boasting some impressive figures, which include being a four times platinum single, and (currently) one of only six Linkin Park songs to have over a billion streams on Spotify, are just minor footnotes when discussing the lasting impact of powerful songs such as 'Numb', and just two years after Linkin Park had gone global with 'In the End', they were doing it all over again with their second album's standout song.

* * *

After almost a year away from the stage, Linkin Park returned in late-February 2003. The *Meteora* tour cycle began with the LP Underground Tour, where material from the new album was debuted in front of audiences largely made up of fan club members who were offered free access, and the first of sixteen shows took place in Milan, Italy. In between, the band played a secret show put on by BBC Radio 1 at Nottingham's Rock City, and they recorded several performances for *Top of the Pops* for future broadcast to promote later single releases. The mini tour concluded in America, where two special shows took place at the Wiltern Theatre in Los Angeles on the night before, and night of the album's release.

The Underground Tour was a warm-up for the second instalment of Projekt Revolution, which got under way on 9 April in University Park, Pennsylvania. Linkin Park was joined by the Swedish nu metal band Blindside, fellow nu metallers Mudvayne and hip-hop star Xzibit, although a handful of dates had to be cancelled along the way for reasons including bad weather, Chester suffering a throat infection, and scheduling conflicts due to Linkin Park filming the music video for 'Faint'. The band debuted 'Nobody's Listening' in their set, as well as the *Reanimation* version of 'P5hng Me A*wy', and although their standing could have afforded them a more elaborate stage show by now, the sextet continued to humbly perform in front of their original *Hybrid Theory* backdrop.

After Projekt Revolution, Linkin Park was already gearing up for their tour of Europe when, on 30 May, Chester was admitted to a Los Angeles hospital. The news wasn't broken by the media until five days later, but when it was, it caused alarm among fans who sought to find out the severity of the singer's condition. The reports stated Chester had experienced severe back and abdominal pain; after extensive tests, doctors believed the cause to be some kind of parasite, or an intestinal disorder. Most importantly, Chester's illness was not life-threatening. Understandably, Linkin Park had no other choice but to cancel their European run, which allowed Chester plenty of time to recover at home after his release from hospital on 10 June, and to build up his strength ahead of the band's next set of scheduled dates, which happened to be part of the super tour of 2003.

In support of Metallica's polarising eighth album *St. Anger* (those damn drums!!), the thrash metal titans launched the second edition of Summer Sanitarium in Pontiac, Michigan, on Independence Day. After Chester's hospital stay, there were fears Linkin Park would have to pull out of Summer Sanitarium, but that was not the case and the band joined the insanely star-studded line-up alongside Limp Bizkit, Deftones and Mudvayne. The band's set consisted of the same seventeen songs for each show, which now included 'Figure.09' and 'Numb', after both songs had been given their live initiations during a warm-up show at The Joint in Las Vegas on 27 June, as part of the Boost Mobile Pro of Skateboarding Championships.

Summer Sanitarium ran across America and Canada from 4 July to 10 August, and the tour gave Linkin Park their first taste of performing in stadiums. With two studio albums and a remix album already under their belts, the band decided to document their latest monumental moment by recording a live album and DVD. They may not have been the headline act, but the responses to their sets during the early part of the tour gave Linkin Park all the encouragement they required to film a couple of shows for a CD and DVD release, which dropped later in the year on 18 November under the title *Live in Texas*. The DVD was made up of concert footage from the band's consecutive shows at Houston's Reliant and Irving's Texas stadiums on 2 and 3 August, while the fully mixed and mastered audio CD contained only twelve of the songs performed during their set, with the rest being purposely held back for future release as single B-sides, or for inclusion on later *Underground* albums.

In the second half of 2003, Linkin Park returned to Europe to headline the Leeds and Reading festivals, and to play a handful of shows to partly make up for the cancellation of their previous overseas visit because of Chester's hospitalisation. Next, they flew over to Australia and then Asia, before an autumn tour began in the UK and ended in America with some radio-sponsored Christmas events. The tour cycle continued well into 2004, with an extensive North American run where Linkin Park brought along Story of the Year, Hoobastank and P.O.D. as support, and international dates including a headline spot at the UK's Download Festival, and for the first time, one-off shows in Indonesia, the Philippines, Hong Kong, Thailand and Singapore. For the year's Projekt Revolution, Linkin Park expanded the event into a fully-fledged festival, with a bigger line-up that was spread across two stages. On the Revolution Stage, Wu-Tang Clan rapper Ghostface Killah headlined, but it was newer acts such as the Welsh screamo band Funeral for a Friend, the Canadian hardcore mob No Warning, and Orange County punks Autopilot Off who thrived the most from performing to some of the biggest crowds in their careers at that point. On the main stage, ska punks Less Than Jake, who were belatedly added to the bill after Limp Bizkit reportedly refused to be the opening band, The Used, Snoop Dogg and Korn all laid waste before Linkin Park entered the fray, performing another jampacked setlist where they opened with 'Don't Stay', and ended with the now customary 'One Step Closer'. Among all the fan favourites from *Hybrid Theory* and *Meteora*, there was also room for a cover of the Nine Inch Nails song 'Wish', the *Reanimation* version of 'Wth>You', and the snappy hip hop medley of 'Step Up'/'Nobody's Listening'/'It's Goin' Down'.

As Projekt Revolution represented the final tour of the *Meteora* cycle, the final show promoting the album followed on 11 September at the Estádio do Morumbi in São Paulo, Brazil. As part of the annual Chimera Music Festival, the show was Linkin Park's biggest yet as they performed in front of approximately 80,000 people. In the space of just four years, the band had transformed from being an opening act playing in tiny clubs, into one who was regularly headlining arenas and now stadiums, and the São Paulo show brought an end to another spectacular period in Linkin Park's career.

First and foremost, they had successfully navigated the perilous obstacle that is commonly known within the music industry as 'second album syndrome', and even though *Meteora* didn't match *Hybrid Theory* in the sales department and the general consensus among fans and critics to this day still gives the debut album an edge over its follow-up, *Meteora* did earn Linkin Park their first number 1 record (it also topped at least ten other national charts, including in the UK). It had also spawned another megahit in 'Numb'. Their position among rock's elite had been confirmed, but more importantly, the fresh sounds and elements Linkin Park had incorporated into *Meteora* had opened the door to a whole world of exploration in the future.

*   *   *

On 14 June 2004, the band released the fifth and final single from *Meteora*. 'From the Inside' had failed to chart anywhere in America at the beginning of the year, and touring aside, it seemed that promotion of the second album had run its course. But as Linkin Park presented their newest batch of songs to Warner in late-2002, the band demanded that at some point, 'Breaking the Habit' had to be a single. It didn't have to be the first single or even second, it just had to be one of them.

'Breaking the Habit' is the culmination of a six-year idea Mike had, where in that time he could never get its balance right. The idea was in the lyrics, but during repeated efforts he would always deem the words too dark or melodramatic, and many a time he would put the idea on hold and focus on other songs instead. While writing for *Meteora*, Mike came up with an electronic piece that he planned to use as an interlude, but when he played it for his bandmates, he was implored to turn it into a full song. Back at home, Mike began writing some lyrics for the track, and in the space of only a couple of hours he found what he'd been searching five years for. His original idea had finally revealed itself, and it was just how he'd imagined it.

There is no need to look any further than the song's title to identify its overbearing theme, and with Chester supplying solo vocals on the track, some mistook the lyrics to have been written by him. But they weren't, and the traumatic effects of addiction and the physical and mental scars that remain thereafter, are a big part of why Chester had such a hard time recording his vocals for 'Breaking the Habit', having been through those exact same things himself. Chester found such a heavy connection to each line, and he was even reduced to tears the first time he read what Mike had written. He was aghast that his bandmate had tackled a subject that encapsulated so many, but in this instance seemed to zone in on Chester and Chester alone. Chester and Mike's personal bond had grown as strong as their professional one. The time they had spent together on endless roads and in uninterrupted skies, during one-to-one recording sessions and going late into the night in studios, or just by hanging out in a more relaxed environment, had given them plenty of time to talk, to confide in one another, and to recount stories from their past which at times revealed their deepest darkest secrets. Mike may not have even met Chester when his lyrical concept first arose in his mind, but knew him extremely well when it came to writing the final verses and chorus that would prove crucial to the song's lasting identity. They are hard-hitting and were sure to strike a nerve with many a listener, but what Mike had written came with great sensitivity, and never once were his words throwing scorn on people for their past transgressions.

Musically, 'Breaking the Habit' is the true manifestation of Linkin Park's sonic ambitions. From day one they had never been a band to conform to a single genre, and while *Meteora* generally follows the guidelines laid out by *Hybrid Theory*, all the band was searching for was that one song that allowed them a chance to break away from the sound that everyone expected of them. 'Breaking the Habit' is void of heavy guitars, and instead the finger-picked notes sway the emphasis onto the smooth but dynamic electronics. There is a digitally manipulated beat, and even live strings. Mike had written some string progressions on his keyboard, but he knew they had to coalesce with the enormity of the rest of the song. To do be able to do that, Mike turned to David Campbell, who took those keyboard parts and reworked them with cellos and violins, before bringing in ten musicians to play the parts live. The results are dramatic but enthralling, and during mixing, Linkin Park and Andy Wallace overlaid the musicians to give off the sound of an entire orchestra on the final recording.

For all its palpable differences, however, 'Breaking the Habit' still has that Linkin Park sound. Whether it was hearing the song for the first time on the album or much later on the radio, it was understandable that some were forced to do a double take, but Chester's delicate vocal soon grew familiar, and the poignant lyrics, tender melodies and effective scratches (which Joe took from the same sample that acted as the basis for 'Points of Authority') brought a further sense of awareness that 'Breaking the Habit' was indeed a Linkin Park song.

An instrumental demo titled 'Drawing' can be found on the *Underground 9.0: Demos* album, and a later version that also has Mike on vocals was included on the *Underground XIV* collection in 2014, both of which possess a distinctive element that made the rest of the band want to extend the interlude into the gem it eventually became. Even after the song was finished, it took some time for Chester to feel able to perform it live, in fact it wasn't until Linkin Park headlined the Smoke Out Festival in San Bernardino on 15 November 2003, almost eight months after *Meteora* had debuted, that 'Breaking the Habit' was given its live introduction. That didn't mean Chester didn't like the song, though. He loved it, and it would become his favourite song in the band's catalogue. 'I'm almost pissed off that we wrote it because I like it that much,' he said during an LPU chat later in 2003. 'If someone else had written it I could play it all the time, but if I do that people will think I am a narcissistic punk.'

Every music video the band had filmed thus far was distinctly different from one another. 'Crawling' and 'Numb' correlated their lyrics with equally affecting visuals, while 'One Step Closer' and 'In the End' had sub-plots that weren't so easy to decipher. All the videos did however, at one point or another feature performance shots. The video for 'Faint' stood out for its orchestrated live feel, and its clever focus on Chester's scream lyric of 'I won't be ignored'. The cameras are intentionally positioned behind the band for much of the video, which was filmed in a secret location in downtown Los Angeles. The audience is made up of a thousand raucous LPU fans who jump, mosh, scream and sing along in an almost cult-like state of worship, while their favourite band play before them on a dimly lit stage. Their silhouettes are exposed by a wall to wall set of blinding spotlights, the reasoning behind it extremely significant. The video's concept was created by Mark Romanek, which explores the frustration that inspired 'Faint' in the first place, of wanting to be acknowledged instead of feeling ignored. The 'Faint' video is a million miles away from the big budget clip of 'Somewhere I Belong', which follows a dream sequence where ordinary objects such as paintings and toys come to life, but the common ground that each video shares is in the importance of Linkin Park having a visual aspect that is equally on par with the music.

For 'Breaking the Habit', the band went all out in making its video their biggest production yet. Joe assumed the role of director, having come up with the concept that highlights the struggles people have when they are trying to break their own habits. First, he considered filming a live action video, before he decided to lean towards making a manga-like mini movie. To create the stylisation, Joe teamed up with the Japanese studio GDH, and the project was overseen by Kazuto Nakazawa, who directed the animated sequences in Quentin Tarantino's *Kill Bill: Volume 1* movie. The video's three fast-moving stories surround a crime scene where police are investigating the death of a man whose body is found on the roof of a car (later revealed to be Chester), a girl in a deeply emotional state who self-harms, and a woman who returns home to find her husband committing adultery. The video's final sequence has Linkin Park performing 'Breaking the Habit' on the same rooftop that Chester is shown to have jumped from earlier on, and with the frontman now back among the living, the performance releases some of the tension that played out in those earlier scenes. The video was a huge project to undertake when you consider 'Breaking the Habit' was the fifth single to be taken from *Meteora*. For any other band it would have felt like they were trying to flog a dead horse, but Linkin Park's belief in the song from the very beginning meant that it was never likely to have been charged with a simply constructed release.

At the VMA's in 2004, the 'Breaking the Habit' video won the Viewer's Choice Award, which underlined its popularity since first debuting on the MTV network, and with over 378 million views on YouTube to-date, it is one of Linkin Park's most popular promo clips. As a single, the song topped both the Modern and Mainstream Rock Tracks charts, and reached 20 on the Hot 100. Being able to create a song like 'Breaking the Habit' was an important moment for Linkin Park, and that people had taken it to their hearts with the same kind of adoration that 'One Step Closer' and 'In the End' were met with meant that for the first time, the band could begin to comprehend a future outside of rap rock. By the time they began work on their next album, the possibilities of which direction Linkin Park might go seemed absolutely endless.

Fig. 6

World's Collide

Thanks to their spot on Summer Sanitarium, Linkin Park were beginning to excel in the stadium environment, and while many a show on the *Meteora* cycle had featured unforgettable performances, it was the tiny stage inside the Roxy Theatre on 18 July 2004 that created another seismic moment in the band's already remarkable career.

The show didn't feel as big as it does when looking back on it today. It was, after all, just two acts from contrasting worlds playing mashups of their songs, in what was supposed to be a one-time only deal. But as the evening developed, it was clear that those worlds weren't so far apart as they first seemed. The show was intended to be the first in a running series being spearheaded by MTV, as part of what they were calling *Ultimate Mashups*. The network's idea was to bring together rock and hip-hop artists to mashup just one or two of their own songs, and then perform them live in front of an exclusive crowd and a host of TV cameras. It was a compelling concept, and MTV had more than enough pull to attract big-name artists from both genres, regardless of whether the mashups would be any good or complete clusterfucks.

At the time, mashups were becoming ever popular, almost like a viral sensation but long before the term was coined to describe a universally circulated YouTube video, an Instagram Reel, or a TikTok. As the internet and computer technology continued to expand, where the various programs and software's catered for virtually everything the consumer desired, any aspiring DJ could now turn their hand to creating remixes and mashups.

A landmark moment came in February 2004, when the producer everyone now knows as Danger Mouse released *The Grey Album*, which consisted of throwing Jay-Z's rap vocals from 2003's *The Black Album*, over music from The Beatles' 1968 double LP, universally known as *The White Album*. Danger Mouse hadn't sought permission to use the copyrighted material, as his sole intention was to create a passion project that was not meant to profit him in any way. But when he uploaded the material online, music websites soon caught wind of the album and because it was so good, they began to promote it, and various online stores even began to sell it. Music piracy was rife at the time, and *The Grey Album* became a viral sensation as its content continued to be downloaded hundreds of thousands of times on a daily basis. Whether it was his secret plan all along or not, the album put Danger Mouse on the map, and his expertise in deconstructing and re-amalgamating one, two or sometimes three tracks into one was quickly noticed by others, which in turn made Danger Mouse a highly sought after producer. Before long, he was working with the rapper Prince Po, Gorillaz and later on rock acts such as The Black Keys and the Red Hot Chili Peppers.

The response to *The Grey Album* may have proved significant in helping MTV come up with the idea of starting their own mashup show, and even though *The Black Album* was being promoted as Jay-Z's retirement album ahead of him taking up the position of president at Def Jam Recordings, the hip hop star was one of the first to be contacted by MTV to discuss his potential participation in the *Ultimate Mashups* series. When he was asked which rock band he would consider wanting to work with, he assuredly name-checked Linkin Park.

Years before, Mike spent a lot of time in his bedroom with a sampler to create his own mashups. He would fuse Depeche Mode with Wu-Tang Clan, Nine Inch Nails with the Jackson 5, and the Smashing Pumpkins with Jay-Z. He was already a big fan of Jay's work, and when the phone call came that one of his heroes wanted to work with him and his band, Mike jumped at the chance. In 2004, Jay was one of the biggest rappers on the planet, at times even being mentioned in the same breath as Tupac and Biggie when discussions arose on who was the best ever. At the same time, Linkin Park was one of the biggest rock bands in the planet, and for two artists of such stature to join forces for the very first episode of *Ultimate Mashups* could not have presented MTV with a better way to get their show off the ground.

To test the waters, Mike started creating mashup demos in Linkin Park's tour bus studio while the band was trekking across America. Not long after the release of *The Black Album*, Jay also put out an acapella version, partly so fans could embrace the depth of his lyrics more clearly, but also to encourage

DJs to use his vocals in their own mashups. Mike used those acapellas and added them to Linkin Park instrumentals, before remixing parts here and there, and looping patterns if it helped to further compliment Jay's vocal flows. Upon hearing the demos, Jay was impressed by Mike's assertiveness and production talents, and the two remained in frequent contact through email and trading files as they continued to work on the potential tracks. MTV had struck gold, but there was no way they were prepared for the sheer gravity of what Mike had in mind for the collaboration. He knew that if Jay-Z and Linkin Park created dynamite, it would be impossible for MTV to ever be able to top it. Performing one or two mashups onstage was one thing, but what if Jay-Z and Linkin Park made more, and recorded them in a studio? What if they then went and released the whole thing as an official album?

Collision Course could have been seen as a publicity stunt by two of the biggest artists in modern music, but only by those who were blissfully unaware of the credibility and work ethics that both Jay and Linkin Park shared. Since debuting with *Reasonable Doubt* in 1996, Jay had released a studio album in each calendar year up to and including 2003, and Linkin Park had done four albums in four years, if you include *Reanimation* and *Live in Texas*. In NRG Studios, there was instant chemistry between the two artists, and a lot of fun was had during the recording of *Collision Course* between 16 and 19 July, either side of the Roxy show. Brad, Chester, Dave, Joe and Rob were all into Jay's music, not necessarily on the same scale as Mike's fandom, but as the documentary that came as part of the *Collision Course* package revealed, everyone got on like a house on fire. Any egos were left at the door, which made for a courteous and light-hearted environment, but when it came to taking care of business, everyone in the room was professional and focused.

Six mashups were recorded, which was enough to comprise an EP. From Jay's side, he took three tracks from his most recent *Black Album*, and one each from the equally stellar *Vol. 2…Hard Knock Life*, *Vol.3: Life and Times of S. Carter*, and *The Blueprint* records, while Linkin Park selected their big hitters of 'One Step Closer', 'Papercut', 'In the End', 'Points of Authority', 'Faint', 'Numb', and 'Lying from You'. When mashed together, the results were rather impressive. Jay's East Coast bars, often accentuated by complex lyrical detail, double entendres and hefty doses of braggadocio, but always fuelled by the rags to riches narrative that had driven his work from the beginning, were fused with Linkin Park's intensely emotive verses and choruses. To better suit their parts alongside Jay's ruthless rapping, certain sections of Linkin Park's songs were updated for the project, like Mike's verses on 'Lying from You', 'Papercut', 'Faint', and 'In the End'. Chester re-recorded his backing vocals on 'In the End', and on the 'Papercut' chorus, before he laid down some entirely new vocals on Jay's 'Encore' track. For Jay's '99 Problems', which already had a solid rap rock crunch to it, Mike re-recorded the first verse with his own vocal, while Jay himself saw the benefit in updating his own bars on 'Jigga What'. Each of the changes gave the mashups a more coherent vibe, which allowed Linkin Park to play along to Jay's domineering leads. Alternatively, the band's heavy rock elements, those moody keyboard entries, and Joe's pulsing beats at times lead Jay's performances to sound more reflective, certainly in comparison to how he came over on his own original recordings, which makes for a more wholesome listening experience.

As interesting as the coming together of Jay-Z and Linkin Park sounded on paper, the prospect was also extremely exciting. Jay was undoubtedly the bigger name of the two, however Linkin Park's credentials were beginning to supersede their partner in crime by the time their two worlds collided. Jay had amassed an impressive eight number 1 albums, but none of them had sold anywhere close to what *Hybrid Theory* had. Furthermore, Jay had never scored a hit single of his own, only on tracks in which he'd featured, while Linkin Park had only just missed out on the summit of the Hot 100 with 'In the End'. From listening to *Collision Course* though, and watching the behind-the-scenes documentary and the Roxy performance, there was no rivalry between the two acts, nor was there any jealousy of each other's accomplishments. The mutual respect and admiration they had for one another went a long way in developing the mashups, which were mostly cohesive in their final forms, and brought to life with effortless ease. From the opening burst of 'Dirt Off Your Shoulder'/'Lying from You', to the rousing closer of 'Points of Authority'/'99 Problems'/'One Step Closer', everything Jay and Linkin Park planned for *Collision Course* had masterfully come to fruition. The fun they had in the studio filters into those recordings, and there is a swagger that melds two combustible artists into an act that sounds like they have been working together for years, before Mike's pristine production supplies the stamp of authenticity that the EP required to be taken seriously, and not just considered a publicity stunt or cash grab.

No one in the Roxy crowd knew about a prospective EP when, after Linkin Park rifled through a few of their own songs, Jay joined the band onstage to perform their six mashups. The show actually took place twice on that 18 July evening because MTV messed up the lighting set up, but no one in attendance cared if it meant they got to witness a little piece of history all over again. Despite squashing the network's hopes of ever being able to host further episodes, *Collision Course*, which wasn't released until 30 November 2004, did have MTV's seal of approval, and their '*Ultimate Mashups* Presents' sticker sits proudly on the EP's front cover. Distributed through Jay's own Roc-A-Fella label, Linkin Park's Machine Shop imprint, and also Warner and Def Jam, *Collision Course* became the first EP since Alice in Chains' *Jar of Flies* in 1994 to top the Billboard 200. In its opening week it sold over 368,000 copies in the US, and as a double platinum record, *Collision Course* stands as one of the most successful EPs of all time. The sole single from the project, 'Numb'/'Encore', followed two weeks later, and its accompanying music video contains a mashup in itself of the Roxy performance, and footage from the accompanying documentary. The track reached 20 on the Hot 100, and in the UK it obtained the unusual feat of spending the longest time in the top twenty without ever actually getting inside the top ten. For thirteen weeks it floated between those nine positions, where its peak placing of 14 matched what 'Numb' as its own song had previously achieved.

Collision Course was a rather historic release back in 2004. The majority of mashup albums that came before it had pissed off record labels and copyright holders and were relegated to bootleg status, regardless of how internet famous they became. *Collision Course*, however, was the first of its kind to combine two multiplatinum artists who had the backing of their respective labels to be able to go out and do it. With a green light, they had retrieved their original master tracks, filtered in new parts and rearranged others, and gave everything a polished and professional gleam through Mike's scrupulous production.

In 2012, Linkin Park found themselves on the end of their own unofficial mashup album, when the unknown producer Blaze Audio released the cheekily titled *Collision Course 2*. The album spans thirteen tracks and runs for fifty-five minutes, with each mashup combining a well-known song of Linkin Park's with those of the rap phenomenon Eminem. The album is brilliantly put together and it's arguably as good as Danger Mouse's *Grey Album*, although it did come at a time where even better software made it far easier to create mashups than in the years before.

The original *Collision Course* is *the* ultimate mashup album though, and it came at a time when both artists were at the peak of their powers. It was certainly a more significant release for Linkin Park, who continued to bump shoulders with the biggest names in the industry. Having people like Jay-Z wanting to work with them showed just how admired the band was outside of the rock genre and not just within it, which was a rare feat that very few bands had the chance to experience over the course of their careers. As prosperous as their union with Jay-Z had been, *Collision Course* also provided a fitting end to Linkin Park's rap rock exploits. The band wanted more, and with a whole other world of sounds and styles out there for them to experiment with, now seemed as good a time as any to draw a line under an incredible first chapter in the Linkin Park's career. What came next offered new opportunities, and the chance to expand their musical horizons in a way that no one could have ever anticipated.

Turn My Mic Up, I Got to Say Somethin'

Chester's funereal serenade of 'In this farewell, there's no blood, there's no alibi…' poignantly bridges the gap between the end of one era, and the beginning of another. The opening line of 'What I've Done', the lead single from *Minutes to Midnight*, acknowledges Linkin Park's many successes of the past, while also signifying the clean palette the band had to work from ahead of their eagerly anticipated third album.

By the time *Minutes to Midnight* finally arrived, it had been four long years since *Meteora*, where for the most part, Linkin Park as a collective retreated into the shadows after their tour cycle concluded in September 2004. The band was burnt out and in need of some deserved rest and time spent with loved ones, but for Mike, the space in his schedule meant he could finally work on his solo album. He'd considered doing something on his own for a couple of years, and in getting Fort Minor off the ground, it allowed him to fully express his love of pure hip hop. In no way did it mean he'd outgrown Linkin Park, he just wanted to explore another creative outlet, and one where he could share his own stories more thoroughly.

Released on 22 November 2005, *The Rising Tied* goes against the stereotypes of mainstream hip hop. Each song is driven by live instruments, all of which Mike played, and he created all the beats and samples too. Getting to grips with the ins and outs of the music industry had served him well, and the confidence Mike had gained meant he could take the reins and record and produce the whole thing himself. He did, however, call upon Jay-Z, who is credited as an executive producer, and Brad, who served as his A&R, for advice on which songs should make the final cut and form the most cohesive track listing. The album also features a litany of guests, all of whom Mike had met in recent years and felt comfortable in asking the likes of Styles of Beyond, Black Thought, Common, Holly Brook (AKA Skylar Grey) and others to deliver some virtuosic verse and chorus bars.

Upon its release, *The Rising Tied* received critical acclaim. No longer was Mike only being touted as the rapper guy from Linkin Park, he was now being recognised as a serious hip hop artist. 'Where'd You Go' is highlighted by a set of deeply personal lyrics written from the point of view of Mike's wife Anna, which tell of the loneliness she feels when her husband is away on tour. 'Kenji' explores the heart-rending tale of Mike's family heritage, and the racial profiling that led to his father and aunt being sent to an internment camp in the wake of the Pearl Harbor attacks in 1941. The piano-led track is hard-hitting in every sense, and none more so than in Mike's aggressive rhyming, where hints of anger and sadness help paint a vivid portrait of the desperate plight that many Japanese Americans endured during World War II. Elsewhere, lighter-hearted moments come best when they are accompanied by some bounce and swagger, like on the trash-talking battle tracks of 'Petrified', 'Cigarettes', and the previously touched upon middle finger salute of 'Get Me Gone'.

The Rising Tied peaked at 51 on the Billboard 200, which was nowhere near the heights Mike had been used to with Linkin Park, but the success of the album came in him finally being able to create his own solo record. It's made up of venomous alternative hip hop, but it also has just the right amount of reflection and poise to avoid there being any feelings of self-indulgence. Singles-wise, 'Where'd You Go' became a hit upon reaching 4 on the Hot 100, while the motivational anthem 'Remember the Name', which is tempered by some dramatic strings, went quadruple platinum thanks to its frequent use in NBA, UFC and WWE programming, as well as in multiple TV and movie trailers.

The album remains the only one to come from Mike's Fort Minor alias, which was inspired by the music of his youth. He intentionally steered clear of the pitfalls hip hop had fallen into by 2005, where it had seemingly lost some of its originality, and the new artists coming through were more reliant on a pop hook and splintering into other genres. *The Rising Tied* brought back some of hip hop's excitement and intrigue, and while the album is nowhere near perfect, it was everything Mike had intended it to be.

* * *

In 2005, Linkin Park played just two shows throughout the entire year. Early on, the band founded their Music for Relief charity, after witnessing the destruction caused by the earthquake and tsunami that struck the Indian Ocean on Boxing Day 2004. They were no strangers to doing their bit for charity at this point, as earlier in 2004 they had donated $75,000 to the Special Operations Warriors Foundation, a non-profit organisation who provided college scholarships and education counselling to children of US Armed Forces personnel killed in the line of duty. And during Projekt Revolution, $5 from every ticket sold for the Tampa date had been donated to aid those affected by Hurricane Charley, which struck Florida in the middle of August. Just a few months later, Music for Relief was set up to provide aid for survivors, to assist in disaster response, and to support long-term recovery efforts. Linkin Park had long embraced the spirit of collaboration, but launching their own charity which enabled partnerships with others was an admirable move. In four years, the band had accomplished so much and been afforded many privileges, and now they were in a position to be able to give back.

In raising money for the victims of the tsunami, benefit concerts took place at the Wiltern Theatre in LA on 17 January, and at the Arrowhead Pond in Anaheim on 18 February. The second show fell under the banner 'Music for Relief: Rebuilding Southeast Asia', in which Linkin Park performed alongside The Crystal Method, Story of the Year, and the headlining No Doubt, among others. The band's fifty-minute set consisted of twelve songs, where after playing six of their own, they brought out Jay-Z for a surprise performance of the entire *Collision Course* EP. The ecstatic crowd was a far bigger one than had been able to fit into the Roxy Theatre for that first mashup show, and even more eyes were cast on the two acts when they regrouped at the Live 8 spectacle on 2 July. To coincide with the twentieth anniversary of Live Aid, and preceding the G8 summit which was due to begin in Scotland four days later, Jay and Linkin Park were personally invited to perform at the Philadelphia event by U2 frontman and Live 8 co-organiser Bono, who had noted a distinct lack of hip hop artists on its bill. Outside the Museum of Art on the Benjamin Franklin Parkway, and in the same city where Live Aid had been held twenty years before, Linkin

Park again played their own mini set before Jay came out to perform the *Collision Course* mashups.

Live 8 bestowed Linkin Park their largest ever crowd for a single show. Being ticket-free, the event allowed people to come and go as they pleased throughout the day, and across the eight hours of Live 8, the Philadelphia crowd was estimated to be somewhere upwards of 800,000, while others reported the figure could actually have gone well over a million. It was a special show for Linkin Park; at regular occurrences the band members could been seen staring out into the endless crowd, where people were partying and supporting both the band, and the Live 8 cause, which was to raise awareness of global poverty. That Linkin Park had been headhunted to perform in Philadelphia was another notch on their belts, and their crossover appeal was now at the point where everybody seemed to know who they were. Furthermore, the band was now being recognised not only for their musical efforts, but for their humanitarian contributions too.

Since its inception, Music for Relief has responded to over thirty natural disasters and has raised millions of dollars towards relief efforts. In 2008, Linkin Park teamed up with Habitat for Humanity to assist in rebuilding homes for those affected by Hurricane Katrina, and in the aftermath of New Orleans being decimated by the historic tropical cyclone in late-August 2004, Chester jumped on a rerecording of Mötley Crüe's classic 1985 ballad 'Home Sweet Home', which was released as a benefit single to help raise funds for the city's victims. On 10 September, ReAct Now concerts were also held across the US to support the relief efforts of the Salvation Army, American Red Cross, and America's Second Harvest, and although Chester had been due to perform at the Los Angeles event, he decided to fly to Nashville and perform with the hair metal legends, and to record vocals on the updated 'Home Sweet Home' at Northstar Studios. He and the Crüe then moved on to Ocean Way Studios, and with the assistance of a twenty-six-person gospel choir and string section, Chester laid down a haunting vocal that embodied the despair that was being felt by the entire population of New Orleans.

* * *

By the summer of 2005, Linkin Park should have been preparing to begin work on their next album. They had plenty of stems of ideas dating back to the *Meteora* cycle, and with a move away from rap rock already predetermined, the album was going to be their most important yet. Instead, they spent the rest of the year at loggerheads with Warner Bros. Records.

The band's charitable contributions just about provided a positive deflection on everything that was going on behind the scenes, where in May, the Warner Music Group launched a $750 million Initial Public Offering (IPO). The company wanted to sell shares to raise capital, and to cut around $250 million in costs, which spelt trouble for the artists on Warner's roster, who stood to make not a single cent in the revenue share. Linkin Park spoke out the loudest, and made their frustrations clear from the beginning, as they felt Warner's move would mean all the band's future work wouldn't be so efficiently marketed and promoted. The final straw came when they were asked to perform at the New York Stock Exchange to celebrate the public stock offering, where it seemed they were being used as a pawn to attract potential investors. In a phone call with the *New York Times* who were reporting on the developing story, Brad spoke of how being asked to play the show exemplified just how out of touch Warner was with Linkin Park. 'It doesn't make any sense to us why we would play a show at the New York Stock Exchange,' he said. 'I don't know what was going through their minds.'

After the band went public in declaring their desire to sever all ties with Warner, despite them still having four albums left on their existing deal, Warner and Linkin Park entered into negotiations. With the talent agency The Firm fighting their corner, Linkin Park demanded a $60 million advance, and they proposed a joint venture deal in which they would split their profits instead of receiving royalties. Warner fired back with a counteroffer of a new five-album deal, worth $3 million per album. Linkin Park stuck to their principles over profit; they had made their record label a lot of money in recent years, even after the difficult beginnings in which they had their creative freedom stifled, and of course there was the unsubtle plot to oust Mike before the ink on his contract had dried. Linkin Park, like every artist on Warner's roster, deserved to be appropriately compensated for their art.

Eventually, an agreement was reached in December 2005, and when it looked like the band would indeed be moving on, a press release confirmed that Linkin Park had signed a new five-album contract, with an increased royalty rate estimated to be around 20 per cent. And for their next album, the band would receive a $15 million advance. That no other Warner artist received a similar offer appeared to emphasise the sheer pull that Linkin Park had at the time, and having the balls to stand up to their bosses and fight their own corner ultimately paid off. They might not have secured a win in the profit-sharing stakes, but they had successfully navigated a fraught situation that wasted so much of everyone's time; with the drama over, they could now turn their attention back to the music, and that all important third album.

*   *   *

'It doesn't sound like rap rock,' said Rick Rubin, when confidently sharing his thoughts on *Minutes to Midnight* ahead of its release. Linkin Park spent over fourteen months writing and recording their third album, having enlisted Rick, a master producer, to create an atmosphere that challenged the band in different ways. This time they had no creative boundaries, just a freedom that let them go in whichever direction they pleased. There was just one rule Rick demanded Linkin Park abide by: do not fall back into the past.

Rick Rubin had done it all, long before he was asked to co-produce *Minutes to Midnight* alongside Mike. From popularising hip hop in the '80s to reviving rock and metal in the '90s, Rick had worked with everyone from the Beastie Boys and Run-D.M.C. to Slayer and the Red Hot Chili Peppers. By the time Linkin Park came calling, he'd also steered the nu metal acts System of a Down and American Head Charge to proverbial greatness, having produced their early records and signing both bands to his American Recordings label. When it came to working with Linkin Park in 2006, Rick was well aware the band was done with the nu metal sound that had brought them great success, and his encouragement in keeping them on a forward path was vital in the band being able to capture the atmospheric and progressive nature that courses through their third opus.

Minutes to Midnight was predominantly recorded at Rick's famous Laurel Canyon mansion in the Santa Monica mountains. The location offered a new kind of working environment for Linkin Park, who were no longer stuck within the suffocating confines of a traditional recording studio and cut off the rest of the world. Instead, the band was relaxed, and the independence they had in being able to roam The Mansion and its grounds meant they could let those creative inspirations come to them in their own time. And whenever they required a little pick me up, all they had to do was stare out at Los Angeles beneath them, a city that not too long ago had taken Linkin Park to its heart and embraced the band as native sons.

The finishing touches to the album were done at the usual haunt of NRG, well over a year after the band had begun to explore their close to 150 song ideas. Many of them had started off as individual seeds, created by each member who, after Rick supplied them with hard drives and Pro Tools rigs, recorded their ideas in their home studios. Previously, they had preferred to perfect a song musically before adding the vocals, but Rick had them laying down rough mixes with a partial vocal, or even just a hum or a scat, to form a base point. If the track sounded promising then Linkin Park would continue to evolve it, and if it didn't, it was scrapped on the spot. Rick repeatedly impressed on the band the importance of making music that was exciting to *them*. It didn't matter what kind of style they experimented with, or how the music sounded, nor whether their fans would seize it with the same infatuation they had for 'In the End', or 'Numb'. Linkin Park could have written another *Hybrid Theory* or *Meteora* in their sleep, but they had really come of age in the years since and things that didn't matter to them before mattered to them now. It's partly why *Minutes to Midnight* was such an interesting album to categorise upon its release, because every song sounds completely different to the next. Regardless, they still have that unequivocal Linkin Park feel to them, and it's a more thoughtful Linkin Park, who were now exploring a wider array of themes in their songs and lyrics.

Personally, the band continued to search for that fine line between a healthy family life, and being part of one of the biggest bands on the planet. They had wives, partners, children, and in Chester's case he'd recently started his life over again. On New Years Eve 2005, the singer married Talinda Bentley, a former Playboy model turned veterinary student, within months of the couple first meeting. By the middle of 2006, they had already welcomed a son and adopted another into their quickly expanding family, and the stars, it seemed, had realigned for Chester after a difficult period. By the end of the *Meteora* cycle, Chester's drinking and drug intake had spiralled out of control, which played a big part in his and Samantha's separation and eventual divorce. His relationship with his bandmates had also deteriorated, and the downtime after *Meteora* didn't do Chester any favours whatsoever, where in the small Santa Monica apartment he was now occupying, the singer entered a sustained period of self-destruction. The inspiration behind some of Linkin Park's biggest songs, like 'Crawling', had come from Chester's past battles with addiction and depression, and now those same unhealthy traits were threatening to undo all the hard work he'd put into trying to commit to a life of sobriety. A great deal of drinking followed before Chester finally found the courage to seek help, having been faced with an intervention from his band of brothers and who supported him during counselling sessions and a stint in rehab. Having a new family gave Chester all the ammunition he needed in recommitting to sobriety, and by the time Linkin Park and Jay-Z was collecting their Best Rap/Sung Collaboration Grammy for 'Numb'/'Encore' at the 2006 awards ceremony, where they also performed the mashup alongside Paul McCartney (the performance incorporated the Beatles' 'Yesterday' into the mashup), Chester looked back to his best, with renewed vigour and a lust for life.

Moments of reflection from that time in Chester's life are found on *Minutes to Midnight*, with further themes inspired by the band's eyes being opened to a world that appeared to be going backwards rather than showing any signs of progression. Their charitable work with Music for Relief, and their involvement in Live 8 had awoken a new perspective, and now Linkin Park was using their music to bring more attention to things they felt so strongly about. Throwing in some politically charged lyrics stemmed from a collective frustration with their own nation's incompetent regime, where for the first time Mike and Chester incorporated some sporadic swearing to highlight their vexation. It meant that *Minutes to Midnight* became the first Linkin Park album to feature a 'Parental Advisory' sticker on its cover.

Minutes to Midnight slots nicely into the alternative rock category, where an emphasis on heaviness is replaced by subtle melodies to create sprawling moods. There are guitar solos, extended epics, and of the twelve tracks that form the standard release, only two feature Mike's rapping. In fact, the album finds Mike recounting on his renowned hip hop style and moving into cleaner singing, and all these firsts are what make *Minutes to Midnight* such an interesting and refreshing album.

'What I've Done' was the final song to be composed and recorded, and remarkably it came together in only two days. It's the big anthem Linkin Park was searching for, and one that binds the album together. The song is nowhere as intense as 'One Step Closer' and 'Somewhere I Belong', the previous albums' lead singles, but 'What I've Done' still has that big time feel to it. The guitars emit a classic rock vibe, and they are loud when they need to be before they retreat to allow the introspective nature of Chester's ode-to-the-past lyrics to take centre stage. The spooky piano melody provides a mournful sway, before a trademark Linkin Park chorus puts forward the song's hit credentials. 'What I've Done' is fitting of the stadiums the band would soon be calling a regular hunting ground, and its hook brings a degree of familiarity among a wider sea of change, where any other song being put forward as the first single could have sounded too disjointed in unveiling Linkin Park's ambitious makeover.

The lasting memories of *Minutes to Midnight*, however, come from the exploration of new styles, which would have been impossible to predict just a couple of years before as Linkin Park continued to rap rock their way around the world. The solemn 'Leave Out All the Rest', which explores humility, is built around delicate strings and spacious synth waves which allow the song's sumptuous guitar melodies to blossom at their own pace. Chester's lyrics, which ask for help and forgiveness, provide a heaviness that the music is never programmed to orchestrate, while 'Shadow of the Day' shares a similarly bleak outlook, but also in a way Linkin Park had never previously utilised. Feeding off an ethereal and rhythmic electronic undercurrent and a soothing bass drive, the song revels in Chester's stunningly fragile vocal. His lyrics, which contemplate how one day the sun will set for all of us, highlights the emotional maturity and insightfulness he and his band are now bringing to the table, where each guitar note, every aching orchestral flourish, and Brad's first guitar solo on a Linkin Park track, transcribe the sentiment of the contemplative lyrics into spine-tingling music.

Songs like 'Leave Out all the Rest', 'Shadow of the Day', and most certainly the epic masterpiece of 'The Little Things Give You Away', are unlike anything Linkin Park had written before. They didn't want to repeat history, nor make a trilogy of the same kind of album. There were some reservations that the LPU might shun their latest repertoire of songs, but those fans were also growing up, and some of them too were now outgrowing nu metal. In recent years, the movement had dramatically receded from the mainstream, and many of its leading bands were expanding on their own sound and moving further away from the angsty rap metal or groove-based music with which they had emerged onto the scene. The shift in these bands' dynamics lent support to the idea that there was always room for creative manoeuvre, and moreover, they and Linkin Park owed it to themselves to write the kind of songs that pushed them to greater lengths, in order to achieve ultimate fulfilment.

'The Little Things Give You Away', the album's stunning closing track, is the epitome of Linkin Park wanting to push themselves to greater lengths, and in its six-plus minute running amasses the most pristine combination of everything they set out to accomplish on *Minutes to Midnight*. The song was born from Rob's drum seed, before Mike wrote the tender but tense acoustic guitar verse leads, and Brad the piano parts. Chester's vocal, which favours a range of thrilling harmonies over the antagonistic screams and snarls he more commonly relied on in the past to get his points across, hover over the acoustic guitar and a palpitating beat. The singer taps into the frustration he felt in the aftermath of Hurricane Katrina, and launches a direct attack on George W. Bush and his administration's failure in appropriately responding to the disaster. The then-US president also bears the brunt of Linkin Park's ire on the album's most savage track, 'No More Sorrow', where the use of an EBow in the intro signals the warning alarm for a vicious tirade of pummelling guitars, wiry bass, and a crushing drumbeat. On 'Hands Held High', Mike investigates the effects of war and misplaced power, and while the song feels primed for a melodic vocal, it features one of only two rap performances on the entire album, which Mike delivers with the same passion and intensity that he lent to the Fort Minor track 'Kenji'. Mike has the incredible ability of investing in every word of every bar or line he raps or sings, and on 'Hands Held High', where the full-band gang vocal of 'Amen' makes for a powerful and collective stance in itself, the true effectiveness of his delivery comes in the reverberating pipe organ and marching snare that reinforces his performance.

While *Minutes to Midnight* was being created, the Iraq War continued to amble on into a third year and by now, Bush's verbal slip-ups ('Bushisms', if you will) had turned his tenure of power into a bit of a joke. But where 'No More Sorrow' and 'Hands Held High' say what many American's were thinking at that time, 'The Little Things Give You Away' acts as a direct letter from Linkin Park that highlights what they felt was one of Bush's biggest failings. The abject disappointment in Chester's wounded vocal was inspired from personally visiting New Orleans a year after Katrina, only to find the response to the disaster had been desperately insufficient. The lyrics paint Chester as one of the city's victims, where the chilling line of 'All you've ever wanted, was someone to truly look up to you/and six feet underwater, I do' is tinged with the same sadness that had served to drive his guest vocal on 'Home Sweet Home' some eighteen months prior. 'The Little Things Give You' grows in stature with every ensuing segue, and after its mood-altering synth breakdown, Brad's emotional guitar solo steers the track towards to its big finale, where the eruption of an atmospheric wall of sound brings *Minutes to Midnight* to its colossal climax. In covering such a theme, the instrumentation could easily have been fraught with danger, but instead Linkin Park employ their newfound control to exude their emotions with a richness that lands a punch equally as big as any heavy riff or vicious scream could have achieved.

Elsewhere on the album, Chester broaches his failed marriage on the musically upbeat 'In Pieces', which features an unexpected reggae or ska-like staccato guitar riff and another dazzling guitar solo from Brad. On the pop-tinged 'Valentines Day', which finds Chester reflecting on just how off course his life became after he and Samantha unceremoniously parted ways, peaks with an emotional burst of melodic rock, before the band favourite 'In Between' thrives off its sparse production, and was voted onto *Minutes to Midnight* over songs containing far bigger arrangements. The apology letter track is built around some more sorrowful strings and a hazy sample, and it's the first in which Mike assumes the lead vocal, where his honesty was deemed far more suited over Chester's own take in seeking to preserve the song's original integrity.

Among all the new styles and sounds explored by Linkin Park, there are still flourishes of their past iteration. 'Given Up' is powered by the same kind of raw and punky aggression as 'Faint', which supports the disgust in Chester's rabid vocal as he revisits his recent troubles with addiction. In a moment of further exasperation during the song's recording, and at a time when the band was struggling to come up with an idea for its punchy bridge, Mike had Chester repeatedly draw out his anguished cry of 'Put me out of my misery'. This culminated in an irate Chester letting out the most ferocious scream you're likely to ever hear, and one that lasts for a staggering eighteen seconds. In the fullness of time, the scream sealed Chester's legendary status, and even though it had been completely inadvertent, Mike thought it was the most epic thing he'd ever heard. He was adamant that the scream had to remain on the track, and while Chester realised he would have to do it during every live performance of the song moving forward, the scream serves as one of the album's moments, and one of Chester's most renowned vocal accomplishments of his entire career.

One of the main priorities Linkin Park had when working on *Minutes to Midnight* was to simply enjoy the process, and nowhere is that more evident than on 'Bleed It Out', which withstands the pressure of its aggressive overtone. The track was recorded towards the end of the album sessions, and it projects the party atmosphere in the studio where the band's make-up team, photographers, and security were all invited in to record themselves cheering in tandem. 'Bleed It Out' carries the same structure as many of Linkin Park's rap rock-orientated songs and provides another brief period of familiarity on an album that was always going to shirk the responsibility of having to revisit past glories. But 'Bleed It Out' is a different kind of rap rock song; Mike felt its guitars sounded like AC/DC, its beat was reminiscent of Motown, and the groove sounded a little like the Rolling Stones. He also described the song as being the most difficult he'd ever written for the band, because of the endless rewrites of the lyrics. Until now, Mike and Chester's words had never been scrutinised by their bandmates, but another idea of Rick Rubin's on how to switch things up involved everyone congregating in a room inside The Mansion to go over everything the duo had written. It was a particularly unsettling exercise for Chester, because as hard as it was for him to channel his past and put his feelings and experiences down on paper, to have them critically evaluated in a team meeting felt awkward for him. This new way wasn't necessarily the right or wrong way for the band to conduct their business, but if nothing else it gave them a new perspective in how to involve everyone, and make sure they were comfortable in standing behind the lyrics. 'Here we go for the hundredth time, hand grenade pins in every line', raps Mike straight out of the gate, the lyric shaded with frustration and no doubt a touch of sarcasm too, while Linkin Park's maintenance team continue to cheer in the background as the *Minutes to Midnight* sessions drew to a triumphant close.

*   *   *

'I think the title really captured how we were feeling and where we were going in so many different ways,' Chester told *The Star* in April 2007. He was speaking about how naming Linkin Park's third album proved harder than the band first imagined, until Chester watched a TV programme about the Doomsday Clock one evening. First devised in 1947 to represent the perceived threat level of a global catastrophe, which would occur when the clock struck midnight, Chester relating *Minutes to Midnight* with the Doomsday Clock may have seemed a tad overdramatic initially, but you can see why he drew certain parallels between the two.

With the album and an altered perspective, Linkin Park used their status as certified rock gods to not only do what they wanted stylistically, but to deliver an important message that came with a stark warning and a pledge for societal change. Upon their unveiling, the sonically disparate trio of 'No More Sorrow', 'Hands Held High', and 'The Little Things Give You Away' became profound moments in the band's history, because no longer were they solely speaking of their own turmoil, now they were tackling societal issues, and casting a spotlight on the state of humanity on both a large and intimate scale. It was unlikely their messages would reach the people who needed to hear them most, namely the president of the United States of America, but Linkin Park at least carried enough clout for their concerns to be taken seriously by those who did choose to listen. Released on 14 May 2007, *Minutes to Midnight* sold around 623,000 copies in America in its first week and went straight to the top of the Billboard 200. It also went to number 1 in the UK, and on countless other international charts. The album was also the first in which all its singles ('What I've Done', 'Bleed It Out',

01. Chester and Mike, the ultimate vocal combination, at Rock im Park 2014. (*Wikimedia Commons. Photo: Stefan Brendig*)

02. Linkin Park, live in Macau in 2009. (*Wikimedia Commons. Photo: Jase Lam*)

03. Joe Hahn, DJ extraordinaire. (*Wikimedia Commons. Photo: Rebirth Wand*)

04. Linkin Park, onstage in 2013. (*Wikimedia Commons. Photo: Chealse Vo*)

05. Dave and Chester, front and centre, live in Berlin in 2010. (*Wikimedia Commons. Photo: Chiragdude*)

06. Brad and Mike, guitar slaying Rock im Park in 2014. (*Wikimedia Commons. Photo: Stefan Brendig*)

07. Chester Bennington. An icon in his element.
(*Wikimedia Commons. Photo: Jakub Janecki*)

08. Dave, bringing the bass. (*Wikimedia Commons. Photo: Stefan Brendig*)

09. Mike taking the lead at the o2 Arena in London in 2017. (*Wikimedia Commons. Photo: Drew de F Fawkes*)

10. Joe conducting the crowd in Singapore in 2011. (*Wikimedia Commons. Photo: suran 2007*)

11. Brad, ear cans and all, in London in 2014. (*Wikimedia Commons. Photo: Drew de F Fawkes*)

12. Mike on piano duty in Buenos Aries in 2012. (*Wikimedia Commons. Photo: Noranja*)

13. Rob supplying the rhythm and groove in Stockholm in 2007.
(Wikimedia Commons. Photo: Rickard Laurin)

14. Brad, Mike, and Dave, paying tribute to Chester at the Hollywood Bowl on 27 October 2017. (*Wikimedia Commons. Photo: SuperVirtual*)

15. Linkin Park, with Emily and Colin, press photo upon their triumphant return in 2024. (*Wikimedia Commons. Photo: James Minchin III*)

16. Emily and Mike, instant chemistry, at the o2 Arena in London in September 2024. (*Wikimedia Commons. Photo: Luca Dell'Orto*)

'Shadow of the Day', 'Given Up', and 'Leave Out All the Rest') charted on the Hot 100, with 'What I've Done' performing the best in debuting as high as 7 on the Hot 100.

Minutes to Midnight has perhaps aged more gracefully than any other Linkin Park album. The songs were built to last forever, and in retrospect, the themes the band cover on the album are as relevant today as they were back in 2007. From the very beginning, Linkin Park has always demonstrated the ability to change people's lives with their music, but on *Minutes to Midnight* it was their voices that were heard louder than ever before as they issued some of the most powerful and pertinent statements of their entire career.

Intermission

Sean Smith (The Blackout)

In 2003, the post-hardcore outfit The Blackout formed in Merthyr Tydfil, Wales. With the release of their debut album, *We Are the Dynamite*, in 2007, the six-piece became one of the hottest bands in the UK rock scene, and it was during that album cycle that The Blackout received the call to join Linkin Park on five European dates in the summer of 2008. Interviewed especially for this book, the band's co-vocalist Sean Smith, discusses just how influential Linkin Park and *Hybrid Theory* was to him when growing up, and to The Blackout in their formative years, while also looking back on those European tour dates, of which their show in Greece was particularly eventful.

As a kid, I was into hard house and happy hardcore, before I found Stereophonics, who were based around seven minutes from where I lived. Then I came across Lostprophets and Limp Bizkit, and they changed my entire view on music. I fell in love with nu metal. And how could you not fall in love with Linkin Park? *Hybrid Theory* was a fucking unbelievable record, a wall to wall banger. Every song was fantastic, and I remember being blown away by it the first time I heard it.

I think what set *Hybrid Theory* apart was its phenomenal songwriting throughout. There's not a skip on it, and at the time nu metal was so hit and miss with albums that had a couple of good singles, and then you would have bonkers shit that was obviously just filler. A lot of nu metal albums for me kind of fell apart after four or five songs, but *Hybrid Theory* was punch after punch after punch of fantastic songwriting, brilliant melodies and great aggression. I was also really drawn to the band through their lyrics, which perfectly encapsulated mine and many millions of other people's teenage and early twenties' angst. They were so poignant, and we'd all had similar feelings to the lyrics on Linkin Park's records.

I've enjoyed everything the band has ever done, and I understood why they would keep changing up their sound because the term 'nu metal', like the term 'emo', has a derogatory lick to it. Linkin Park shifted away from nu metal because it became tarnished and diluted by a load of crap bands later on, but Linkin Park was some of the best writers of nu metal and I enjoyed *Meteora* as well, but I completely understood why they moved away from their original style on *Minutes to Midnight*, and it worked for them. For me, they've never put out a bad record, and even when an album perhaps wasn't what you wanted it to be, it's easy to look back now and realise it was actually exactly what it was supposed to be.

Linkin Park influenced so many bands who came out after them, and they still influence newer bands coming out today. Everyone in The Blackout were nu metal fans first, and when we originally started out before we became The Blackout, I was DJing (I've always loved DJs in bands, and when I heard Mr Hahn's work on *Hybrid Theory*, it blew me away), and I was also the screamer. I was basically Mr Hahn but with Chester's screams. We're a dual vocal band with a bit of singing, a bit of screaming, and now and again a bit of rapping as well, which is all very reminiscent of Linkin Park. I don't think our sound made it blatantly obvious that we were influenced by them, but we definitely were. We just loved them, and I still love them to this day.

In June 2008, The Blackout jumped on five dates of Linkin Park's European tour promoting *Minutes to Midnight*. We were so excited that we got lots and lots of merchandise printed, and of all the five dates we worked out we probably played to something like 150,000 people, and we sold just fourteen T-shirts. That was the power of Linkin Park, the fact that the fans were only there for them. When we were offered the shows, I remember our booking agent saying, 'It's Linkin Park's first ever gig in Greece', and I was thinking, 'A club show with Linkin Park, this will be fucking amazing. I can't believe I get to do this!', and when we turned up it was an 18,000 capacity open air festival site. That band was just massive everywhere.

We couldn't believe we got asked to play, and we were chuffed to do it. We played in Spain, Lithuania, Latvia, Greece and Germany, and we had a great time. The Linkin Park fans were awkward with us at first, and in Greece a couple of people were throwing plastic bottles at us, so after the song I said, 'Listen, if you want to hit us, you've got more chance if you all throw them at the same time! For this next song, for one song only, if you want to throw a bottle, throw a bottle', and I spent three and a half minutes basically being a goalkeeper to my drummer, palming bottles over his head. At one point I remember looking over at my guitarist at the perfect moment that half a bottle full of water hit his guitar and sent the water directly up into his face, and I was like, 'Yes! This is amazing!'. At another point when we were playing the Greece show, and when I'm having fun, sometimes I'll spit onstage, I turned to my right, spat, and in slow motion I saw my spit cartwheeling through the air towards Chester's wife, who was watching us from the side of the stage. Luckily for me it dipped at the last moment and landed on the floor in front of her. I thought we'd ruined our own tour, but I looked up and she was smiling, and I thought, 'Thank god for that!'. I also got to meet Chester backstage in Greece when he came and thanked us for being there, and I was thinking, 'Don't be stupid will you, I would've pulled my arm off to be here.'

Linkin Park was fantastic to us, and I have a lot of respect for that band. I think we saw Mike out and about now and again but it was very rare to see the other guys, however Chester made a point of coming to see us and say hello. They had Linkin Park World backstage, where you had to be in Linkin Park or have passes to get into that area, and we had to walk around it to get to our dressing room. That's how I ended up meeting Pharrell Williams, because our dressing rooms were like portacabins and it was The Blackout next to N.E.R.D., and then across from us was Ville Valo's band, HIM.

That tour and Linkin Park's performances was the first time I thought, 'Oh, this is another level, this is a step up from everything I'd seen previously.' They were great live, they always have been, and even just watching their crew during soundcheck was interesting. I was so into the band that I just wanted to see how the workings of everything went on, and most nights they let us watch from either the side of the stage, or at the front. Linkin Park were just powerhouses. Hit after hit after hit. And Chester's voice was absolutely fucking incredible. Literally one of the greatest vocalists to have ever committed to record, and who was just as good live. Linkin Park was an absolutely enthralling band.

When Chester passed away, I was going through a dark time myself. The Blackout had ended, and I was kind of lost in a depression. Hearing that someone you look up to and respect goes and does something like that makes you question your own life really. I know we don't know what everyone's going through behind closed doors, but to people on the outside, that's the singer from one of the biggest bands in the world, like, if it can affect him, why isn't Sean – formerly of The Blackout, who is now a nobody because I've just spent the best part of twenty years making this band, only for it to fail… what am I doing?

Luckily, I kind of got through my own issues, but I just remember being devastated by Chester's death. Generally, the whole world stood still when they received the news. It was just a shock to everyone, and instantly we went back and listened to *Hybrid Theory*, and if you look at 'One Step Closer', Chester was telling us from day one how he felt. It's mad to look back at all his lyrics now and be like, 'Wow, this almost feels like a cry for help that we all ignored because, maybe the music was too good?' I felt like the whole world let him down. I think some people thought it was just an angsty act to sell records, and then it turns out it wasn't, and we all should've done more. I don't know what that 'more' is, but I feel like he was let down by the whole world.

Chester was a pivotal voice and frontman in our scene, from fashion to the way he sang, to the way he screamed, to the way he jumped off drum risers. People were ripping him off around the world. He's the one that loads of people wanted to be like, and I don't know if there's another vocalist in nu metal who was as influential as Chester Bennington was to the world. There wasn't another vocalist who was copied as much, loved as much, and revered as much as Chester. Often imitated but never duplicated.

Fig. 8

Across This New Divide

'I am Optimus Prime, and I send this message so that our pasts will always be remembered. For in those memories, we live on.' As the end credits were set to roll on the second instalment of Michael Bay's live action *Transformers* movie franchise, the supreme commander of the Autobots in their battle with the Decepticons' enduring speech is played out over futuristic-sounding synths, and an ascending drum pattern. The music sounded spacious and rather saturnine, and it sounded extremely familiar.

'New Divide' had arrived two weeks before *Revenge of the Fallen* stormed global box offices. After 'What I've Done' had successfully driven the first *Transformers* epic curtain call in 2007, Linkin Park was asked to contribute to the explosive sequel. 'New Divide' was specifically recorded for *Revenge of the Fallen*, in what was a rare example of the band writing a song that fitted a pre-existing story, while also working out how to maintain the spirit of that story by staying true to their own intentions. In places, 'New Divide' and 'What I've Done' sound alike, chiefly in the delivery of Chester's soaring and melodic vocal, although the later track's prominent rock edge is far heavier than its predecessors. 'New Divide' was designed to match the intensity of the film it was promoting, and along with its mighty hook and lyrics that speak of washing memories clean to then start afresh, the thick layers of synths tie in with Brad's punchy guitars and Rob's looser drumming to create a fascinating sonic texture. There's even a rather mechanical-sounding breakdown that was intentionally crafted to emulate the transforming effect the franchise has been centred on since its animated inception in 1984, and it provides the latest radical shift in Linkin Park's electronic capabilities.

The power of 'New Divide' is also transmitted into the movie's score, where Steve Jablonsky incorporated some of the song's elements into other musical pieces, such as 'Nest'. And Linkin Park's involvement didn't stop there; on 22 June 2009 they were invited to perform a special concert outside the Mann's Village Theater in Westwood, immediately after the venue had hosted the film's US premiere. In front of a close-knit audience who'd either won tickets to the show via KROQ radio, or obtained them through the LPU, Linkin Park's six-song set began just after 10pm and concluded with an incredible first live performance of 'New Divide'.

Other big name artists were reportedly considered to contribute a song to spearhead *Revenge of the Fallen*, but when Linkin Park presented 'New Divide' to Michael Bay, they were confident that their cut had the winning formula. The band's first standalone single was an instant hit and went straight in at 6 on the Hot 100, which at the time was their highest ever debut on the chart. The song was just huge everywhere, and that first performance of 'New Divide' as part of a mini street party on the corners of Le Conte and Braxton was filled with so much energy, that it confirmed the song wasn't just a smash hit single, but that it was already well on its way to becoming an all-time great in Linkin Park's catalogue.

*   *   *

By now, the tour cycle for *Minutes to Midnight* was long over. Linkin Park had been all over Europe, Australia, New Zealand, and in America they had revived Projekt Revolution after a two-year hiatus. For the first time, the spectacle was taken over to Europe for four dates in June 2008, where the UK leg at the Milton Keynes National Bowl was filmed and later released as a live album and DVD, titled *Road to Revolution*.

Before Linkin Park resumed work on their next album, they were requested to do one more tour to further promote 'New Divide'. Its immense popularity in the second half of 2009 showed no signs of wavering, and of the seventeen shows that made up the unofficially dubbed 'International Tour', or the 'New Divide Tour' to some, six of those dates were notable for Chester pulling double duty. It had taken him four years to finally get his side-project fully in motion, from its early inception as Snow White Tan in 2005, to the full awakening of Dead by Sunrise in the middle of 2009. During the early stages of writing for *Minutes to Midnight*, Chester came up with some ideas that weren't a stylistic fit with Linkin Park, but he liked them enough to consider them for a potential solo venture. Chester's preliminary song ideas were written on an acoustic guitar, before they would then be transformed into full-on rock tracks. Snow White Tan, as it was known at the time, was an avenue that gave Chester full creative licence to further explore and share his own feelings by putting them to music that had the same grunge, punk and new wave aesthetics that had inspired him over the years. 'There was a lot of freedom in the fact these were my songs and this was my thing,' he told ARTISTdirect in October 2009, preceding Dead by Sunrise's debut album, *Out of Ashes*. By the time the album was recorded, Chester had a full band to supply the wall of guitars, driven beats and subtle swathes of electronics that were required to bolster a track. In bringing his acoustic demos to life, Chester worked with Ryan Shuck and Amir Derakh, his close friends since the early days when both Linkin Park and Orgy were coming up and taking the nu metal movement by storm. Post-Orgy, Ryan and Amir had reinvented themselves under the name Julien-K, an electronic rock outfit of which Chester was a big fan. An earlier version of the Dead by Sunrise album was recorded and shelved when Chester returned to Linkin Park for *Minutes to Midnight*, but in July 2008, the side-project was woken from its slumber. Alongside Chester, Ryan and Amir, Dead by Sunrise's line-up was completed by Antony Valcic on keys and synths, Brandon Belsky on bass, and Elias Andra on drums, and after being recorded and mixed in the first quarter of the year, *Out of Ashes* was released in October 2009 via Warner Bros. Records.

By then, Dead by Sunrise had already sewn their live seeds on six of Linkin Park's summer 2008 tour dates. Mike was a big supporter of the band, and of Chester for doing something of this own, and he invited Dead by Sunrise to jump on stage during Linkin Park's encore break to play a mini set. It was impossible for fans to react to Dead by Sunrise with the same excitement they had for Linkin Park because at the time, *Out of Ashes* hadn't been released. But what was apparent in Chester's vocal performance, and how he commanded the stage and crowds during those short sets, was that the frantic grungy jousts of 'Crawl Back In', 'Fire', and 'My Suffering' hadn't just stemmed from a side-project that fed a new creative outlet, but each song was part of Chester's ongoing healing process.

Those songs, and the others that make up *Out of Ashes*, are more straightforward in their approach to virtually any Linkin Park song, but that is exactly how Chester wanted them to be. There are strong flashes of Stone Temple Pilots and Nirvana during the heavier moments, complete with grit, determination, and a lethal dose of punk attitude. When given the room to glisten, the electronic elements evoke The Cure and Depeche Mode, while the vulnerability of 'Too Late', and the stunning love letter to Talinda, 'Give Me Your Name', beautifully warp under the pressure of Chester's fragile vocal.

Out of Ashes, both figuratively and musically, finds Chester overcoming the self-destructive pattern in which he was fully immersed at the peak of his post-*Meteora* relapse. The album is a kind of memoir put to music, in which its themes and lyrics overwhelmingly explore addiction, lost love, new love and depression. At a time when it still felt taboo for men to openly discuss their struggles with mental health, Chester continued to use the platform he'd made for himself with Linkin Park to lay his cards on the table and let the whole world in on his feelings and thought processes.

The one and only Dead by Sunrise album didn't set the charts alight (it peaked at 29 on the Billboard 200 and then promptly plummeted), but the goal for Chester had never been about achieving mainstream success with the project. He already had that with Linkin Park, and then some. Chester was aware that the ideas he had for the songs weren't suited for Linkin Park, but it didn't matter because he was finally in a place where he could branch out and go it alone. *Out of Ashes* was the result, and the collection of songs provided the therapy Chester required to maintain some distance from his turbulent past, while also enabling him the strength to keep moving forwards. No hit single or certified album could have given Chester that same sense of emotional release.

Fig. 9

Try to Catch Up Motherfucker

For all the success Linkin Park had experienced with *Hybrid Theory*, *Meteora* and *Minutes to Midnight*, none of those albums were met with the same critical acclaim as *A Thousand Suns*. The band's fourth opus, released in September 2010, was praised by journalists for its ambitious material and its unique genre-bending approach. So, if *A Thousand Suns* received such universal approval from those whose jobs it was to provide unbiased opinions, why did the album have such a polarising effect on Linkin Park's own fans?

The catalyst for this division began with, ironically, 'The Catalyst'. The track was released a few weeks before *A Thousand Suns*, and it could not have been any farther away from how Linkin Park had sounded a decade prior, or even three years prior in all fairness. *Minutes to Midnight* presented a huge departure from the rap rock of *Hybrid Theory* and *Meteora*, but its foundations were at least still built around rock. 'The Catalyst', however, which almost suffocates under the weight of progressive electronica, was a lot harder to digest for some.

As *Minutes to Midnight* neared its completion, the band realised they still needed a song with big hit potential, and 'What I've Done' was the belated creation that served as such and achieved exactly what it was intended to do. Of the nine full songs on *A Thousand Suns*, there was no outstanding choice for a lead single, and no one song that assumed any kind of hit potential. This time, though, there was no return to the studio to rush-write another song for the sake of mainstream grandeur. 'The Catalyst' isn't necessarily the centrepiece of *A Thousand Suns*, even if its eventual reveal is pre-empted on a couple of the album's earlier interludes. It does, however, embody the core of the album's intentions. It, like the record, makes far more sense when you listen to *A Thousand Suns* in its entirety, and you can at least see why Linkin

Park felt 'The Catalyst' being the lead single would suitably demonstrate the band's latest aural transformation.

Early on, *A Thousand Suns* was intended to be a concept album, and that's how Linkin Park promoted it in the run-up to its release. It was going to be a rather heavy album too, if the demos that were later shared on the *Underground XIV* compilation in 2014 are anything to go by. But somewhere along the way the concept idea became one with multiple arcs, and the music shed its raw rock prowess and transitioned into a post-apocalyptic soundscape full of electronica, synths and noise. The only obvious similarities between the new album and *Minutes to Midnight* was in the themes explored, as Chester and Mike continued to build on the intellectual growth that helped birth 'Hands Held High' and 'The Little Things Give You Away'. By 2010, Barack Obama had entered the White House as the 44th US president, and although there was now a bit of optimism for the country's future, Chester and Mike chose to focus on the fear that many Americans were still feeling on the back of George W. Bush's reign. The Iraq War went on, a period of economic downturn had led to the Great Recession, and while the overarching idea of *A Thousand Suns* revolved around nuclear warfare, the album moved forward without an obvious narrative and instead explored an assembly of abstract topics.

'The Catalyst' leads with the undertones of war and oppression, and the very first line in the song of 'God bless us, everyone/We're a broken people living under loaded gun' finds Mike and Chester picking up where they left off on *Minutes to Midnight*. But it's how the theme was carried that surprised and confused a lot of fans, as mad flourishes of sharp synth waves, frazzled scratches, and programmed beats were displayed without any kind of rock edge. Even in its second half, where the band use uplifting music to mask the fear and desolation of the song's storyline, some refused to be swayed by Linkin Park's latest sonic semblance and promptly shunned 'The Catalyst', and the upcoming album it was tasked with promoting.

Work on *A Thousand Suns* began in 2008, while Linkin Park was in Europe promoting *Minutes to Midnight*. In between shows, the band, or primarily Mike, entered Sono Studios in Nouzov, Czech Republic, and Tritonus in Berlin, Germany, to work on early ideas. In 2009, the six-piece spent the entire year building on the demos and undertaking jam sessions, where no direction was off limits to them and inspirations, no matter how off-kilter they seemed, were investigated to their end. Mike called the approach 'a weird mix of perfectionism and chaos', and choosing to work with Rick Rubin again helped keep the band on their toes and out of their comfort zones.

The album's title was lifted from J. Robert Oppenheimer's famous quote following the first atomic bomb test in 1945. Considered the father of the atomic bomb after overseeing its development and use by the US Army on Hiroshima and Nagasaki during World War II, Oppenheimer's quote, which referenced the Bhagavad Gita Hindu scripture, features in the second track/interlude 'The Radiance', where his voice is sampled over a heavy industrial beat. The quote: 'If the radiance of a thousand suns were to burst at once into the sky, that would be like the splendour of the Mighty one… Now I am become death, the destroyer of worlds', seemed to share Linkin Park's own thoughts on the moral implications of nuclear weapons, which was considered as some early inspiration to base their fourth album around. Oppenheimer isn't the only historical figure to appear on *A Thousand Suns*. On the fierce and politically charged 'Wretches and Kings', Mario Salvo's 'Bodies upon gears' speech from the American activist's 1964 Sproul Hall sit-in opens the track, and on the interlude 'Wisdom, Justice, and Love', Martin Luther King's 1967 declaration against the Vietnam war, known as 'A time to break silence', plays out over a moving piano pattern. As historically significant as these speeches were, Linkin Park felt they resonated just as strongly in the current climate, and they said things the band didn't quite know how to put into words themselves. But in providing the speeches with a backdrop of mechanically modified moodiness meant their inclusions weren't just playing important roles in supporting the album's themes, they were solidifying its emotional core too.

There was, however, a lot that Linkin Park did have to say, and on the savage hip hop driven 'When They Come for Me', the band takes aim at their own critics. Containing booming tribal beats and a chorus made up of middle eastern chanting, Mike's scathing rapping touches on the backlash Linkin Park received upon leaving their rap rock roots behind ('Everybody wants the next thing to be just like the first'), and in a way foreshadows those same negative responses to 'The Catalyst', and *A Thousand Suns* upon their releases. 'Wretches and Kings' references Public Enemy both lyrically and in its aggressive hip hop, where Mike and Chester lead the call for social resistance and the toppling of those in power. Featuring layers of warping synths and crunching samples, the track could easily have been lifted of *Reanimation*, while Brad's screeching guitars provide further venom on one of the album's standout songs. The viciousness of Chester's rage-fuelled rapping on 'Blackout' is not so much aimed at anyone in particular, but stems from Rick Rubin's idea to have him freestyle when the song's lyrics were proving difficult to construct. Having Chester 'rap' instead of Mike creates an interesting role reversal, and the techno blasts that follow are equally as ear-catching. With their inclusion, 'Blackout' transcends into a haywire dancefloor jaunt, and Joe's sampling of Chester's screams to create a cacophony of stutter edits only adds to the song's strange but likably heavy approach. Most of the album's tracks were written in parts, and the way they segue into their next movement supports the impressive balance *A Thousand Suns* has in floating between chaos and serenity. 'When They Come for Me' and 'Blackout' both progress into epic finales based around either a guitar or piano melody that offer temporary resolutions, while the lullaby-like 'Robot Boy', a song of hope and indifference, ascends on the back of a climactic synth solo.

Despite the heavy electronic emphasis on *A Thousand Suns*, not every song yields under the pressure. 'Burning in the Skies' is a lush alternative rocker that contains some of the same tendencies that pulse throughout *Minutes to Midnight*. It's a rare Linkin Park song in that it features fingerpicked guitar, and with its ambient pop rock drive, programmed beats, and spine-tingling piano, the album's first full track casually masks the tension that is soon to consume *A Thousand Suns*. 'Waiting for the End' follows a similar approach, although its summertime vibe sways with a tentative hip hop backbone and some interesting reggae-style rapping from Mike, which works well with Chester's soaring lead and chorus refrains.

Both of these songs were justifiably released as singles because they sit somewhere between pop and the lighter edges of rock, while 'Iridescent', the album's fourth single, channels the best moments of 'Burning in the Skies' and 'Waiting for the End' to enter epic level balladry. The track offers some light among the album's overbearing gloom, and attempts to present a resolution to what Linkin Park and much of the world appeared to be searching for in 2010: hope among chaos and sadness. Throughout *A Thousand Suns*, Chester and Mike's vocal interplay is astonishing, and arguably more cohesive than on any previous album including *Hybrid Theory*. Whether their vocals are overlayed or they take it in turns to sing the leads (Mike's singing voice is exceptional on this record), they are always there to support one another and add to the emotional aspect of the songs. 'Iridescent' is no different, and Mike's compelling verse leads are perfectly shadowed by Chester on an inspiring chorus that implores everyone to let go of their sadness and frustration. In further impressing the song's mighty hook, Linkin Park present their message of unity with a rousing gang vocal, a further facet the band brought to their latest album for the first time. While 'Iridescent' could, and quite possibly should, have been the album's closing track, that responsibility falls to 'The Messenger'. In stark contrast to everything that comes before it, the song is rid of all its electronics and serves as Linkin Park's first ever acoustic number, with only a smattering of piano and a harmonium providing further modest textures. It's a bit of a flat way to end *A Thousand Suns*, but the idea of 'The Messenger' is to offer some hope for the future, and Chester does just that with a raw live vocal and a folky chorus line of 'When life leaves us blind/Love keeps us kind'.

* * *

A Thousand Suns emerged at a time when indie was the leading rock sub-genre in the mainstream, and bands like Coldplay, The Black Keys, The Killers and Kings of Leon were anywhere and everywhere. Linkin Park didn't follow trends, though, they set them, and while it's easy to look back now and consider *A Thousand Suns* as the next rational step in the band's sonic progression, an album like their fourth was a huge shock to the system in 2010.

'Breaking the Habit' demonstrated that Linkin Park could go fully electronic and get away with it, but that was just one song slotted in the middle of a smash hit rap rock album. Everyone knew what the band was capable of, but very few, if any, really thought they would go and write a whole album that explored such a style, and something that was largely void of any rock sensibilities. As appreciative of their fan base as they'd always been, Linkin Park held the keys to their own destiny, and after Mike had spoken of listening to a lot of Nine Inch Nails, Radiohead, Tool and several electronic artists in the early stages of writing *A Thousand Suns*, it shouldn't have been so surprising that what followed was an amalgamation of experimental prog. In promotional interviews before the album's release, the band remained tight-lipped on what people should expect, and while no one expected a song like 'The Catalyst', the criticism that was aimed in its direction appeared to be far more subjective than it was objective. 'The Catalyst' wasn't a bad song at all, it was just… different. And so was *A Thousand Suns*.

As digital downloading and streaming became a new and popular way of consuming music, people's listening patterns also began to change. Listening to single tracks and curating playlists catered for shorter attention spans, which at the same time weakened the appeal of full-length albums. Pre-*A Thousand Suns*, Linkin Park was asked by Warner if they would consider releasing a set of EPs instead of another full-length, and while the band flatly refused, they knew *A Thousand Suns* was going to be a hard sell. Promoting it as a concept album was the best way to support its cohesion when listened to as a complete piece, from beginning to end. Its narrative may have been less penetrable than that of a traditional concept album, but as the multiple interludes move seamlessly into the tracks they are tasked with paving the way for, the end result becomes a winding soundtrack that is built on cutting-edge experimentation, and the realisation of Linkin Park's sonic ambitions.

Despite the love/hate relationship that came with *A Thousand Suns* upon its release in September 2010, the album still debuted at the top of the Billboard 200. Its first week sales of 241,000 were almost 400,000 less than what *Minutes to Midnight* had done in its own opening week, and while the sharp decline could have pointed to the scepticism that surrounded *A Thousand Suns* upon its release, it could equally have been down to the fact that digital sales were now vastly exceeding physical ones.

A Thousand Suns was no instant classic, but in the years since its release it has gone on to amass quite the cult following. Repeated listens are required to unearth every tiny aspect that went into its creation, because there is simply too much going on to absorb everything in one go. At the time of its release, certain album reviews even likened *A Thousand Suns* to Radiohead's

Kid A and Pink Floyd's *Dark Side of the Moon*, both of which have long been considered prog rock classics. For *A Thousand Suns* to be mentioned in that same space gives a tiny indication of just how genre-defining Linkin Park's fourth album was considered to be, and what it has ultimately become. It was a bolt from the blue that posed an alternative to the indie rock boom, and in sticking to their own principles, Linkin Park's biggest career risk was one that more than justified their latest trip into the experimental wilderness, regardless of how divisive the album had proven to be.

*   *   *

Amid a stunning backdrop of the Kremlin and the nine multi-coloured onion domes of St Basil's Cathedral, Linkin Park strutted onto the stage to a cacophony of noise. A ravenous crowd was already bouncing to the electronic crunch of the band's walk-on intro, before they launched straight into another immaculate performance of 'New Divide'.

Linkin Park was following in the footsteps of Paul McCartney, the Scorpions and the Red Hot Chili Peppers in playing a concert in Moscow's Red Square. Over many years and centuries, Red Square has been the setting for mass demonstrations, riots, parades, speeches and even public executions. On 23 June 2011, Linkin Park held their own demonstration, and for a couple of hours on a blissful summer evening, the band and their devoted crowd was united in a shared love of music, expression and *Transformers*. If Red Square had a roof, it would've been blown off within seconds, as the six-piece kicked off their set with 'New Divide', the *Revenge of the Fallen* theme song and smash hit single. The show was part of the second European leg of the *A Thousand Suns* world tour, but more than that, it coincided with the global premiere of the third *Transformers* film, *Dark of the Moon*, which was opening the Moscow International Film Festival. *Dark of the Moon* is just as intense as its predecessors, especially during its emotionally chaotic action sequences that present a good vs. evil dichotomy. But compared to *Transformers* and *Revenge of the Fallen*, the overall theme of *Dark of the Moon* offers a more positive outlook. Reiterating the importance of freedom of choice and standing up for one's own beliefs, Linkin Park had just the song in mind when Michael Bay reached out and asked the band to once again contribute to the franchise's soundtrack. 'Iridescent' had been out in the ether for nine months by the time it appeared as the opening track on the film's soundtrack album, but Mike felt the song was a natural fit even though it wasn't as heavy as Linkin Park's previous *Transformers* entries.

'Iridescent' emerges during the final throes of *A Thousand Suns* as a gloriously uplifting ballad. Early on, the song follows a similarly bleak outlook to the short story that inspired it, Mark Twain's *My Boyhood Dreams*, which explores the disappointment of unfulfilled dreams. In keeping with one of the themes of *A Thousand Suns*, 'Iridescent' depicts someone being alone in a place that's been ravaged by nuclear warfare, but as the song progresses it switches its focus towards overcoming adversity, as musically demonstrated by Linkin Park's towering gang vocals, and their inspiring melodies and alt rock instrumentation. Even upon first listen, 'Iridescent' felt destined to be a part of something much bigger and wider reaching, but to do so it required a bit of a makeover.

Backed by Warner's radio team to rework the song, Linkin Park elevated its tempo by bringing in Rob's throbbing drumbeat from the beginning. It was the biggest difference from the album cut, where its first movement is led by some sombre piano chords and Mike's desolate vocal. The 'Energy Up Version', as it was to be called, was created while the band was touring *A Thousand Suns*, and its newfound density came from the flushing of certain parts and instruments to give the track a more direct rock approach. With all the edits, the 'Energy Up Version' shaved a whole minute off the original's running time, but all the vital ingredients remained to preserve its uplifting narrative, and to support the likeminded mission statement of the film to which 'Iridescent' would lend itself. In collusion with the premiere of *Dark of the Moon*, Linkin Park performed the 'Energy Up Version' for the first and only time during their Red Square concert, before the band brought another legendary live show to a close with the one-two punch of 'What I've Done' and 'Bleed It Out'.

Like 'Iridescent', *A Thousand Suns* had been out a while by the time Linkin Park transformed Red Square into their own personal playground. Their setlist was largely made up of their latest album's tracks and segues, like it had been for much of the tour, with the occasional classic thrown in here and there for good measure. As Linkin Park rifled through their latest set of songs, they'd already begun to plot their next album, and having just expanded on their soundscape like never before, their next offering would be one that encompassed a little bit of everything from their past into a short and concise fifth studio record.

Building It Up to Break It Back Down

*L*iving Things marks the shortest period between albums in Linkin Park's career, where just twenty-one months separated the releases of *A Thousand Suns* and the band's fifth album.

Writing for it began in March 2011, while they were touring *A Thousand Suns*, and with the continued development of digital audio software, early ideas such as samples and beats were created on phones, and plugging instruments into laptops meant riffs and even vocals could be recorded on the move. The files were then safely stored until they could be more thoroughly investigated by the band in their own personal studios.

Living Things was the first album to arrive since Linkin Park set out an action plan in which they would attempt to release a new record every eighteen months. As each member moved into the latter stages of their 30s, two-year tour cycles became a thing of the past. Intense spells on the road were becoming less enjoyable, or as Chester called it, 'excruciating'. Chester, Brad, Dave and Mike all had young children born in recent years, and having families that for too long had operated on long distance phone calls and video chats meant that more than ever before, Linkin Park had both a need and desire to spend more time at home. This showed in the touring for *A Thousand Suns*, where the band played around eighty shows which were spread out over eleven months – almost half the time they undertook when promoting *Minutes to Midnight*, and the albums before it. They even dialled back on Projekt Revolution, where the latest, and what would prove to be the last, event of its kind consisted of just four European shows in the summer of 2011.

Spending more time at home seemed to enhance Linkin Park's creative output. With ideas already devised on the road giving them a head start to build upon in the comfort of their own personal spaces, *Living Things* would be the first of three albums the band released in a little under five years. It was decided early on that the band's fifth effort was going to be more energetic and song based. Another concept album like *A Thousand Suns* was never on the cards, where song construction felt more of a priority over actual song creation, and although *Living Things* does have a heavy electronic and synth presence, Linkin Park's signature rock edge makes its welcome return to share the limelight. But this wasn't the band dusting off their nu metal cobwebs, even if some of the songs are rooted in the rap rock style of *Hybrid Theory* and *Meteora*. Other songs tip their hat to the alt rock nuances that palpitate throughout *Minutes to Midnight*, while the electronic overdrive of *A Thousand Suns* was a new custom that Linkin Park was always likely to instil in their next batch of new material. The band's fourth album had in all honesty presented a peak in Linkin Park's sonic creativity, and now finally feeling comfortable in their own skin, their fifth endeavour found them incorporating elements of their entire back catalogue into direct, thirty-six-minute LP.

The louder songs are in no way an attempt to revive a decrepit nu metal scene. Sure, Linkin Park was somewhat going back to their roots on *Living Things*, but in giving their rap rock fusion a fresh and contemporary edge meant the band was in no way trying to revisit their past glories. After *Meteora*, Linkin Park knew that a third rap rock album would pigeonhole them for eternity. In some ways, the nu metal label was never fully discarded, despite their best efforts, but if nothing else their affiliation with the movement had served as a permanent reminder of where they had come from, and how they had succeeded where so many of their contemporaries had failed and disappeared into oblivion.

As brilliantly obscure as *A Thousand Suns* was, and how it overflowed with genre-bending intrigue, there were times where it felt Linkin Park was overcompensating for the sake of it. In creating the album's sonically expanded soundscape, the band pushed themselves to the limit and sometimes over it, to the point where they exhausted their experimentation and there was seemingly nowhere else to go other than backwards. 'For me, it's all about getting back to the real "hybrid theory",' said Mike in one of his blog entries in 2012. 'Not the album of that name, but the idea that the six guys in the band have drastically different tastes in music, and the blending of all those sounds into one is exactly what we built our band upon.' And that is exactly what Linkin Park did on *Living Things*, while also dumbing down on the amount of equipment they used to deliver a more straightforward and less cluttered set of songs. Each one sticks to a specific genre and resists any kind of bending in the middle. They play to the band's strengths, and the regular ebbing and flowing never feels forced. When put together as a complete package, there is a versatility to *Living Things* that while not breaking any new ground, it caters for long-time fans as well as those who had more recently been introduced to Linkin Park, where no matter what album their personal favourite was, *Living Things* contains a bit of something for everyone.

Thematically, Mike and Chester replace the importance of the global and societal issues that served as the heartbeats of their two previous albums with a return to writing deeper, personal explorations. The album's title comes from the very ideas that are expressed within the songs, where each mood is connected through human perspectives, and personal interaction. It means that while the music is typically atmospheric, the songs are often driven by those old feelings of regret, loss and sadness; all familiar topics that for a long time had been a big part of Linkin Park's core identity.

The recording of *Living Things* began in early 2012, once again in the familiar setting of NRG, and with Rick Rubin again occupying the co-producer role. This time, however, his involvement was more sparing, as he made weekly visits to the studio to go over what the band had worked on thus far. Rick offered his input on how the songs were sounding and what required further work, while Mike was given greater control in guiding his bandmates through the majority of the recording process. Chester described Mike and Rick's teamwork as Linkin Park's 'golden ticket', as their union gave the band the freedom to explore new sounds while maintaining complete control of where their creative adventures took them. In Rick allowing the band more space to work on their own, with far less pressure on their shoulders than they'd experienced in the past, it is perhaps a significant reason why *Living Things* doesn't at all feel strained or oversaturated. Of the twelve songs, four fail to reach the three-minute mark, and the lead single 'Burn It Down', is the longest performer at 3:51. Since Rick had begun working with the band, he always made sure they didn't fall back into past habits, but with less guidance it appeared they'd done just that. It isn't necessarily a bad thing in this instance, or a slight on the band or their fifth album, but the measure of *Hybrid Theory* and *Meteora* had been in those sustained assaults that refused to let the listener pause for breath, as one hit followed the next before bowing out in less than forty breathless minutes. After the exuberance of *A Thousand Suns*, and to a certain degree *Minutes to Midnight*, it wasn't a bad thing that Linkin Park opted for a more simplistic approach on *Living Things*, even if its legacy is one built on single moments, and where it feels more like the band is consolidating its position rather than trying to swing for another home run.

In a preview of *Living Things*, Mike uploaded the full track listing in acapella and instrumental form on iTunes on 25 June 2012. It was the first Linkin Park album to receive such treatment, and the idea to do so had been partly inspired by Mike hearing a number of the band's songs being remixed by other producers. As Jay-Z previously did in releasing an acapella version of *The Black Album*, which unbeknownst to him would act as a precursor to his eventual collaboration with Linkin Park on the *Collision Course EP* and usher a whole wave of other mashup creations, Linkin Park was now offering free creative licence for others to mashup their songs too. A prime example of this was Blaze Audio's *Collision Course II* album, which arrived in December 2012 and impressively bonded Linkin Park with Eminem. In addition, the *Living Things Acapellas and Instrumentals* album exposed just how hard Linkin Park had always worked on the full production of their songs, whereby cutting the vocals and music into separate parts meant the complexity of the production could be studied in a way that was more audibly apparent.

In comparison to the negativity that surrounded 'The Catalyst' when it was tasked with previewing *A Thousand Suns*, 'Burn It Down' was greeted with far greater optimism when the *Living Things* lead single debuted in mid-April. With its irresistible synth line and almighty hook, which treads the line between pop and rock like only Linkin Park could do, and furnished with enriching energy from start to finish, 'Burn It Down' offers fine example of the band being able to remain relevant without ever being accused of imitating current trends. Like the album, 'Burn It Down' combines the best of the band's decade-plus career into one captivating song, and its lyrics are made up of personal entries from Chester in the throbbing verses and

Mike in the bridge, which are overlayed with pop culture nuances speaking of one's fall from grace ('We're building it up, to break it back down/We can't wait, to burn it to the ground'). 'Burn It Down' was a big hit in mosh pits and on dancefloors, and it was somewhat a hit in the charts too, where it topped Hot Rock & Alternative Songs, and reached 30 on the Hot 100.

Living Things begins with the breathless 'Lost in the Echo', which redefines Linkin Park's original fusion of rap and rock by giving it a modern twist. Bubbling synths meld perfectly with the band's pre-*Minutes to Midnight* sound, where for the first time in years, Mike brought a rap rock demo to the table that wasn't immediately rebuffed by his bandmates. The song also features a trademark chorus, which is already huge in stature before Chester's resounding screams during the final hook create one of the album's big highlights with the very first offering.

The arena rock vibes of 'In My Remains' and 'I'll Be Gone' press home a portion of *Living Things* that elects for heavy guitar leads. The former has some crisp verses and a catchy chorus playing over thick military percussion, and the latter, which details a broken relationship (with some additional and unusual lyrical metaphors of space travel), is equally as effective due to Brad's driving riffs. The hip hop influenced 'Lies Greed Misery', and the punk tirade of 'Victimized' are brief in their existence but make visceral impacts in the time they hang around, so much so that they would form a reference point in where Linkin Park would go on their next album, while the intricate pop swoon of 'Castle of Glass' offers a nice change of pace. The track was written by Mike during the *A Thousand Suns* sessions as a slow tempo ballad, but it didn't really fit with what else the band was writing for the album. It was then revived by Mike for *Living Things* and was one of the first songs to be worked on, and the addition of some live drums to compliment the soothing strings, subtle samples, and Mike's deeply invested vocal, makes 'Castle of Glass' the most unique entry on *Living Things*, in that it doesn't sound like anything Linkin Park had ever written before.

Following the folk-tinged industrial stab of 'Skin to Bone', 'Until It Breaks' reveals itself to be the most adventurous track on the album, where a handful of discarded demos were pieced together to create a melting pot of jarring transitions, which abandon the traditional ideas of song structure. Mike's decision to combine multiple demos was partly inspired by The Beatles, who did the same thing on their 1969 album *Abbey Road*, as a way to use up some incomplete songs. The track is the closest thing to resembling something off *A Thousand Suns*, and the Fort Minor-influenced track that at some point became a Linkin Park work provides a crash course in fusing industrial hip hop with a clout of mechanical beats and juddering synths. Mike's venomous bars during the 'Apaches' and 'Foot Patrol' segues are temporarily separated by a piano-led Chester cameo, before Brad provides his first ever lead vocal on his previously written 'Three Band Terror' movement, with a soothing glide that brings 'Until It Breaks' to its messy but inventive conclusion.

The two epics on *Living Things* come in the form of the contemplative 'Roads Untraveled', and the closing 'Powerless'. The former is an exercise in patience and grace, where even in its early moments it feels like something big is coming. Its verses contain folk-like melodies, chime patches and sombre piano chords, which continually build towards the song's tipping point, and when it explodes into a colossal *Minutes to Midnight*-esque wall of sound, 'Roads Untraveled' reaches to its enthralling summit. The same can be said for 'Powerless', which was another song that originally stemmed from the *A Thousand Suns* sessions, before it was later reinvestigated for *Living Things*. The track started out as a seven-minute saga, but it felt too long and was therefore trimmed down and given a more compact arrangement. As part of the fleshing out process, its ascending intro was cut into its own track ('Tinfoil'), where its atmospheric samples form the spirited backbone that drives 'Powerless' to deliver the album's grand finale. Chester sings about a self-destructive lover, while he also appears to take into consideration the effects his own addictions have had on the people closest to him ('You held it all/and I was by your side, powerless'). His brittle vocal aches over sweeping electronics and some belatedly incorporated live drums and percussion, before the emotional nature of the song concludes with another swelling bout of full band instrumentation.

Living Things isn't quite the 'predictable earache' that *NME* stated it to be in their review ahead of its release. The album feeds off the raw energy of *Hybrid Theory* and *Meteora*, but it also acknowledges the songwriting and production of *Minutes to Midnight* and *A Thousand Suns*, which makes for an intriguing synthesis of everything Linkin Park had so far explored during their career. Musically, the band's fifth effort feels like a bit of a drop off by their lofty standards, but having to follow *A Thousand Suns* and its radical experimentation was always going to be a tough exercise. But, considering *Living Things* to be more 'straightforward', in the band's own words, is still a long way off what many other artists would consider elementary to be, as the album still possesses a richness in spite of its general schematics.

Linkin Park maintained their run of securing the number 1 album on the Billboard 200 when *Living Things* debuted at the summit with first week physical sales of 223,000. With it, the band set a new record in becoming the first act to have debuted since the year 2000 to achieve five number 1 albums on the biggest US chart, which provided even more proof of Linkin Park's unwavering appeal, even among the constant sea of musical change.

Fig. 11

Even If It Sucks

'Even if it sucks at the end of the day, I'd rather make a loud mistake than be timid and not take any chances.' Mike's statement during an interview with *Vice* in October 2013 echoed those same sentiments he'd long lived by and incorporated into Xero, Hybrid Theory, and ultimately Linkin Park. On this occasion, he was discussing the band's recent collaboration with the electronic house producer and DJ Steve Aoki, on 'A Light That Never Comes'.

In the write-up, the *Vice* journalist comes across as rather unenthusiastic about the song, in which Mike's incessant rap verses that forge some defiance and perseverance against the defeatism that Chester emits during a bounding chorus ('The nights go down/I chase the sun, waiting for a light that never comes'). In true collaborative fashion, the song captures the essences of both its artists; the piano chords are irrevocably Linkin Park as they fluctuate with one of Steve Aoki's trademark heavy basslines, and gyrating synths.

Mike and Steve first began colluding during a Twitter exchange, before 'A Light That Never Comes' grew organically over a number of months as the two artists traded files through email. The results are in no way the kind of electronic rock that Linkin Park had been developing throughout their career, where in this instance 'A Light That Never Comes' is far more befitting of rave environments than mosh pits. Its sound and style party emanated from Mike's belief that rock music in 2013 required some serious innovation and fresh excitement. In his mind, the genre had grown increasingly stale, and the rock world needed a few more Linkin Park's who were willing to try something a little offbeat.

'A Light That Never Comes' opens *Recharged*, Linkin Park's second remix album, which follows in the footsteps of *Reanimation* in delivering new interpretations of the band's most recent material. But where *Reanimation* gave *Hybrid Theory* a bruising hip hop orientated makeover, *Recharged* took

Living Things by the throat and transformed the album into a set of dubstep, drum and bass, and EDM dancefloor booty shakers. Mike had sworn never to make another *Reanimation*, but his mind was altered when he heard a number of remixes by other producers who were giving the *Living Things* tracks new and contrasting identities. In preordering the band's fifth album, a subscription service entitled fans access to a newly remixed track in each month until the end of the year. Some of those, by producers such as Datsik, Killsonik, Vice and Pusha T. were later included on *Recharged* after Mike decided to compile them into a remix album, the majority of which had been created from stems he'd previously sent out.

In May 2012, Mike revealed that Warner had asked him if Linkin Park would consider working with some dance producers during the early stages of *Living Things*, and while the idea at least piqued his interest, Mike strongly considered whether such collaborations would give the impression that the band was jumping on the electronic bandwagon. Korn received similar accusations after their foray into dubstep on their *Path of Totality* album in 2011, which saw them work with big-name producers like Skrillex, Downlink and Noisia. In Korn's case, *The Path of Totality* arrived in the middle of a lean period where the nu metal godfathers were suffering a bit of a personality crisis; something which Linkin Park had never experienced despite their persistence in exhausting the limits of experimentation.

For Linkin Park, an EDM-inspired studio album was not the way to go. A remix album, however, that was something the band could get away with, and that was the general consensus when *Recharged* dropped in late-October 2013, alongside a Facebook game entitled *LP Recharge*, in which players had to solve puzzles to save a planet depleted of natural resources from machines (the game served to raise awareness about areas of the world without reliable power). *Recharged* is in no way loud mistake, not that Mike would have been too bothered if it was seen that way, and the remix album shifted 33,000 copies in its opening week as it snuck inside the Billboard 200's top ten.

Tell Us Again What You Think We Should Be

Just when everybody thought they had Linkin Park all figured out, the band came roaring back in 2014 with the heaviest album in their entire career. When Mike spoke of rock music being in dire straits during his interview with *Vice* in 2013, it was while promoting an album and a song that didn't necessarily reinforce his theory of how the genre required some new invention. In truth, 'A Light That Never Comes' barely had any rock in at all, and it wasn't the song to lead a revolutionary charge. Neither was *The Hunting Party* for that matter, which revealed itself to be a statement of intent rather than a pledge for change.

The album's title matched the desire Mike had in wanting to bring back rock's energy and soul, after it was felt the previously considered *Carnivores* didn't embody the lengths Linkin Park was going to in retaliating against rock's passivity. In this instance, Linkin Park saw *themselves* as the hunting party, who instead of resting on their laurels and waiting for opportunities to come to them, were taking it upon themselves to go out in search of their own. Their sixth album could have turned out extremely different, though, because early on, Mike was writing songs similar to those on *Living Things* and *A Thousand Suns*; songs that continued to be heavily induced with electronics. They were nowhere close to being emblazoned overtures in defining rock's future landscape, but that was the kind of headspace Mike was in at the time as his efforts found him rehashing the likes of 'New Divide', and 'Burn It Down'. If he hadn't called upon Rick Rubin for the producer's opinions on the demos, who knows how Linkin Park's sixth album would really have turned out, but when Rick shared his surprise at how 'poppy' they sounded, Mike was thrown off course.

The demos were written while the band was touring *Living Things*, where only thirty-four shows made up the album's world tour, which didn't count a North American co-headline run with Incubus. When Mike returned to the demos once the tour had ended, Rick's pop diagnosis still echoed in Mike's head and he lost all belief in what he'd been working on, so much so that he binned everything and returned to the drawing board. Little did he know at the time but the inspiration he required, and what would set the album on a different path entirely, would come in the form of a random riff he started playing on his guitar. The riff represented the frustration he was feeling as Linkin Park's main songwriter and master musical tactician found himself in a bit of a rut for perhaps the first time in his professional career. The riff he began playing was angry, it was heavy and rebellious, and it would ultimately lay the groundwork for the album's first single, 'Guilty All the Same'. The riff spearheaded Mike's quest in wanting to reinvigorate the rock genre by bringing back some of the influence the bands of the '90s had on radio. But instead of concocting another slab of *Hybrid Theory* rap rock, Mike decided that a punishing of the senses anti-mainstream attack on the active rock bands continuing to play it safe was required to give the genre its much needed shake-up.

In creating *The Hunting Party*, Linkin Park did use *Hybrid Theory* as a kind of template, and Brad even jokingly called the band's sixth album a 'prequel' to their first. In capturing the energy of the songs, each one was written in the studio instead of taking in furnished ideas that were worked on beforehand. After a long and prosperous relationship with NRG, the band moved over to Larrabee Sound in North Hollywood, while Mike and Rob also eloped to EastWest on the Sunset Strip to work on the drums and percussion. Linkin Park used Larrabee as a compositional tool to seek on-the-spot inspiration, works of spontaneity and happy accidents. With all the ingredients in place, the songs were played and recorded in their entirety to harness the live energy of the performances, instead of relying on overproduction and making them sound too polished. It was a new way of working for the band, who for a long time had recorded everything in separate parts and pieced it all together later. *The Hunting Party* is also the first album Linkin Park created fully in-house, where after three sonically disparate but nonetheless successful albums, the band moved on from Rick Rubin and had Brad co-produce alongside Mike.

* * *

A large portion of *The Hunting Party* was already in place by the time Chester joined his bandmates at Larrabee, having more recently been realising a lifelong dream of fronting Stone Temple Pilots.

The band was one of the most successful rock acts of the '90s, where from their admission into the grunge scene and long surviving its demise, the quartet sold millions of records, scored countless hit singles, and won multiple awards. In Scott Weiland, Stone Temple Pilots possessed one of rock's most flamboyant frontmen, and since their formation in 1989 and signing to Atlantic Records in 1992, the San Diego outfit continually evolved from one acclaimed album to the next by incorporating psychedelic chord progressions, glam and jazz elements, and later traces of jangle pop and shoegaze into their ever-expanding repertoire. But in Scott Weiland, Stone Temple Pilots also had a frontman who was ravaged by addiction, and who was belatedly diagnosed with Bipolar Disorder. At his best, Scott's versatile baritone and wider vocal range was as good as any other rock singer out there, but at his worst, his years of substance abuse resulted in stints in jail, poor live performances, and him becoming a liability that caused the band to call it a day in 2003. When they reunited five years later, Scott and Stone Temple Pilots had a second chance at building on their already impressive legacy, but Scott's issues would sadly return and at the beginning of 2013, he was officially fired from the band.

Scott and Chester bore certain similarities. Their talent was undeniable, but when they were in the midst of addiction, they saw substance abuse as a solution rather than a problem. Scott openly admitted to believing he had a chemical deficiency that only drugs could balance out, and while Chester was never as heavy a consumer as Scott, certainly not in the sense of using heroin to numb himself from the pain of his past, there was likely something in Scott's tortured rockstar persona that Chester found himself being able to relate to.

Chester had first joined Stone Temple Pilots onstage during the Family Values tour in 2001, and getting to perform 'Dead & Bloated' on regular occasions was a dream in itself. But when Chester joined Dean and Robert DeLeo, and Eric Kretz at KROQ's Weenie Roast on 18 May 2013, the show became Chester's initiation as the new frontman of Stone Temple Pilots. During their set at the Live 105 BFD festival the next day, the band debuted a brand new song titled 'Out of Time', the first song written and recorded with Chester, which preceded the upcoming five-track EP, *High Rise*, which was later released in October 2013. Each song on the EP is a predictably thrusting hard rock number packed with the kind of riffs and melodies that Stone Temple Pilots were synonymous with throughout the '90s. Vocally, Chester channels his inner Scott Weiland on the memorable cuts of 'Black Heart' and 'Cry Cry', as his familiar snarl and infectious energy pays homage to the band's iconic singer, while also sustaining the Pilots' legacy in the modern day.

For much of Chester's tenure with the band, the 'Stone Temple Pilots with Chester Bennington' heading never quite felt like the singer was truly welcomed into the fold, and although the 'with Chester Bennington' was finally removed in middle of 2015 as the quartet continued to undertake small tours, Chester amicably departed Stone Temple Pilots in the November to focus solely on Linkin Park. Sadly, Scott passed away a little under a month after. Despite regular periods of sobriety, his latest relapse would be his last, and while on the road with his band the Wildabouts, Scott was found dead on his tour bus in Bloomington, Minnesota on 3 December, aged just 48.

As a sign of respect for everything they had been through and accomplished together, Chester sought the support of his Linkin Park brothers before he took the Stone Temple Pilots gig. Naturally, he received their blessings, and then some. They weren't going to be the ones to stop Chester from taking a chance on a dream.

* * *

Upon returning to Linkin Park, by which time the wheels were already in motion on *The Hunting Party*, Chester was surprised to hear how heavy the material was. It was a pleasant surprise, though, because Chester had always found it easier to write to heavy music, and it didn't take him long to acclimatise to the bludgeoning soundscape that was being laid out in front of him.

The Hunting Party doesn't necessarily represent Linkin Park's strongest songwriting, but it is without doubt their most visceral entry. The band's usual reliance on electronics is buried deep under a torrent of grinding guitar and bass movements, and pummelling drum sequences. After delving into processing electronics in recent years, Brad had now fallen back in love with the guitar, and when he isn't shredding like the Metallica-obsessed teenager of yesteryear, he is reeling off a number of blistering solos. Just as impressive as Brad's guitar work is Rob's drumming, which is so rigorous that he ended up putting his back out during the recording sessions and had to visit a chiropractor. In fully committing to the album, he practiced for up to ten hours a day, as well as working with a personal trainer to meet the physical demands of the song's heavier styles and often faster tempos. Some of his performances were captured in only one or a few takes, and they are all incredibly fierce and on point, while Dave also stepped up to the plate by delivering memorable basslines capable of ingraining themselves in people's minds. Much like At the Drive-In's *Relationship of Command* album had inspired him, the impact of Dave's bass work on *The Hunting Party* cannot be underestimated.

'Guilty All the Same' was released three months ahead of *The Hunting Party*, and the song immediately revealed itself to be the antithesis of what a lead single should sound like. Warner aired similar views as they implored Linkin Park to go with a song that was more melodic and radio friendly, but the band refused to back down because their choice of first single was purely intentional. The inspiration behind 'Guilty All the Same' came from things that pissed off the band as late-30-somethings, whose wider world views now came with a certain amount of cynicism. Beginning with an extended intro full of razorblade guitars, thrashing drums, and a piano riff that tempers the song's fragility, Chester's lead vocal doesn't quite match the overall intensity of the instrumental, but when the hip hop icon Rakim joins in on the bridge, 'Guilty All the Same' has its crowning moment. Along with his sidekick Eric B., Rakim put the hip hop world on notice in 1987 with their seminal album *Paid in Full*. As his career progressed, Rakim's innovative lyrical technique was regularly cited as setting the blueprint for all future rappers, and almost thirty years later, he was still delivering imperious bars on 'Guilty All the Same' as part of a vicious diatribe against corporate greed. (Fun fact: Rakim is terrified of flying, and to record his parts on 'Guilty All the Same', he drove all the way from New York to Los

Angeles. Furthermore, previous performances overseas have even seen him take week-long boat trips rather than risking taking to the air.)

The Hunting Party is the first studio album in which Linkin Park brought in special guests, and as well as Rakim, Helmet's Page Hamilton provides additional guitar and a lead chorus vocal on the bruising alt metaller 'All For Nothing'. System of a Down's Daron Malakian contributes some of his trademark riffage on the frenetic 'Rebellion', which also includes some pacey tribal drumming and off kilter Chester vocals, while Rage Against the Machine axeman Tom Morello swaps his customary funk-fuelled fretwork for something more atmospheric on the soft and sparse 'Drawbar'. The track was born out of a jam session that had no pre-planned direction, and although vocals were recorded, they were later removed to designate 'Drawbar' an instrumental. Unfortunately, Tom ends up being severely underutilised, and as 'Drawbar' plods along to no great effect, this track more than any other on the album feels like an extremely wasted opportunity.

'Keys to the Kingdom' and 'War' strengthen Linkin Park's aversion to the mainstream with a pair of venomous old school punk/metal songs. The first is a prime candidate to open the album with its brisk tempo, demolition job instrumentation, and a chastening vocal effect that makes Chester's screams all the more unnerving, while 'War' sounds like it could have been the wretched spawn of Black Flag, Gorilla Biscuits and early era Bad Religion. The two-minute metallic hardcore banger features some insane one-take drumming, and Chester's extended final scream is as deafening and menacing as any he'd ever bellowed in his career.

For all of Linkin Park's concerted efforts in making *The Hunting Party* as heavy as they could, their knack for writing catchy arena rockers was sure to lead to at least a couple finding their way onto the album. Or three, in this case, where 'Wastelands' proceeds with Mike's energetic rapping over a heavy groove, before the song explodes with an intrinsically melodic hook. The brooding but rather generic 'Until It's Gone' could easily have been featured on *Minutes to Midnight*, as Chester once again sings of past regrets over a powerful rock bounce and smooth electronics, before the anthemic nature of 'Final Masquerade' is built around simmering keys and palm-muted guitars. The song makes for a worthy album closer, had Linkin Park not already given that honour to 'Line in the Sand', where its running time of

6:35 makes it the band's longest ever number. Its expanded intro begins with rumbles of thunder, tempestuous electronics, and Mike's soft and echoey vocal, before the next segue rises with a pounding rhythm section. Various guitar tones and amp setups keep the finale fresh and exhilarating, as the band use the quiet/loud dynamic to great effect in continuing to build the song towards one last bout of metal-inspired instrumentation. 'A Line in the Sand' incorporates everything Linkin Park shoot for on *The Hunting Party*, where their primary focus came in them wanting to deliver power and menace, but with enough melody and intuition to loosely tie in the album with everything that came before it.

* * *

The Hunting Party had only just been released in certain parts of the world when Linkin Park commenced their headline set at the UK's Download Festival on 14 June 2014. Their set was split into two acts, the first of which presented a full playthrough of *Hybrid Theory* in its original sequence for the first time ever. The second act compiled 'Numb' with songs from *Minutes to Midnight*, *A Thousand Suns* and *Living Things*, and while the headline slot posed the perfect opportunity for the band to really drive home the belief they had in their latest album, only 'Guilty All the Same', 'Wastelands', and 'I'll Be Gone' were performed from *The Hunting Party*. On the Carnivores Tour, which Linkin Park co-headlined with Thirty Seconds to Mars in the US, just six songs from the band's latest album were played, meaning to this day, 'Keys to the Kingdom', 'All For Nothing', 'War', the experimentally heavy 'Mark the Graves', and 'Drawbar' have never been explored in front of live audiences.

For the first time since *Hybrid Theory*, *The Hunting Party* failed to earn Linkin Park the number 1 album on the Billboard 200. Selling 110,000 copies in its first week secured a debut and peak position of 3, while none of the album's five singles came anywhere close to cracking the Hot 100. Linkin Park had shunned the mainstream with their sixth opus, and in response the mainstream had shunned Linkin Park. The album hadn't reinvigorated rock like the band hoped it would, and as the current trend of rock acts remained on top by keeping it safe, there appeared to be a changing of the guard taking place. Linkin Park was now being seen as veterans, before any of the band had even reached the age of 40, where in fifteen years, they had released six studio albums, two remix albums, a mashup EP with Jay-fucking-Z, live albums and DVDs, and annual *Underground* compilations. Very few could keep up with the band's incredible output, where even they themselves barely had any time to pause for breath and take stock of everything that had achieved. Fifteen years had flown by in an instant, and for the first time it seemed that Linkin Park's fortunes were on the downturn.

During their surprise appearance at the Ventura County Fairgrounds leg of the Warped Tour on 22 June 2014, Linkin Park's position as elder statesmen became clearer to them than ever before. They were surrounded by a plethora of up-and-coming post-hardcore, pop punk and emo bands, many of whom had cited Linkin Park and *Hybrid Theory* as major influences in steering them on their own musical journeys. In one sense it felt like there was a passing of the torch, not that Linkin Park was washed up or fading into obscurity like a lot of the bands they'd come up with back in the early 2000s. Things just weren't quite the same anymore. The band's seven-song set had them bring out guest vocalists to perform with them, including the rapper Machine Gun Kelly on 'Bleed It Out', Jeremy McKinnon from A Day to Remember, who lent his ferocious pipes to 'A Place for My Head', and Finch's Nate Barcalow who did the same on the rasping bridge of 'One Step Closer'. Over the years, Linkin Park had been used to jumping onstage and joining their own heroes, but now they were giving others a once in a lifetime opportunity to do likewise, such was the band's standing within the rock community.

Linkin Park's influence extended far beyond the tiny 'Main Stage' they had brought with them to Warped Tour, though. Whether it was the reverberation of a glistening synth pattern underneath a barrage of meaty riffs, a vocal dual of piercing screams and whiny emo harmonies, or a chorus so inherently catchy that it brought some light to a song that was being weighed down by propulsive gloom, there was a little bit of Linkin Park to be found in the music of many of the bands who made up the bill. Most of those bands weren't afraid to admit it, either.

I Don't Like My Mind Right Now

Linkin Park had completed only two dates of the second US leg of *The Hunting Party* tour when disaster struck. With some time to spare before the next show at the Bankers Life Fieldhouse in Indianapolis, some of the band, their crew and members of the opening act Of Mice & Men took to the backstage basketball court, during which time Chester went for a layup and came down on a water bottle. The camera that filmed the downtime had missed the original incident, but when it quickly panned round to find Chester writhing in agony on the floor, it seemed his injury was more serious than just a turned ankle.

Chester had endured his fair share of tour mishaps over the years. During Ozzfest in 2001, he was bitten by a Brown Recluse spider while in his tour bus bunk. The footage of the wound, all black and blue and located just above his backside, can be seen in the *Frat Party at the Pankake Festival* DVD, which Chester shows off like a badge of honour. Years later, he spoke of fearing he had cancer when, as well as developing a fever, the poison that flowed through his bloodstream caused lumps to form on his body that were half the size of golf balls. The fever caused Chester to become extremely disorientated, but he went against doctors' orders and finished the remaining dates of Ozzfest while on antibiotics.

In October 2007, Chester broke his wrist during the early moments of a show in Melbourne, Australia, when during 'Papercut' he went to jump off a set of stairs and his foot got caught, and as he fell backwards, he immediately felt his wrist crack upon impact with the stage floor. And in 2011, Linkin Park had to cancel the final date of their *A Thousand Suns* tour when their accident-prone frontman was forced to undergo surgery on a shoulder injury he sustained during the band's recent trip to Asia. Additionally, Chester suffered a severely split lip after smacking himself in the face with a tennis racket, and he even tore one of his nipples off after catching the barbell on a shower door while he attempted to squeeze through it.

By the time Linkin Park took to the stage in Indianapolis on 18 January 2015, Chester had returned from the hospital and had it confirmed that his ankle was broken. The evening's show went on, like they almost always did, and Chester defiantly arrived onstage with the aid of a scooter, before he proceeded to perform to a jampacked audience while on crutches. His vocals were as powerful as ever and his stage presence was as commanding as always, as Chester refused to let the pain deter him from giving anything less than a hundred per cent. He'd dealt with pain all his life, so a broken ankle here or a broken wrist there was nothing he couldn't overcome. Chester never did things by halves, though, and in breaking his ankle he'd also torn almost all the ligaments, which meant urgent reconstructive surgery and the cancellation of the rest of the tour. Those shows were never rescheduled, however, Linkin Park did play some more American dates later in 2015, as well as five stadium shows in China, and ten on the European summer festival circuit.

* * *

As the band drew a line under the *Hunting Party* cycle and prepared to fly home from Europe, Mike chose to stop off in London and meet up with some songwriters. He'd already begun plotting ideas for the next album, and in doing so he was curious to find out how others approached the writing process. Mike had only ever known how to write with the guys in the band, and after years of constantly switching things up from one album to the next, but keeping the majority of the work in-house, Mike was opening himself up to the idea of collaborating with outsiders. He met with Justin Parker, who had written for Rihanna, Seal and pop's latest starlet, Lana Del Rey. Mike also met with Eg White, who in a long and illustrious career had writing credits on songs by Alison Moyet, Kylie Minogue and Adele. Mike spent a few days with both men, to find out how they worked with such big-name artists, and learning just how important mutual respect was in helping build professional relationships.

When Mike returned home, he was certain he wanted to work with collaborators for the next album. And he did, and there were many. In the past, Linkin Park's collaborations had always started with the band having a fully finished song already in place, but this time they were to enter into complete creative partnerships that began at the root, with numerous songwriters and producers including Justin Parker and Eg White, as well as the likes of Ilsey Juber, Jesse Shatkin, blackbear, Justin Trantner, and Julia Michaels.

Maybe it wasn't so much of a surprise that Linkin Park's seventh album became the latest in their discography to feature such a dramatic aberration in sound and style, considering their associates had penned hits for Beyoncé, Justin Bieber, Florence and the Machine and One Direction to name a few. But to follow up the savagery of *The Hunting Party* with… a pop record? A major part of how *One More Light* came to be was in the band learning how to write without any kind of pre-determined sound in mind. It was a method Rick Rubin had encouraged them to trial during *Minutes to Midnight*, where in beginning with a concept and some lyrics and giving them time to blossom, the words then formed the direction in which the music would take.

One More Light is Linkin Park's most personal album, and their most honest, where many of the songs paint vivid pictures of specific times and places through diary-like entries that tackle frame of mind thinking, personal fears, and regret. Previously, Linkin Park had counterbalanced their fragilities by hiding behind musical aggression, however *One More Light* masks its darkness with candy-coated hooks, and sweetly innocent pop melodies. The band had written the occasional pop-centric song before, think 'Breaking the Habit', 'Leave Out All the Rest', or 'Shadow of the Day'. Those songs had been well received, but they had been cast as outliers on albums that were still driven by a harder rock edge, so when Linkin Park presented ten fully committed pop expeditions in one go, with not a rock riff nor a single Chester scream within earshot, *One More Light* was always going to be a challenging listen for fans who were still revelling in the heaviness of *The Hunting Party*.

The first taste of what the band had been cooking up for their seventh album came in the form of 'Heavy', and like all the songs it was born from a simple conversation. More recently, Chester had suffered another relapse. As well as dealing with the war that constantly raged inside his head, he was still processing the death of his father-in-law from cancer when Amy Zaret, a Warner employee for over twenty-five years who helped Linkin Park obtain radio promotion in the Midwest in the early Noughties, also succumbed to the hideous disease. On top of that, Chester still felt a degree of guilt at walking away from Stone Temple Pilots; Scott Weiland's passing from an accidental overdose just weeks after Chester left the band had compounded his self-reproach even further. Chester's myriad problems caused him to begin drinking again – and drink he did, until he couldn't feel a thing – to the point he would blackout before waking up and repeating the vicious cycle all over again. This continued for much of the second half of 2016, until he sought help through an outpatient treatment program. In therapy, he learned to better speak about his problems and about how and what he was feeling, and in being able to work through some of his issues, Chester began to appreciate the good things in his life. He had a beautiful wife, great kids, extremely supportive friends and bandmates who had his back no matter what. Chester also understood how fortunate he was that in fronting Linkin Park, he had one of the best jobs in the world.

When Chester joined Brad, Mike and the songwriting duo of Justin Trantner and Julia Michaels in Sphere Studios one day, he began to speak of feeling particularly overwhelmed by the destructive thoughts permeating his mind. 'Heavy' is the culmination of that honest and open conversation, the song taking its early shape from Mike playing a tender chord progression that lent some support and understanding to Chester's feelings, before Michaels chimed in with one of the album's most indelible lyrics. 'I don't like my mind right now' is that lyric, which inauspiciously begins the song that Mike felt represented the core sound of *One More Light*, and instantly reels the listener in like all good opening lines should do.

'Heavy' grew from being a Chester solo confessional into a powerful duet, where for the first time Linkin Park brought in a female singer to give the sing a different dynamic, and one which acknowledges the themes being explored aren't just felt by one person, but many, and from all walks of life. The band first asked Michaels to do the vocal, but she chose to remain in the background and assist on the chords and melodies (Michaels would actually release her own 'Heavy'-esque song in January 2017, which included the lyric 'When I'm down, I get real down'). When searching for another singer, Mike was put in touch with Kiiara, a rising singer-songwriter signed to Atlantic Records who had scored her first Hot 100 hit in October 2015 with the song 'Gold'. Interestingly, she'd also cited Linkin Park as being one of her biggest inspirations. Kiiara spent seven hours recording her vocals in late-December 2016, and the intricate interweaving of her and Chester's voices work well in expressing the emotional conflict when dealing with those inescapable thought patterns.

One More Light doesn't always portray such a crestfallen outlook, though. In fact, 'Heavy' has its own moment of hope when Chester's self-realisation finds him admitting, 'If I just let go, I'd be set free'. Elsewhere, the storm clouds temporarily part on the unencumbered ballad 'Battle Symphony' ('If my armour breaks, I'll fuse it back together'), and on the folk-tinged closer 'Sharp Edges', in which Chester playfully reflects on ignoring warnings and having to learn the repercussions for himself. The heartening line of 'We learn what doesn't kill us makes us stronger' provides one final moment of affirmation, and it puts earlier songs like the dispirited 'Nobody Can Save Me' into perspective. On 'Halfway Right', Chester looks back on the insanity of his drug-fuelled teenage years ('I never been higher than I was that night, I woke up driving my car'), and he shares his surprise at how the cycle of abuse continues to haunt him so many years later. On the energetic pop rock stomp of 'Talking to Myself', he writes from the perspective of Talinda, as he considers how hopeless his wife must have felt when watching Chester sink deeper into depression and addiction.

Mike's leads are less frequent on *One More Light*, but he shines on 'Invisible', in which he contemplates the effects of disciplining his children, before he offers a half-hearted apology on the tongue-in-cheek 'Sorry For Now', which is again inspired by fatherhood, for all the times he has to leave his kids behind to assume his Linkin Park alter ego ('There will be a day that you will understand'). The anomaly on the album is 'Good Goodbye', a sturdy hip hop number that offers a change of pace and rather interestingly incorporates basketball metaphors when describing trying to escape a toxic relationship. Instead of having just one guest feature on the track (Pusha T. delivers a rather toothless performance during the second rap verse), Linkin Park also called upon the British grime star Stormzy, who, after being on the band's radar for some time, takes his big chance in elevating 'Good Goodbye' in its rousing final third.

It's easy to sometimes forget that even in Linkin Park's heavier years, songs such as 'One Step Closer' and 'Crawling' were wrapped around pop hooks and pop melodies to hold everything together. *One More Light* is no different, it's just more blatantly obvious. The songs are able to glide in their rich production, courtesy of another meticulous process where the band searched high and low for the best sounds, samples, and beats to suit their atmospheres, without any notion of genre. When combined, the swells of warm synths, throbbing beats (both live and programmed), and complimentary guitar chords that sit underneath create a decisive contrast to the regularly combustible subject matter. And when a song does threaten to collapse under its own weight, there is always another sparkling melody that arrives to salvage the situation. From around 150 demos, the ten songs that make up *One More Light* are the ones the band agreed best represented Linkin Park in 2017. Unlike on previous albums, each song is its own statement, and they are given room to breathe without instantly transitioning into the next; their separations from one another intentionally orchestrated to help them build their own emotional arcs.

* * *

It's only natural that Linkin Park fans would want to build a similarly deep connection with every album in the same way they had with *Hybrid Theory*. They'd been doing it for years, dissecting each subsequent release to its bare bones, with surgical-like precision to see if the music could live up to their own expectations, and to the incredibly high standards *Hybrid Theory* had set from the off. Linkin Park's fanbase has always been outspoken, and the relationship between them and the band has long been built on mutual appreciation and respect. Linkin Park knew from the very beginning that not everything they did was going to please everyone, and they had experienced plenty of friction in the past. But the sheer volume of what has to be considered hatred that was aimed in the direction of *One More Light* was something the band had never encountered before. Opposition towards the album wasn't completely unexpected, and a rock band releasing a pop album was always going to set the cat among the pigeons, but the earlier songs that were released had created such a preconceived bias that the fallout became even more explicit upon the album's release, and of all the band members, Chester had the hardest time in dealing with it. If it wasn't enough that he continued to fight the demons in his head, now he was beginning to question whether he was good enough. Whether *he* was enough. The risks Linkin Park had taken on *One More Light* weren't in the pop nuances of the album's sound, but in the intimate revelations that had shaped the songs in the first place. Mike, and especially Chester, had done it many a time before, but never with the same rawness they were expressing this time around, and it hurt Chester to know that the album he'd gone on record as to call his favourite, having poured so much of himself into it, was now the subject of mass ridicule.

Linkin Park was accused of selling out, of following current trends to navigate their way back up the charts, and of seeking monetary gain. After Chester haphazardly invited detractors to 'stab yourself in the face' in a *Kerrang!* radio interview, if that was what people really felt were the band's intentions, the singer took a breath and regathered his thoughts before continuing. 'It doesn't matter if they like it or not. What matters is that you took the chance to do something that you felt was important to you, and that's what being an artist is all about.' Linkin Park never apologised for wanting to experiment with different styles, sounds, and genres, and they weren't going to start now. More importantly, they didn't have to. They never felt the need to justify why they changed course after *Meteora*, or why they were so infatuated with electronics on *A Thousand Suns*, and they didn't have to explain why they were going pop on *One More Light*. In truth, in pushing themselves to even greater lengths as songwriters and musicians, the band had never sounded as cohesive as on their seventh album.

One More Light isn't pop in the traditional sense. It isn't at all cheesy (even if there are a few too many chipmunk vocals for one's liking), nor was it directly manufactured towards achieving mainstream chart success. The album proved that not all pop music can be so inherently flawed, but that it *can* be creative, imaginative and most certainly compelling. After the band's run of number 1 albums had come to an end with *The Hunting Party*, its follow-up saw its creators return to the top of the Billboard 200 ahead of hip-hop's latest sensation Kendrick Lamar, and his critically acclaimed fourth album *Damn*. Getting to number 1 with *One More Light* was just an added bonus, but as Linkin Park celebrated their latest success and another job well done, little did they know their joy would soon be replaced by the most crushing sorrow.

Fig. 14

One More Light Goes Out

'No one really knows what run-of-the-mill depression is. You'll think somebody has run-of-the-mill depression, and the next thing you know, they're hanging from a rope. It's hard to tell the difference.' Chris Cornell's haunting and rather prophetic quote during a 1999 interview with *Guitar.com* came while the Soundgarden frontman openly discussed his own history of mental illness and substance abuse. Throughout much of the '90s, Chris, cited by peers such as Axl Rose, Eddie Vedder and Alice Cooper as having the best voice in rock and roll, had been able to manage his depression and addictions. But during a tumultuous period towards the end of the decade, where Soundgarden disbanded and his first marriage ended on an extremely sour note, Chris' substance abuse found him teetering on the edge. Even at his worst, though, where over the years he dealt with everything from crippling anxiety, extreme agoraphobia, and suicidal thoughts, Chris maintained a self-awareness that his darkest days were just patterns of life, and the next day could always be a better one.

By 2005, Chris was happily remarried, and his latest band, the hard rock supergroup Audioslave, followed up their powerhouse self-titled debut album from 2002 with the equally impressive sophomore effort *Out of Exile*. More importantly, however, Chris had quit alcohol and drugs altogether. Two years later, his commitment to sobriety and helping others in their own addiction recovery processes saw him become the latest recipient of the MusiCares MAP Fund's Stevie Ray Vaughan Award, something which Chester would also be awarded in 2013. Since 1993, the non-profit organisation had provided members of the music community with somewhere to turn in times of financial, personal, and medical crisis, as well as enabling access to addiction recovery treatments. On 11 May 2007, during the third annual benefit concert, Alice Cooper presented Chris with the distinguished award for his own tireless dedication in helping those in need, knowing full well that with the right support, they too could work through their struggles and come out the other side. Chester never hid the fact that Chris Cornell was one of his musical heroes, even after the two men became such close friends. While promoting his second solo album, *Carry On*, Chris joined Linkin Park on a two-week tour of Australia and New Zealand in October 2007, where he and Chester bonded over the hardships they had suffered, and the achievements they had accomplished. They were two extremely talented and influential artists from two of the biggest rock movements of recent times, but they were also two tortured souls. They were both sober, but it wasn't easy to stay that way, and in each other they could confide and lean on one another for support during constant battles they faced on a daily basis.

Chris also served as direct support to Linkin Park on the 2008 edition of Projekt Revolution, where each night he lent his iconic voice to an inspired rendition of 'Crawling', after Chester had done the same on 'Hunger Strike', a song Chris had written for the lone Temple of the Dog album in 1991, which featured members of the grunge band Mother Love Bone, and future members of Pearl Jam. On stage, the chemistry Chester and Chris shared was undeniable, and off it their bond became unbreakable. As their friendship grew deeper their families grew closer, and Chester was immeasurably proud to be godfather to Chris' son, Christopher Nicholas. Chester would later describe Christopher Jr.'s baptism and christening as two of his favourite memories of his entire friendship with Chris.

* * *

As Linkin Park prepared to perform a mini set for *Jimmy Kimmel Live!* on 19 May 2017, the day before *One More Light* was due to be released, the band's excitement for the show and their new album had been replaced by extreme sadness. Chester was particularly distraught, because along with the rest of the rock world he was struggling to come to terms with Chris Cornell's death. On the night prior, Chris appeared to be in good spirits as Soundgarden, who'd triumphantly reformed in 2010, put on a masterful show at the Fox Theatre in Detroit as part of their latest North American tour. The band's set featured many of their biggest songs, like 'Black Hole Sun', 'Fell on Black Days', and 'Rusty Cage', and during their final song of the night, the spectacularly heavy composition 'Slaves & Bulldozers', Soundgarden incorporated a refrain of Led Zeppelin's 'In My Time of Dying'. They had done so on many occasions in the past, but on that night in Detroit, its inclusion ended up being far more poignant than anyone could have imagined at the time. Within an hour or so of Soundgarden leaving the stage, where the band's respected frontman smiled and waved and thanked his fans for coming out, and telling them he would see them again soon, Chris Cornell was found dead in his MGM Grand Hotel bathroom with an exercise band around his neck.

Linkin Park's *Jimmy Kimmel* set was supposed to include an on-air performance of 'Heavy', but in wanting to pay tribute to Chris, they instead played their latest album's stunning title track. The stripped-down ballad, percussion-free and made up of only looped piano and emotive guitar chords to support Chester's spine-tingling vocal, is a song that offers care and support to those going through the grief of losing a loved one. Mike had written the song with Eg White, about the late Amy Zaret, whose passing from cancer had hit the entire band hard. 'One More Light' is the only full song title track in Linkin Park's career, and it became such because the band felt it was too important to just be an album track. It was, after all, a song of condolence, and its enduring line of 'Who cares if one more light goes out? Well I do' is heavy enough on its own, but when Chester sang it to honour one of his closest friends during that *Jimmy Kimmel* performance, it felt even more gargantuan. His voice trembles, and at times it breaks. Towards the end he can't even bring himself to repeat the chorus at all, and the pain on his face is clear for all to see as he sits on a stall, dressed in all black and wearing a pair of shades that do little to hide the tears in his eyes. That same day, Chester wrote a moving open letter to Chris on Twitter, in which he described the grunge star's talent as 'pure and unrivalled', and his voice as 'joy and pain, anger and forgiveness, love and heartache all wrapped into one'. Chester's grief had barely subsided when he performed an emotional rendition of Jeff Buckley's 'Hallelujah' (originally written by Leonard Cohen) at Chris' funeral on 26 May. In front of a diverse array of celebrities, from A-listers such as Brad Pitt and Christian Bale, to rockstars like Dave Grohl and Jimmy Page, Chester sang his favourite song of all time with Brad beside him playing the guitar chords, as a final goodbye to someone he called a hero, and someone he said he felt like he'd known his whole life.

Chester carried his grief with him as Linkin Park embarked on a European tour to promote *One More Light* at the beginning of June, headlining various festivals before the band finished up with some UK dates. After playing London's O2 Arena, Linkin Park took over the Brixton Academy for the first time since 2003, right before *Meteora* had sent the band into the stratosphere. The intimate Brixton show was billed as 'One More Night in London', and it consisted of a twenty-seven-song set where Stormzy was on hand to rap his part on 'Good Goodbye', and The Bonfire's Jon Green played guitar on 'Nobody Can Save Me', having previously recorded on the studio version of the track. The European tour should have concluded at the Manchester Arena on 7 July, but the show was cancelled following the tragic terror attack that had taken place in one of the venue's main entrances two weeks earlier. As fans began piling out of an Ariana Grande concert, where parents waited to collect their children and others moved towards the car parks, train station and food exits, a suicide bomber detonated a nail bomb which killed twenty-two people, injured over a thousand others, and caused significant damage to the arena's foyer area. At Linkin Park's Barclaycard Arena show in Birmingham on 6 July, which instead became the final stop on the tour, a typically enthralling performance saw Chester dedicating 'One More Light' to the victims of the Manchester attack. Ahead of the song, Chester spoke of unity, and of love conquering hate: 'We don't care what you look like, we don't care where you come from, we don't care what you believe in, we love every single one of you out there and nothing will ever change that.'

Chester's words epitomised everything he was about, and everything Linkin Park was about. From day one the band had been an open book. They could be the loudest and angriest-sounding band at times, but as human beings they were honest, loyal, kind and appreciative of the position they found themselves in to be able to give back to those less fortunate. Never once had they forgotten who had helped them get into that position in the first place, 'The best fans on the planet', as Chester described them. Whether it was before or after a show, and no matter if they were tired, sweaty and in need of some time to decompress, the band always came out to meet their fans and talk to them, to smile for photographs, sign CDs, posters and sometimes even body parts.

The Birmingham show wasn't a particularly momentous one in terms of prestige, nor did it allow the band to tick off another box in their list of career-defining moments. It was just another Linkin Park concert in which they gave a hundred per cent as they rifled through songs spanning their entire seventeen-year history, which ended with a typically rapturous performance of 'Bleed It Out'. As piercing feedback reverberated behind them, each member remained onstage to salute their audience, who were just a tiny smidge of the much wider Linkin Park community. The band shook outstretched hands and fist-bumped others in the front rows. They waved, blew kisses and bowed many times over, Linkin Park as humble as they had always been. Chester seemed more animated than the others in showing his own appreciation. Even as a certified rock god who possessed one of the most powerful voices in the history of the genre, and who had the personality to match, it seemed he still relied on the adoration of crowds around the world to make him feel like he belonged. No one knows if he ever truly believed just how much he meant to his fans, and to his bandmates and peers, but we all know the truth. Chester was enough.

Just two weeks after the Birmingham show, where he was smiling from ear to ear as he left the stage for the final time, Chester Charles Bennington lost a fight that his words and music had helped so many others to win. 'Shocked and heartbroken, but it's true,' wrote Mike on his Twitter just after 3pm later that day. Everyone was hoping the developing news story was just one big mistake, a tasteless hoax even, but Mike's despairing tweet confirmed that Chester was indeed gone, and on what would have been Chris Cornell's 53rd birthday. Like his close friend, Chester too had committed suicide by hanging.

No one saw Chris's death coming, but Chester's seemed even more unfathomable. Three months earlier, he'd spoken of not being able to see himself enduring those the same battles with addiction and depression like he had in the past, the reason he stated: 'because I have such good friends'. On the outside at least, Chester appeared excited for the future. He'd told his bandmates that their most recent European tour had been the best tour Linkin Park had ever done, and he was looking forward to the three-month run across North America that was due to begin in Mansfield, Massachusetts on 27 July. Outside of Linkin Park, Chester had been making moves to revive Grey Daze for a twentieth anniversary show, and to rerecord some of their early material for a future release. And outside of music entirely, Chester remained deeply committed to his family.

In the days prior to his death, Chester, Talinda and their six children took a trip to their cabin in Sedona, Arizona, which was set among steep canyon walls and vast pine forests. The Bennington clan were at one with nature, and each other. Chester then returned to Los Angeles early for some work commitments, while everyone else stayed behind at the cabin. Upon leaving, his kissed his wife and children in what was supposed to be a 'goodbye for now', but what sadly ended up being a goodbye forever. A photoshoot was reportedly planned for Linkin Park on the 20 July, and a music video for the second *One More Light* single, 'Talking to Myself', was set to be released that day, but when Chester's housekeeper found his body in his Palos Verdes Estates bedroom early that morning, nothing the band had in their itineraries mattered a jot anymore.

Later, Linkin Park founded the One More Light Fund, an offshoot of Music for Relief, to raise money and awareness in combating suicide within the rock community. Talinda founded her own charity too, the 320 Changes Direction, which set out to educate individuals on the signs to look out for in people suffering with mental health and addiction issues. In an interview with *CNN* almost a year after Chester's death, Talinda admitted that having never gone through depression herself, it made it harder for her to recognise when her husband was struggling, and to be able to relate to how he was feeling. In such instances, it can be near enough impossible for someone to read the warning signs, especially when those warning signs can be masked by a false smile or a disingenuous laugh, and transmitting a happy exterior that stifles the inner turmoil which one chooses to keep hidden from others. Talinda told *CNN* that as she became more educated in what kind of signs to look out for, she learned of the red flags Chester had exhibited, but which had sadly gone unnoticed by her at the time.

Chester's last relapse had occurred some six months earlier, but with the help of an outpatient treatment program, where, in learning to be more open with how he was feeling had plotted the foundations for 'Heavy' to become Linkin Park's biggest hit in years, it seemed Chester had left his latest slide in the rearview mirror as he became more positive for what was to come next. Towards the end of his life, however, he was resisting the urge to drink again. While downplaying the obvious parallels between Chester and Chris Cornell's deaths (some considered whether Chris' suicide had been the catalyst for Chester's own), Ryan Shuck told *Rolling Stone* in early August 2017 of how Chester had confided in him that he was enveloped in an 'hour-by-hour battle' with his alcoholism, and it seems the pressure of abstinence and ultimately bowing to it became too much for Chester to bear anymore. Even though it was only a trace amount, a toxicology report found alcohol in Chester's system, while the investigation into his death confirmed an empty bottle of Stella Artois was found in the bedroom's en-suite bathroom, and a half-empty pint glass of Corona sat on a nightstand near Chester's body.

The outpouring of love after his death was testament to Chester's character and his talent, where from far and wide people not only paid tribute to the musician he was, but to the man he was too. Words like 'gracious' and 'humble' were used to describe him. He was called a 'beam of light', and he was noted for his smile, intelligence, and his hard work and commitment. Musicians from bands including Black Sabbath, Guns N' Roses, KISS, Metallica, Mötley Crüe, Disturbed, Papa Roach and System of a Down all shared their own personal eulogies, some of whom highlighted just how seriously mental health issues should be better addressed. Chester's legions of fans paid their own kinds of tributes too, and whether it was through holding vigils that allowed others a place to be able to come together and share their grief, or through displaying fan art, or photographs or simply writing of their memories of Chester and just how much he had inspired or even saved them with his lyrics and music, the outpouring of emotion towards Chester quickly turned into a celebration of his incredible life.

Everyone was wounded, but none more so than Chester's family, close friends, and the remaining members of Linkin Park. Each of them had shared only single words, sentences or photos to express their pain before they collectively uploaded an open letter on their Facebook page on 24 July. In the letter, they described Chester's absence as 'a void that can never be filled – a boisterous, funny, ambitious, creative, kind, generous voice in the room is missing'. While the band retreated from the spotlight to privately deal with their loss, Linkin Park's music experienced a substantial uptick in sales and streams, as people went back and listened to songs and albums that Chester had poured his heart and soul into. All those years of lyrics had never seemed more relevant, and now they were being extensively studied like never before. According to Nielsen Music, *Forbes* reported that US sales had risen a whopping 5,300 per cent in the wake of Chester's passing, which also attributed to the impact that downloads and streaming had in giving people easy and instant access to music. In the UK, all seven of Linkin Park's studio albums, as well as *Reanimation* and the *Collision Course* EP, charted inside the Top 100 in the week beginning 28 July, three of which climbed back inside the top ten (*Hybrid Theory* at four, *One More Light* at five), and *Meteora* at seven), while Dead by Sunrise, and Chester's contributions to Stone Temple Pilots were also re-evaluated by his devoted supporters.

It's understandable why people would want to go back and study Chester's lyrics and go in search of any clues that could point to a reason why he chose to cut his life so terribly short. Some consider *One More Light* to be filled with lyrical cries for help, but had Chester not sang about those same struggles for years? On 'Nobody Can Save Me', the first song on the album of which its title already paints a depressive picture, Chester's very first lyric reads, 'I'm dancing with my demons/I'm hanging off the edge'. Yet, seventeen years earlier, he'd already been 'one step closer to the edge'. Beyond any shadow of a doubt, Chester meant every word he ever wrote, said or sang, but more importantly he felt them too. His lyrics not only helped others in such a profound way, but they were just as therapeutic for the man who was writing them. That they were then accompanied by absorbing melodies and killer hooks, and turned into songs that became megahits or part of chart-topping albums was just a bonus, and a reward for Chester being so open and honest. It was what helped him become a voice for the voiceless, and the voice of an entire generation.

No one will ever know why Chester or Chris Cornell took their own lives, but that is often the way with suicide. Sometimes there simply are no answers. It's what makes the loss of those who feel that suicide is the only way out all the more gut-wrenching, and it can make us wish we could have done more while they were still with us. But all we can do is honour them posthumously and keep their memory alive, like how Linkin Park honoured Chester's memory in the only way they knew how, through the power of music and performance. On 27 October 2017, the band regrouped, brought their fans together, and invited a revolving door of musical friends for a tribute concert at the Hollywood Bowl. Dubbed 'Linkin Park and Friends: Celebrate Life in Honor of Chester Bennington', the three-hour YouTube livestreamed event featured soaring renditions of the band's biggest songs, as well as video clips from musicians who couldn't be in attendance but who wanted to share their own memories of Chester. There were also pieces of archive footage depicting Chester's playful character, while on-screen graphics between performances promoted mental health awareness. After weeks of rehearsals with the planned guests, to iron out all the creases in the song arrangements and everything in between, Linkin Park was joined by Jonathan Davis from Korn, Bring Me the Horizon's Oli Sykes, Ryan and Amir from Dead by Sunrise, Daron Malakian and Shavo Odadjian from System of a Down, and Blink-182 (there were many more) for heartwarming collaborations where their sole purpose was to honour their friend and peer. An estimated 1.4 million people tuned into the livestream, and today its viewing figures stand at over 25,000,000.

It was an emotional night for everyone involved, but especially for Brad, Dave, Joe, Mike and Rob. In their open letter to Chester, they described their love for making and performing music as 'inextinguishable', and after three months of processing their grief, they finally felt ready to get back onstage and do what they did best. Only this time, they didn't have Chester standing to the left or right of them, nor was he there to launch himself off Rob's drum riser, or wrap an arm around Mike's shoulder as they laid waste to another enthralling live performance of 'Papercut'. This was a whole new experience, and while they regularly relied on the assistance of others throughout the show, the standout moments came when it was just Linkin Park and the 17,500 fans in attendance. No guest spot compared to the band performing the instrumental of 'Numb' while the entire crowd faithfully sang the lyrics in tandem, or when they did the same on the choruses of 'In the End'; their collective voice so loud and pure that Chester could hear them and be proud of the legacy he'd left behind. 'One More Light' presented another powerful juncture, which Mike sang to a backdrop of phone lights that illuminated the Hollywood Bowl and perfectly demonstrated the song's theme of togetherness in the midst of loss. 'One More Light' had grown from honouring Amy Zaret into a widely praised tribute to Chris Cornell, and now it had taken shape as the official anthem of remembrance for Chester. The song had been released as a single earlier in October, and it came with a music video directed by Joe and Mark Fiore, which compiled a litany of behind the scenes footage of Chester from over the years. He is seen in recording studios, greeting fans, helping out with Music for Relief and performing live around the world, where he was at his absolute best and firmly in his element.

Following 'One More Light', the time felt right for Mike to perform a song he'd written as his own ode to Chester. It too was a ballad, titled 'Looking for an Answer', in which Mike sang of how he could have said or done more to help his friend, while hoping he was now in a happier place and finally at ease with himself. Like the professional he is, Mike powered through the song, even if at times his emotions threatened to get the best of him. There had been the occasional vocal break or lump in the throat moment earlier in the evening, sometimes during a song, or in the middle of a speech, but as the twinkling keyboard chords rang out in front of an audience who stood in a captivated silence, Mike's stunning vocal did himself and the song he'd written about his close friend absolute justice.

The concert raised significant money for the One More Light Fund, where no matter how many times the mental health captions appeared on screen, the importance of promoting awareness could not be underestimated. Later in the evening, Talinda took to the stage and gave her own speech. First, she thanked friends, family, Linkin Park and the fans for all the support she'd received in the days, weeks and months since Chester's passing. Then she spoke passionately about how mental health should be equally as recognised as physical health, and of her 320 Changes Direction initiative, where the '320' part of the name was inspired by Chester's 20 March birthday. As she signed off ahead of Linkin Park's encore, on a night that had been about one man, but also to raise awareness of a common issue that so many experience at one time or another in our lives, Talinda said what everyone else was thinking as she implored us all to help break the stigma and overcome those vicious cycles of despair. 'Fuck depression,' she said. 'Let's make Chester proud.'

Fig. 15

Going Underground

Most artists who have been around as long as Linkin Park tend to have a vault full of unreleased material, most of which never gets to see the light of day for one reason or another. In Linkin Park's case, their copious amounts of dusty hard drives have long held an abundance of hidden gems, and in recent years the band has begun to share even more of them with the world.

Previously, the Linkin Park *Underground* albums were a gift that kept on giving between 2001 and 2016. From the first release that presented a limited reissue of the *Hybrid Theory EP*, and for fifteen consecutive years after, demos, instrumentals and live recordings spanning every era of Linkin Park up until *One More Light* have further bolstered the band's expansive library. The bloodthirsty rap rock track 'QWERTY' was recorded just days before Linkin Park flew out to Japan in the middle of working on *Minutes to Midnight*. They'd planned to incorporate a new song into their sets that had killer live energy, and after Mike and Chester finalised the lyrics on the flight over to the Far East, 'QWERTY' went down well with fans across those four shows, some of whom recorded the performances and uploaded them online for others to hear what Linkin Park had been working on for their third album. Ultimately, 'QWERTY' proved to be too heavy for the alt rock leanings of *Minutes to Midnight*, even after the song was reworked in the studio with Rick Rubin, but that later version ended up appearing on the *Underground 6* album, which was released in December 2006, as well as a chaotic live recording from the band's show in Chiba.

The catchy piano rocker 'What We Don't Know', and the electro-punk of 'Across the Line' were also close to completion before being cut from *Minutes to Midnight*, and they appear on *Underground 9.0: Demos*, and *Underground X* respectively, and as the years moved on, Linkin Park continued to unearth deeper cuts from the past. The 1997 Xero demo 'Coal' hints at what the song could have become with a little more work, while the rough but buoyant duo of 'Blue' and 'So Far Away', both recorded in 1998 when the band was known as Hybrid Theory, are songs that showed promise as the band continued to build some early chemistry with Chester now part of their line-up. Other nods go to 'A.06', which stemmed from the *Meteora* sessions. There are at least three versions in existence, including the thunderous instrumental used to promote the sophomore album in a TV commercial before its release, and another in which Mike raps over a barrage of distorted guitars and bell-like synths. 'Sold My Soul to Yo Mama' is another flashy instrumental created almost solely by Joe, in which he samples 'Points of Authority', and the 'Ppr:kut' remix from *Reanimation*, while the hip hop exercise 'Standing in the Middle' emerged from Mike, Motion Man and Kutmasta Kurt recording a second track together after they had completed work on their 'Enth E Nd' remix.

In 2008, Mike, Brad and Chester appeared on the Busta Rhymes single 'We Made It', which was presented as 'Featuring Linkin Park'. It was the first time since *Collision Course* that the band had collaborated with a rapper, and the hip hop-heavy number, which later featured on Busta's 2009 album *Back on My B.S.*, includes a stellar set of bars from Mike, and an anthemic Chester chorus, before Brad delivers a 'Papercut'-like guitar refrain.

In a further example of Linkin Park's philanthropy, the band took their unfinished *Minutes to Midnight* demo 'Not Alone', and turned it into an electronic alt rocker for the *Download to Donate for Haiti* benefit album, in which its proceeds went towards relief efforts in the aftermath of the earthquake which struck the Caribbean in January 2010. Complete with new lyrics, the track floats with pure melodies, nimble guitar chords, and a programmed beat, as Chester delivers a heartfelt vocal like he'd provided to 'The Little Things Give You Away', and his 'Home Sweet Home' collaboration with Mötley Crüe, when also helping to document the effects of natural disasters.

The final *Underground* album was released in 2016, by which time the more recent compilations had featured a plethora of *A Thousand Suns*, *Living Things*, and *Hunting Party* demos. Most of them are only in instrumental form, some driven by heavy guitars and drums, and others that are more electronically charged. Still, they provide fascinating insights into just how many ideas Linkin Park toyed with in the early stages of writing an album, as well as the extreme lengths they went to in documenting them all, regardless of whether they ever planned on expanding them or not.

*   *   *

Linkin Park was stuck in limbo after Chester's death. The whole world wanted to know what the future held for the band, if there was even a future at all, but as one year passed and then a second and a third, there were no signs of a comeback on the horizon. Some of the band members had spoken of their desire to continue on, and to write new music and return to playing shows, but they didn't know how or what that would look like without Chester's irreplaceable voice and unerring presence.

The *Underground* albums in all reality had barely scraped the surface of what Linkin Park still had hidden away, and as more and more people longed to hear Chester's voice on previously unheard material, the twentieth anniversary of *Hybrid Theory* posed a good time to dust off those hard drives again and take a trip down memory lane. *HT20* was announced in September 2020, while much of the world remained in lockdown mode after the Covid-19 outbreak earlier in the year. Alongside a digital release containing a staggering eighty tracks, extravagant deluxe and super deluxe boxsets were also produced, featuring vinyl reissues of *Hybrid Theory* and *Reanimation*, and for the very first time the *Hybrid Theory EP*. There were also multiple DVDs, an eighty-four-page book full of never before seen photos and interviews, lithographs, posters and even a replica two-track Street Team cassette sampler. The majority of demos and rarities had already been shared online over the years, or on *Underground* albums, but there was significant excitement surrounding the inclusion of the long sought-after 'Pictureboard', which until then had never been released in any shape or form.

'Pictureboard' is a very early Xero track written by Mike and Mark, which grew in prominence after Chester joined the band. He recorded his own vocals on the song, and at some point in early 2000, Linkin Park performed the scratch-heavy rap rock track live on just one occasion. During a handful of shows in 2001, the band played a snippet of the track as an interlude in between songs, where at the time fans gave it the unofficial title of 'Be

Yourself' because of Chester's shortened vocal refrain. The interlude was performed too well for it to be an improvised jam, which only added to fans' curiosity of what the piece was and where it came from. Over the years, Mike had mentioned the song's existence, and even without a studio recording ever being released, 'Pictureboard' developed a cult-like following. In 2009, fans began to salivate at the prospect of it finally getting a long overdue unveiling, when it was set to be included on the *Underground 9.0: Demos* album, but at the last minute it was removed because the song featured a Barry White drum sample in the verse beat. 'You guys think it's like this imaginary holy grail of a song. It's really not that great,' said Mike during an *LPAssociation* podcast in 2015, when speaking of how trying to get the sample cleared was more hassle than it was worth. Eventually, 'Pictureboard' got its release as part of the *HT20* collection, and while it didn't quite live up to the hopes and expectations that came from its years in mystical solitude, the song's energetic bursts and the quieter trembling verses capture a band who was raw and up for the fight, but who were still searching for a formula that suited their combined influences and personalities.

'She Couldn't' is another track given its first official release on *HT20*, some eleven years after it was first discovered by fans when a copy of an eight-track *Hybrid Theory* demo was sold on eBay. Nothing was known about the song at the time, but the demo evokes a moody prowess that is transmitted through sleek synths, vocal loops, and trip-hop beats. 'She Couldn't' revealed a huge stylistic departure from everything else Linkin Park had written and recorded for *Hybrid Theory*, where the intention was to purposely try something that wasn't built around distorted guitars. The song runs for well over five minutes, partly because of its extended instrumental breakdown, which ultimately foreshadowed the band's genre-bending exploits in the years to come. 'In searching for our "first sound", we set the groundwork for our later evolution', wrote Mike in 2020, when 'She Couldn't' was announced as an immediate download for those who pre-ordered the *HT20* boxset.

During its latest rebirth, *Hybrid Theory* returned to the charts at 12 on the Billboard 200, and the boxsets sold over 66,000 copies. It may not have been new music, but *HT20* was the first Linkin Park release since *One More Light*, and the first since Chester had passed. The burning question still remained on whether the band would continue, but Linkin Park didn't have to write another song ever again if they didn't want to, and their enduring popularity proved that. They were still one of the biggest bands in the world, one of the most followed artists on all social media platforms, and their songs were still being streamed thousands of times every day. Their prolonged period of studio inactivity hadn't made them any less in demand, and it remained that way as their next album approached its own twentieth anniversary. This time however, sifting through those hard drives would uncover something bigger than any member of Linkin Park could have anticipated.

*   *   *

No one was prepared for a song like 'Lost', where even from the short teaser that preceded its release, an irrevocable voice was still singing of the same mental frailties that had taken him from the world six years earlier.

'Lost' kickstarted the twenty-year landmark of *Meteora* in February 2023, and Linkin Park celebrated it with another sprawling boxset. They hadn't planned on doing another one, not after the amount of work that had gone into creating *HT20*, but its success, and having found so many long-forgotten gems from their second album cycle, made it clear that *Meteora* deserved the same treatment as its predecessor.

'Lost' was the final song to be cut from *Meteora*. The band deemed its electronic undertones, its compellingly melodic chorus, and Chester's painful lyrical admissions all sounded too similar to 'Numb', and with only one spot up for grabs on the final track listing, one of the two songs had to go. By all accounts there wasn't much in it, but Linkin Park decided to keep 'Numb', and in hindsight it was a smart decision. But, 'Lost' also had 'megahit' written all over it, from its tingling melodies to the fluctuations of quiet and loud and then back again, all the while conducted by Chester's deftly intimate vocal during the verses, before it soars on the colossal hook. Extracts of the song had been showcased back in 2003 on the *Making of Meteora* DVD, where eagle-eyed viewers had spotted a lyric sheet for 'Lost', and also in an *LPTV* episode covering Linkin Park's time on Summer Sanitarium. 'Lost' would have been great in 2003, but in 2023 it was massive. The song may have been twenty years old but it still sounded fresh, and it was popular, so much so that 'Lost' was the biggest song of 2023 on Billboard's Rock

Airplay, where it topped the chart for over TWENTY weeks. It also went to number 1 on Mainstream Rock for eight weeks, while a 38 on the Hot 100 gave Linkin Park their biggest hit on the chart in over a decade. Still, Linkin Park was continuing to show the younger bands how it was done.

While 'Lost' is effectively a demo, Chester's vocal is fully mixed, and it's his greatly missed presence that makes the song so special. The wider reaction to another unreleased Linkin Park song was always going to be overwhelming, where with jubilation came an equal measure of sadness as everyone sought to reacquaint themselves with an old friend. It's why a host of YouTubers and TikToker's around the world shared their first listen of the track in reaction videos, many of whom were unashamed to show their faces on camera with tears streaming down their faces as every line reopened old wounds. 'Lost' hits differently to any other Linkin Park song, a large reason being because Chester sounds so alive and, well? While its subject matter is still mired in the same hopelessness that carried so many other tracks from the past, it was also in being the first true posthumous song the band had released since Chester's death that gives 'Lost' a completely different kind of aura.

The fact that 'Lost' was unearthed by complete accident seems rather incredulous, but that's how Mike came across it. He was specifically searching for another song from the *Meteora* sessions, 'Fighting Myself', which follows the hit single on the track listing of the *Lost Demos* disc. The flow of the track, and its grinding guitars, sound similar in places to 'Hit the Floor' and features another painful Chester admission during the staccato chorus ('Fighting myself, I always lose'). Of the other new additions, 'More the Victim' glides with its pop melodies, rich waves of synths, and an up-tempo beat, and the industrial crunch of 'Massive', a song Chester wanted to include on *Meteora*, contains a rare-at-the-time lead singing vocal from Mike.

After the *Meteora* boxset, it seemed to those on the outside that Linkin Park had reached a point where they felt content to go their separate ways, especially when the band released *Papercuts*, their first hits compilation album, in April 2024. As well as many (but not all) of their classic tracks, 'Lost', 'QWERTY', and the previously unreleased *One More Light* outtake, 'Friendly Fire', were also included on the album. It certainly felt like a line was being drawn in the sand, as the seventh anniversary of Chester's passing approached and apart from Mike, the rest of Linkin Park became less and less active on social media. *Papercuts* was a further reminder, if anyone really needed it, of just how good Linkin Park was at turning their hand to any style and genre of music. From 'Crawling' to 'Faint', 'Papercut' to 'Breaking the Habit', and 'One Step Closer' to 'New Divide', almost everything the band touched turned to gold, and they had the accolades, the chart successes, and the record sales to back it up.

It felt, in watching from afar, as though Linkin Park was bowing out in one final blaze of glory, and *Papercuts* was like an end-credit sequence at the conclusion of a sprawling epic. The band's career had been like that for over twenty years, where in that time there had been unprecedented highs, desperate lows and a heartbreaking loss that overshadowed everything that came before it. No one would have blamed Linkin Park for calling it quits there and then, because they had nothing to prove, either to themselves or to anyone else.

A career-spanning compilation album seemed as good a way as any to bow out on their own terms. But Linkin Park wasn't done yet.

Fig. 16

Beginning (Again) at Zero

rom Zero is an album born from resilience and resolve. It took years to come to fruition, where before the songs could blossom from faceless ideas, the biggest hurdle came in Linkin Park rebuilding themselves, as a band and as human beings, after their tragic loss. The album's title tips its hat to both the past and the present, in acknowledging where it all began in the late-'90s as Xero, and in symbolising a new and exciting era in the here and now.

Linkin Park's eighth album arrived on 15 November 2024, seven-and-a-half years after their last, and just over two months after the band made their sensational comeback with a livestreamed concert at Warner Bros. Studios in Burbank, California. But it was a different Linkin Park who took to the stage on that Thursday 5 September afternoon, which only featured three of the original six members. One of them couldn't be there for obvious reasons, but viewers were immediately left wondering why Brad and Rob were nowhere to be seen either. Mike, Dave and Joe were joined by Colin Brittain, Alex Feder and at the beginning of the second verse of the opening song 'The Emptiness Machine', Emily Armstrong. It still sounded like Linkin Park, though, even if some of the old songs the band performed were in a slightly different key to suit the strengths of Emily's voice, and the trio of new additions to the line-up brought renewed energy, and a dynamic extension of Linkin Park's multifaceted aesthetic.

From Zero features those same characteristics. It has all the hallmarks of the original Linkin Park sound, but it also includes fresh formulas and styles that cater for the band's stringent creative enterprise. How Linkin Park was able to return more than seven years after Chester's death is a long and winding story that involved a great deal of soul-searching, many in-house discussions, and a lot of writing sessions with outside collaborators. It took over five years, with a global pandemic in between, for the band to find the answers they were searching for, and to be able to get into a position where they could consider a future without Chester. When Linkin Park did return in 2024, it was the beginning of one of the biggest rock comebacks in years.

* * *

During a short interview with *Wired in the Empire Show with Mike Z* on 30 March 2024, Orgy frontman Jay Gordon was talking about his own band's career when he mentioned working on the 'Pts.OF.Athrty' remix for *Reanimation*. He then sang the praises of Chester and Linkin Park, before casually adding how he'd heard, 'They got a girl singer now'. The interview went viral because of that one quote, and because of the media frenzy Jay had mistakenly created, he was forced to come out and say his comments had been taken out of context. But, when *Billboard* reported a month or so later that the William Morris Endeavour booking agency (WME) had started taking offers for tour and festival bookings in 2025, it seemed something was finally brewing in the Linkin Park camp. In that same article, *Billboard* also claimed that sources were indicating the band was indeed leaning towards bringing in a female singer, and those who had considered Jay Gordon's remarks as pure hyperbole were now wondering if he knew something that everyone else didn't.

So, if Linkin Park was to have a female singer, who were the frontrunners? Evanescence's Amy Lee was the first name on a lot of people's lips and keyboard fingertips, as music blogs, social media channels and fan chatter all discussed the possible contenders. Linkin Park and Evanescence had first crossed paths in 2002, when they were recording their *Meteora* and *Fallen* albums at the same time at NRG Studios. Evanescence was a little late to the nu metal party, not that they wanted to play up to that scene at all. First and foremost, they were a gothic metal band, and *Fallen* was going to be a deeply personal album for Amy. When she was just 6, she lost her 3-year-old sister to an unidentified illness, and *Fallen* found Amy unloading her lingering grief, and years of teenage angst, into a set of catchy hard rock songs that possessed haunting, and at times darkened, twists. The authenticity of her work came under immediate threat, though, when Evanescence's record label, Wind-up, demanded that two thirds of the album's tracks include male rapping vocals.

Wind-up wanted to market the band in the same space occupied by – and it has to be said, dominated by – Linkin Park. There were very few female-fronted bands in that scene either, and Wind-up didn't mince their words when they told Amy that a male voice was needed to turn Evanescence into a more credible proposition. Initially, Amy threatened to give up on her dreams and return home to Little Rock, Arkansas. Her decision to cut and run was partly inspired by a conversation she'd had with Chester at NRG, when she told him how her record label was trying to make Evanescence sound like Linkin Park. Chester told Amy to stand her ground, which she did for a while, until a compromise was made in that only one song on the album would include a male rapping part.

Mike was first asked to feature on the post-bridge of 'Bring Me to Life', a song that already had hit potential with or without a proposed guest spot. Mike wasn't aware of Evanescence, or what the band even sounded like, and with Linkin Park working on only their second album, he preferred to keep his 'rap thing' for his own band instead of branching out and incorporating it into someone else's music. Needless to say, Mike passed up the offer. In the end, Paul McCoy from the Christian hard rock band 12 Stones supplied the rap vocal, and Wind-up promoted 'Bring Me to Life' to the moon and back. The song became Evanescence's breakthrough hit and the biggest song of their entire career, going to number 1 in the UK, top five on the Hot 100, and winning a Grammy for Best Hard Rock Performance in 2004.

Linkin Park and Evanescence were never closer than during their time at NRG, but even then the two bands were only on casual speaking terms. Evanescence became one of the biggest rock bands in the world on the back of 'Bring Me to Life', and *Fallen* ended up being certified diamond in the US. Despite constant line-up changes, Amy has remained the heart and voice of Evanescence, as well as a beacon of inspiration for all female musicians who have tried to break into a male-dominated rock scene. So it wasn't completely out of the question that Amy Lee could have been earmarked to lead Linkin Park's second coming; except it wasn't her.

In an April 2024 interview, she was asked about her potential involvement with the band, and she denied having any knowledge of the rumours that had started swirling, so with Amy out of the reckoning early on, the following months threw up more names like Bonnie Fraser from the Australian pop punk band Stand Atlantic, and Jennifer Weist from the German punk group Jennifer Rostock. Both singers had performed with Mike before; Bonnie as part of an all-star Aussie line-up of musicians who played a live-in-studio rendition of 'Bleed It Out', and Jennifer onstage in Berlin during Mike's world tour for his 2018 solo album, *Post Traumatic*, where she screamed her lungs out on 'A Place for My Head'. Or could it have been Halestorm's Lzzy Hale who, on the day that Linkin Park's mysterious 100-hour countdown was due to expire on 28 August 2024, had uploaded a piano and vocal cover of 'Crawling'? After four days of waiting and wondering, we were left none the wiser when the countdown ended with the simple message: 'Be part of something. September 5th. LinkinPark.com.' And then the timer began to rise once again.

* * *

Compiling the *Hybrid Theory* and *Meteora* boxsets helped keep the remaining members of Linkin Park engaged with one another. There were no immediate answers of where the band was going to go, or whether they could fill the gaping hole that Chester had left behind.

Mike, Dave and Joe had started writing together again in 2019, and at the time they had no specific project in mind. It certainly wasn't for Linkin Park. If anything, it was just three friends hanging out again and trying to rediscover a creative space where they could write music for the sake of writing music. There were no expectations other than to see where their ideas took them, but the process was slow and staccato, and as some of the ideas began to swirl around them, there wasn't enough momentum for anything to be carried forward.

The trio came together again later in the year, but this time it was to work with a number of collaborators, one of whom was Emily Armstrong. Emily was the lead singer of the LA punk/post-grunge band Dead Sara, who had two full-length albums behind them, and a third on the way. Emily Marcia Armstrong was born in Los Angeles on 6 May 1986, to parents who were prominent members in the Church of Scientology. By the age of 11 she was already a big music fan and writing her own songs and playing the guitar. Next, Emily developed a powerful singing voice, which extended to delivering some piercing screams that were inspired by hearing Chester's thunderous bridge on Linkin Park's breakthrough single, 'One Step Closer'.

Her early musical inspirations had been rooted in 1960s folk, where Joni Mitchell and Fleetwood Mac's Stevie Nicks were two important songstresses that a young Emily greatly admired. She was also into grunge, and acts such as Nirvana, and the female-dominated L7, and upon its release, *Hybrid Theory* became an album that Emily would play on repeat. Her first musical performances came as a solo folk singer, and as part of several school bands, and music became such a motivation in her life that Emily decided to quit education and focus on a career doing what she enjoyed the most. Alongside Susan Medley, who later went by the stage name Siouxsie Medley, Epiphany played their first show at The Mint in LA in March 2005. Not long after, they renamed the band Dead Sara, which rather comically came from a misheard song lyric in the Fleetwood Mac track 'Sara' (Emily and Susan thought the line began with 'Dead Sara…', when it was in fact 'Said Sara…'), but it would take four years and a revolving door of bass players and drummers before Dead Sara was stable enough to really move forward.

Even during her struggles with breaking her band through, Emily's charisma and vocal prowess was being recognised around Los Angeles. In 2009, she was brought in by Courtney Love to sing backing vocals throughout Hole's entire fourth album, *Nobody's Daughter*, and in 2011, Emily was name-checked by Jefferson Airplane's Grace Slick, when asked which contemporary female singer she most admired. Around that same time, Dead Sara was also endorsed by Dave Grohl, who came out and said the band should be the 'next biggest rock band in the world', and in 2011 they finally got their breakthrough with the single 'Weatherman'. They then released their self-titled debut album a year later, followed by *Pleasure to Meet You* in 2014, and then the Atlantic Records-distributed EP *Temporary Things Taking Up Space* in 2018. By the time Dead Sara announced their third album *Ain't It Tragic* in 2021, the quartet had signed to Warner Bros. Records.

Although they were effectively labelmates, Emily was unknown to Mike when some of his friends, and even Rob, had recommended he should meet her. In 2019, he and Emily came together for the first time for a three-day writing session, and post-Covid he invited her to return and write with the rest of Linkin Park, which now included Brad being back in the creative fold. Mike had continued to work with others in that period, but nothing he was doing felt as exciting to him as what he'd done previously with Emily. She had an infectious personality and she was easy to get along with and, just as Chester had been able to do, Emily could emote what she was singing in a way that others could only do in a performative sense. Emily also had a brilliant rock voice, and as she and Linkin Park continued to work together, basic ideas with no pre-determined direction or endgame slowly transcended into songs that were immersed in the band's DNA. To consider the songs anything other than Linkin Park songs would have been a disservice to the guys who'd written them, but by doing everything under a blanket of darkness and keeping their work secret from the outside world gave them the freedom in which they could work at their own pace, without setting themselves or anyone else up for disappointment if nothing came to fruition.

Mike was a believer in Emily from the beginning, and as time passed he could tell that his bandmates also saw what she was able to bring to the music. When Joe raised the idea of having Emily demo lead vocals on some of the song ideas, her voice was found to be a natural fit with the music, and it seemed Linkin Park had finally found a way of moving forward with someone who had all the tools to lead the band into a new era.

*   *   *

Colin Brittain, born Colin Cunningham in Pensacola, Florida, on 29 December 1986, was already a successful writer and producer when he first met Mike during a group writing session in 2021. What instantly drew them to one another was their shared outlook on music, where, like Mike, Colin was a skilled multi-instrumentalist who from a young age had learned to play the guitar, piano and his instrument of choice, the drums.

Colin was raised in Nashville, Tennessee, and as his father played in a country band, that was the music Colin was brought up on. When he discovered Rage Against the Machine, however, his sound base became rounded in rock and hip hop. As a fan of Nirvana, Blink-182, Green Day, the Notorious B.I.G. and Tupac, the musical differences inspired Colin into wanting to get into music production, and by the age of fifteen he was recreating samples and sounds from other songs, one of which just so happened to be 'Faint', by a certain Linkin Park.

More recently, Colin had written and produced a number of hit songs and albums for artists across all genres. Like Mike, his musicality also knew no boundaries, and whether it was playing the drums or the guitar, working behind a production or mixing desk, or writing songs from scratch, he and Mike's compatibility was what led to Colin being invited to write with Linkin Park. At the time, there was no hint of him becoming a fully-fledged member of the band, nor was Emily a shoo-in either, but as Linkin Park's reconstruction continued to gather pace, there were a couple of core positions that required filling.

Rob had already expressed his desire to walk away from the band, although the writing had been on the wall for some time. Fans were quick to notice his lack of involvement in the promotion of the *Meteora* boxset release and the *Papercuts* compilation, and contact between he and the rest of his bandmates had dwindled down to radio silence. When Rob confirmed he would not be getting back behind the kit, Colin was offered the full-time role of becoming Linkin Park's new drummer, as well as being signed up as a co-producer. Accepting the offer to join Linkin Park was a no-brainer for Colin, and while he did eventually land the drumming gig, his guitar skills also made him a prime candidate to fill the space that Brad was about to leave behind on the live stage. In the years since Chester's death, Linkin Park's inactivity had given Brad plenty of time to consider what was most fulfilling to him, and he'd realised that where he thrived most was in the studio. In wanting to focus on that aspect of the band, Brad decided to step back from the demands of touring and performing live. He would remain an official member of Linkin Park though, and record with the band in the studio, while also putting a great deal of energy into planning their live shows and creating setlists, as well as developing their concepts.

Colin was considered for the touring guitarist position, but his drumming talents made him a more viable option to fill the seat Rob had now vacated. At this time, Linkin Park was yet to meet Alex Feder, who was born on 20 November 1983 and raised just outside Washington D.C. Alex had taught himself how to play the guitar and the drums in high school, and in 2002 he co-formed the indie band The XYZ Affair, who independently released two EPs and a studio album before coming to an abrupt halt in 2009. That's when Alex chose to switch coasts and relocate to Los Angeles, where he began a solo career under the name Leonard Friend, and work as a touring guitarist for the Spanish pop singer Enrique Iglesias. Later, he performed with another LP, the rock singer Laura Pergolizzi, and as part of Miley Cyrus' backing band, before Alex met Mike and the rest of the guys in Linkin Park for some collaborative sessions in 2024. The sessions revealed Alex to be a strong songwriter, and an innovative guitar player who could tackle various styles with relative ease, and it was he who Brad hand-picked to take on the role as Linkin Park's touring guitar player.

Emily was officially welcomed into the band around September 2023, where her arrival came with the full support of her Dead Sara family. Even though she and Colin were a generation younger than Mike, Brad, Dave and Joe, they weren't rookies by any stretch of the imagination. They were both seasoned pros who had a wealth of experience behind them, and they were also able to bring a different perspective to Linkin Park; one which would help the band flourish in its new configuration.

* * *

On 5 September, Linkin Park was joined by an audience of LPU members and mailing list subscribers who were bussed to Warner Bros. Studios under police escort. It was miraculous that virtually everything the band had been doing for the last five years had been kept under wraps, but somehow they had pulled it off and now it was time for the world to bear witness to their long-awaited rebirth.

For the thousand or so people in attendance and the millions joining them in watching the livestream around the world, the sixty-minute concert that followed was liberating for the fans, and for Linkin Park. The band looked reinvigorated. They were smiling and having a lot of fun, and from the camaraderie between Mike, Dave and Joe, and the new recruits of Alex, Colin and Emily, the bond they had formed behind closed doors was unmistakable. On a stage that offered a 360° view of the band, and with an LED ceiling and lasers establishing a scintillating visual experience as well as an audible one, Linkin Park came out fighting with formidable renditions of 'Somewhere I Belong', 'Crawling', 'Numb', and 'One Step Closer'. During a mid-show break, Emily's vocal on a piano version of 'Lost' was haunting, while soaring takes of 'In the End' and 'Papercut' further highlighted Mike and Emily's imperious chemistry and their meticulous vocal transitions. Mike then announced the band's first set of tour dates, some of which would take place later that month, and the release of a brand new album entitled *From Zero*. The album's lead single 'The Emptiness Machine', which opened the show and made for the perfect introduction for Emily to take to the stage ahead of the second verse, was released on streaming there and then, as was its music video.

After bringing their set to a close with a typically pulsating performance of 'Bleed It Out', Linkin Park left the stage to rapturous applause, and Mike took the time to walk along the barriers to greet some of the fans, many of whom were evidently overwhelmed by what they had just witnessed. The show was a huge success. It was in part a celebration of everything Linkin Park had accomplished over the years, but it was also a tribute to Chester, who was sadly no longer around to be able to sing the songs that everybody knew and loved. Linkin Park could easily have returned with an arena or stadium show, but by choosing the intimate setting of Stage 30 at Warner Bros. Studios, it allowed the band to find their feet and shed any ring rust at their own pace. For one hour, they put on an emotional, powerful and triumphant performance, where with each song that passed by the weight of the world on their shoulders became that little bit lighter. By the time they left the stage, any doubts Mike, Dave and Joe may have had about bringing back the band were gone, and the explosion of energy that Alex, Colin and Emily had brought with them made for exciting times ahead.

*   *   *

There is often scepticism when any band announces a new singer to replace one who for so long was revered by millions. It had happened when Ronnie James Dio and Ian Gillan were both tasked with filling the shoes of Ozzy in Black Sabbath. It happened when John Corabi came in to replace Vince Neil in Mötley Crüe, and when Sammy Hagar took over from David Lee Roth in Van Halen. It has happened before, and it will happen again. But when that band is Linkin Park and the singer in question is Chester Bennington, whoever came in to replace the irreplaceable was going to be up against it from the start. Any male singer would have felt that same insurmountable pressure, like Chester had felt upon joining Stone Temple Pilots, so imagine how it was for Emily, who came in to sing songs that, thanks to Chester's undisputable genius, were admired the world over not just for how they sounded, but because of the pain and emotion that went into them.

From the moment Emily joined Linkin Park, she kept herself grounded. In preserving the integrity of the band and to honour the legacy Chester had left behind, Emily knew that the best way to do both of those things was by remaining true to herself. Most importantly, she had to identify what songs like 'One Step Closer', 'In the End', and 'Numb' meant to her as a singer, and not just as a fan who grew up listening to them over and over again. Fans of Dead Sara already knew of the impressive control Emily had in her voice, and the more Mike, Brad, Dave and Joe worked with her, they too saw the same star quality she possessed.

Linkin Park didn't need nor want a tribute singer. There were too many of them out there already, performing in cover bands or uploading their vocal covers on TikTok and YouTube. They didn't want someone who was going to sing Chester's parts in the same way as he had, and in Emily, the band knew she could bring a new dynamic to the older material with a female's perspective. Furthermore, Linkin Park had long explored the space between genres, and as they finalised the new songs which would comprise *From Zero* and rehearsed their older material in preparation for future live shows, every session made it more apparent that Emily's voice was built to cover every aspect of the band.

* * *

Like *Living Things*, *From Zero* features a little bit of every era of Linkin Park, as well as some exciting modern flavourings. 'Heavy is the Crown' is a *Meteora*-style roof-raiser built upon Mike's trademark verse rapping and Emily's huge singalong chorus, and the fifteen-second scream she emits on the song's thrashy bridge feels like a massive statement of her own intent.

Down-tuned guitars and a bombardment of scratches are brought to the *Hybrid Theory*-esque 'Two Faced', where its lead riff comes straight out of the 'One Step Closer' playbook, and Emily keeps her 'screamy pants' on for the hardcore-infused 'Casualty', and the biting punk essence of 'IGYEIH' ('I Gave You Everything I Have'). As good as Mike sounds vocally on the album (he doesn't look any different to what he did back in 2000, either!), it's Emily who shines brightest throughout *From Zero*. Her raw and gritty rock tones set the heavier songs on fire, just as her softer and melodic touches lend themselves to the vulnerability of the atmospheric alt pop of 'Over Each Other', the summertime vibe of 'Stained', and the endearing relationship ballad 'Good Things Go'.

Linkin Park worked with a number of outside songwriters for their eighth album, including Mike Elizondo, who assisted in the creation of 'Heavy is the Crown', and the album's most experimental track, the murky and industrial-tinged 'Overflow'. Elizondo had briefly been a member of Linkin Park in the late-'90s after Dave had gone on tour with Tasty Snax, but when he received an offer of becoming part of Dr. Dre's core creative team, Elizondo couldn't turn down the offer and he went straight into performing on Dre's iconic *2001* album as a multi-instrumentalist. He also recorded on Eminem's *Marshall Mathers LP*, before moving into songwriting and production and earning credits on a wide-ranging number of songs and albums by the likes of Snoop Dogg, Busta Rhymes, 50 Cent, Maroon 5 and Avenged Sevenfold. Other collaborators on the album include Timeflies' Cal Shapiro on 'Stained', Nick Long from the band Dark Waves and former *X Factor* contestant Bea Miller on the galloping alternative thrust of 'Cut the Bridge', and Jon Green and Matias Mora on the tension-filled ballad 'Over Each Other'.

By the time *From Zero* arrived, 'The Emptiness Machine' had already excelled in the charts. The lead single, which features primitive vocal interplay between Mike and Emily that builds towards the song's emphatic climax, scored Linkin Park's best debut on the Hot 100 since 'New Divide' by reaching 21. It also topped the Hot Hard Rock Songs chart for fifteen consecutive weeks, before enjoying a further ten weeks at the summit a short time later. Part of the song's success was down to the curiosity surrounding the band's new singer, who some knew from her time in Dead Sara, while others were less familiar with Emily and her musical credentials. A large proportion of

Linkin Park's fanbase welcomed her with open arms, but others were less certain of her appointment. Having anyone other than Chester singing alongside Mike on classic Linkin Park tracks felt wrong, and whether it was down to a stubborn refusal to give the new incarnation of the band a chance, or a bullish selfishness in not wanting them to succeed in their quest of continuing to create, the reaction to Linkin Park's big return was immediately met with a degree of backlash akin to *Minutes to Midnight* killing off the band's rap rock era, or when they went pop on *One More Light*.

Further questions were raised regarding Emily's background in Scientology, and a miscalculation she'd made in 2021 when attending a court appearance by her former friend and actor Danny Masterson, who was on trial for rape charges. With Chester's own history of sexual abuse, some launched a scathing attack on Emily, and the rest of Linkin Park for choosing her as their new singer, which cast a dark cloud over what had been an extremely positive few days since the band had returned to the stage and released a brand new single. In all fairness to Emily, she was quick to come out and draw a line under the controversy by confirming she'd cut ties with Masterson after the one and only court appearance she attended, as well as condemning all abuse and violence against women. Emily deserved the benefit of the doubt, and it seemed the main issue people had with her joining Linkin Park was that she simply wasn't a guy. 'There were people who lashed out at Emily and it was really because she wasn't a guy,' said Mike in a July 2025 interview with *The Guardian*, before adding how the fans were 'used to Linkin Park being six guys, and the voice of a guy leading this song'.

Despite those early minor hiccups, Linkin Park moved on and performed a handful of shows around the world ahead of the *From Zero* release, and after the media tension died down, it was the band's music that deserved to be the subject of people's broader discussions. *From Zero* clocks in at just under thirty-two minutes and is therefore Linkin Park's shortest album to date. Even so, they never planned to play their comeback safe, and the razor-sharp songwriting and oversized hooks helped steer *From Zero* to the top of the album charts in fourteen different countries including Australia and the UK. Upon its release, Linkin Park became the first band to occupy the entire top ten of Billboard's Hard Rock Songs since the chart began in 2020, and as of June 2025, *From Zero* has sold almost 1.5 million physical copies, and its tracks have been streamed over 1.5 billion times on Spotify alone. Most importantly of all, Linkin Park sound like they are simply having fun again which, after the grief and uncertainty they had experienced for so long, must feel far more rewarding than any other accolade that has followed.

The music video that was filmed for 'Two Faced' best represents the band's playful chemistry in their current iteration. Dressed in black suits and ties, Emily and Mike feed off one another's energy by laughing and smiling, and dancing and pulling faces throughout; the video far less serious than the heaviness the song emits, and the scolding lyrics that speak of betrayal and manipulation. The short skits between some of the song transitions offer the same carefree attitude, even if they lead into a sonic rager that takes them down a more serious path. It's in these moments that you can't help but feel delighted for Mike, Brad, Dave and Joe, and also for Colin and Emily, who get to be part of something far bigger than what Linkin Park has become as a band.

The album's sumptuous closer, 'Good Things Go', found some questioning whether the song was written with Chester in mind ('Sometimes bad things take the place where good things go'), and while it's actually about relationships and offers a lot of introspection and emotion, the way Mike and Emily present their back-and-forth vocals over melodic guitar chords, a looped beat, and ascending electronics, provides a stunning end to *From Zero*, while signifying the fully-realised crystallisation of Linkin Park's current form. It's good to have them back.

Tye Zamora (Alien Ant Farm)

Tye Zamora, interviewed especially for this book, is the former bass player of the platinum-selling rock band Alien Ant Farm, who rose to prominence in 2001 with their major label debut album *ANThology*, and their cover of Michael Jackson's 'Smooth Criminal', which became a hit around the world. Alien Ant Farm toured with Linkin Park on the Street Soldiers tour in early 2001, and again in Europe in 2003. They were also both nominated for a Best Hard Rock Performance Grammy in 2002.

In 2000, there was a bunch of bands coming up around LA, and we were playing with Incubus, Hoobastank, Snot and System of a Down, but I don't remember hearing the name 'Linkin Park' until there was a buzz about them with 'One Step Closer'. I'd seen the name 'Hybrid Theory' before in magazine ads for shows, and it was only later that I found out that Linkin Park was previously known as Hybrid Theory.

The first thing I noticed about the band was that whole electronic side to them, which I thought was pretty cool. They had this DJ, and they were using samples and beats and playing along to them. I noticed their structure and the way they did everything, with having Mike and Chester both as frontmen, one guy that was rapping and the other guy that's singing his ass off. I thought there were a very intriguing band, but what I really noticed about them was that I felt like they were kind of soundtrack-y, and not so much a rock band. I think that kind of set them apart. Their music was a little more orchestrated, and they weren't just writing riffs like the bands who were trying to be like Korn and Deftones. I don't want to take away from those other bands, but I wouldn't say Linkin Park was a super riff-y band. They were writing music that was a little bigger, and their sound was more spread out. They did make use of that half-step drop that the bands before them used, I noticed they did that a lot and it was kind of their hook, and that is what I thought made them sound like nu metal, or at least influenced by the nu metal bands.

As 'One Step Closer' was blowing up, we had just finished recording our *ANThology* album and we were putting our song 'Movies' out on KROQ, and then we got invited to do the Street Soldiers tour. We were the openers, then it was Taproot, and then Linkin Park. It was our first national tour as a signed band, and it was also our first bus tour, because we actually had a budget and we were able to get a bus so we could travel with everybody else. Our introduction to the Linkin Park guys was either at the St. Louis or Minneapolis gig, and while we were playing, I think it was Chester who stuck his head out of the drapes behind the stage and watched us the whole time. Anybody in the venue, especially from the balcony, could see him as clear as day, watching us from behind his drummer's kit. After that, Chester always hung out with us. He was on our bus, and he was always in our dressing room, because he got to drink and smoke. We got really close with him on that tour, and we were very fortunate to spend a lot of time with him.

We kind of came in hot with those guys. We were able to drink and party and do whatever we wanted to do, and we had to figure out that Linkin Park, other than Chester, weren't really about all that. I don't know if their tour manager Bob Dallas was trying to run a tight ship, but we weren't prepared for that and we did all kinds of stupid stuff around them. They thought it was funny though, and they had a good time watching us being complete idiots. They were nice to us, they didn't kick us out of dressing rooms, and we would just walk in with alcohol, full on ready to go. We just didn't know they weren't like that. They were kind of dry.

I remember we gave Mike shit at the end of the tour when he came on our bus to have a drink, and we were all, 'Where the hell have you been?' Chester was like, 'He doesn't do this kind of stuff', just busting Mike's balls about it, and Mike was like, 'Hey, I drink. I hang out', and we were like, 'Yeah, right, on the very last day? Whatever, dude.' I think that band knew exactly what they were doing and what they should be doing right when they started in the game, and I don't know where that came from because that is usually something you learn over the years. But I wouldn't put Chester in that same category. I think he was kind of the odd man out, wanting to do the stuff that we were doing. He was a friendly guy, and he loved everybody. It was usually us, the Taproot guys, and Chester together, and the rest of Linkin Park were on their bus. They did hang out with us, but not like Chester did. He was happy, and he probably felt lucky he was there. At least it came off that way. He seemed very humble, and it's really cool to be around somebody like that. But all the guys were great, and we loved their crew. We learned how tour managers run things through going out with Linkin Park, and I would say they introduced us to the touring business and the way it has been ever since. I know our drummer was tight with Rob, and Brad, 'Phoenix,', and Joe were really nice guys, and I felt like they were rooting for us, that they were always on our side and wanting us to succeed, and they would've helped us in any way they could.

In 2002, 'Smooth Criminal' was nominated for the Best Hard Rock Performance Grammy alongside P.O.D., Rage Against the Machine, Saliva, and Linkin Park. At that point we were on tour, and we only saw home for about a week. Our record label wanted us to be at the awards ceremony, and I know I didn't care to go. I'd rather go and spend time at home with my family and decompress a little bit. The label flew us home for the Grammy's anyway, but we didn't end up going, which probably made us look really bad for not representing them. When the nominations came out, we were stoked, but we all knew that Linkin Park was going to win. I never thought we were going to win, and if it had happened, we would've been super surprised, but the momentum of Linkin Park and that genre at the time, they were unstoppable. I think if 'Smooth Criminal' had been our own song then I would've been more hopeful, but Linkin Park was up for their own material ('Crawling'), and I don't think you ever give an award to somebody that didn't write the song. Not for a category like that anyway, because at the time it was a pretty big deal to be your own original rock band. Bands before us used covers as a stepping stone, like Limp Bizkit had done with 'Faith', and Marilyn Manson with 'Sweet Dreams (Are Made of This)', but for us, 'Smooth Criminal' ended up encompassing our whole catalogue and it kind of killed us because we couldn't live up to it. I guess we picked too good of a cover.

When we toured with Linkin Park again in 2003, they were just as flawless, but I felt like they had it from the beginning anyway. The difference I noticed between them in 2001 and 2003, besides knowing all the songs at that point and them having had so much success, was that they were the first band we toured with or were friends with that actually had production. They had a stage that looked like something else, with props on it and set design, and they looked so cool onstage. As far as with the guys, it was exactly the same as before. There were no egos, in fact we were probably even cooler to each other. They were closer with us, more comfortable, and it felt like we were seeing old friends.

Even though we all got along and hit it off, I didn't feel like we were super connected with the rest of the band on that first tour. We had the pleasantries, and we were fine, and they liked to laugh at us doing stupid stuff, like when our singer Dryden was dancing around naked outside their bus, or when we blew fireworks at them and they all got together at the front of their bus and were just laughing, but when we saw each other again in 2003 it felt different.

We'd seen them and hung out at awards shows in between, but in Europe it felt to me like they gave a shit about us way more. Maybe we'd earned their respect a little more by then.

Linkin Park have always been the same kind of guys. Every time they walked into a room, you got what you got. I never felt like they had any kind of ego, and I know some of them were definitely the bosses of the organisation, but I appreciated that, and they never seemed like they were too big for themselves. They were always good guys creating good music, and they are one of the bands you're happy for when they get big and successful, and I hope it continues for them.

When they came back in 2024, I saw everything on social media when it started and I thought, 'Good for them'. Throughout their entire career they've been plagued with naysaying, and I've always felt for them because they always wanted to step out and do something bolder and a little more out the box. I always respected them deeply for that, and I don't think it ever killed their popularity. Every single time they did something different, it validated them even more. And when Emily came in, I thought it was kind of cool because people are getting more open to female singers in metal. I felt like if they had brought another guy in, and Chester was in the same seat with Stone Temple Pilots, you're going to be constantly compared even down to the look. When I saw Emily, Linkin Park got to separate themselves even further away from Chester, and to me, it was more like, 'We're not trying to replace you, we're just doing something completely different', and I thought that was really respectful. They're just doing something where they don't have to worry about those comparisons, and to give themselves the ability to move on.

Chester was an absolute sweetheart. He's one of the sweetest guys I've ever met. The last time I saw him was when he was with Stone Temple Pilots, and I was doing a gig with Godsmack on the same festival bill. I'm really good friends with the guys in Stone Temple Pilots because the DeLeo brothers produced our *truANT* album in 2003, so I was welcomed into their camp to hang out. Chester and I spent a good half hour or so sitting there one-on-one, just talking and bullshitting away from everybody else. Those kind of times were when you realised what a genuine person he was. I've had people I considered friends that are of his status, that when I talked to them they looked past me or looked around as if they were looking for someone better to talk to, but Chester was not like that at all. He was always genuine, you always got a good conversation out of him, and you always got smiles, laughter, and hugs.

Watching videos of him now ends up turning into a reminiscence, and I know it's harder for a lot of people than it is for me, but it's something I'm still very sensitive to. I was devastated when Chester passed, and I'm still devastated. I tear up just thinking about it. I don't know if there's been anything in the music world that tore me up as bad as that. I'm glad I got to see him again. It was such a good moment that we had together, and we had it just to ourselves. It reassured me what a quality person he was. I've got a bunch of videos of us messing around and being stupid together, and some of them are on our *BUSted* DVD. I always spoke highly of Chester with my parents, and my mom especially has a love for him because in the videos I would always ask him to say hi to her. I don't know if she ever met him or not, but when we see anything that has something to do with him, it's not only me going, 'Oh man, there he is', but it's also my mom going, 'Aww, there's Chester'. It's sweet, and I love that he had that effect on people. Anytime that anyone sees him or sees his face, they just get happy.

I miss the guy, and I've missed him for these many years so far. I know he's a big shadow that the band is going to have to live under, but I hope the fans and everybody else can separate it and let them be who they should be. Like Chester, Linkin Park has a soft spot in my heart, and I know all of us in Alien Ant Farm felt the same way about them, and we all love them dearly.

Fig. 17

Legacy

Linkin Park's legacy expands far beyond the music they have created, the accolades and awards they have received, the records they have smashed, and the artists they have influenced. At a time when rap rock bands were becoming more commonplace, Linkin Park burst onto the scene by doing it completely different to how Rage Against the Machine and Limp Bizkit had before them. Instead of sticking to the mould, Linkin Park broke it, by pioneering their own sound that utilised electronics, the bending of multiple genres, and by presenting a double-barrel vocal charge unlike anything else that was around at the time. More importantly though, it was what the band had to say and how they said it that really struck a chord with nu metal fans all over the world, and thanks to Linkin Park's crossover appeal, listeners of other genres too.

As combative as their music is, where on certain occasions they can be as primitive as any other rock or metal band out there, Linkin Park's fractious tones are often parlayed with emotionally resonant lyrics. The pain, anger and mental torture that Mike, and more regularly Chester, sang, rapped or screamed of has always been documented with such raw honesty, and it went a long way in forming a powerful connection between the band and their fans. In the early 2000s, speaking about one's mental health felt extremely taboo in rock music. Linkin Park weren't the only ones singing of their personal struggles, but whether it was down to the profusion of melodies and pop hooks that shone among abrasive rhythm sections and moody riffs, or something else entirely, the masses seemed to find it easier to tap into the Agoura six-piece's music than they did the likes of Staind, or the slightly less accessible Korn, for example, both of whom were just as open with expressing their own inner turmoil on tape.

In Chester, a whole generation of music fans who were experiencing their own traumas, or who felt isolated and lost in an expansive world had found their idol. He was someone who possessed an incredible voice, and who wasn't afraid to use his painful past to try and fuel a better future. That he was just an ordinary guy who was as goofy and whacky as he was intelligent and empathetic made Chester all the more appreciated and respected, and even though he was just one part of a six-pronged behemoth of a band, where each member was as talented as the other, it was Chester who stood loud and proud and offered a beacon of hope to millions of lost souls who struggled to find their place, and some inner peace.

Linkin Park's willingness to address sensitive topics would pave the way for many future artists to do the same, and twenty-five years on there is a much greater openness in discussing those topics inside the music community, and outside of it too. Even so, there is still a stigma that refuses to completely rid the shackles, and after Chester's death, mental health remains a hot topic of debate. There are many of us who in one way or another are trying to help preserve Linkin Park's, and more Chester's, legacy. One of them is Jack Davis, who in 2019 founded the UPRAWR Mental Health Foundation. The charity is the latest extension of his UPRAWR brand, which in its early days helped define the UK's alt and emo culture in running weekly club nights at The Asylum in Birmingham, and in other venues across Britain. UPRAWR Studios, and their very own music publishing company followed, before Chester's passing inspired Jack to want to do his bit in raising mental health awareness and provide support to those in need. 'The UPRAWR Mental Health Foundation exists because of Chester Bennington,' Jack begins.

> His death was a devastating moment that deeply affected the alternative community – and it was the wake-up call that pushed us to act. Chester's loss made it painfully clear that something had to change. We set up the foundation to provide free mental health support to people in the alt rock scene, because too many felt like they had nowhere to turn.

The foundation is committed to building itself through music-oriented events, and its biggest and boldest attempt yet came in the form of 1000 Lights on 18 August 2024. It was no coincidence that the setting for the event happened to be the very same one that played host to Chester's last ever concert on 6 July 2017, the now renamed Birmingham Utilita Arena.

But how could a relatively small and underfunded charity excel in an arena environment – by inviting 1,000 guitar and bass players, keyboardists and drummers to play together to the music of Linkin Park.

But that was only part of the monumental event, which was led by the 'house band' L1NKN P4RK, who themselves had formed in the wake of Chester's passing to play tribute shows and raise money for charity. Joining the band onstage were members of established British acts like The Blackout, Bullet for My Valentine, Dream State and Holding Absence, for a riveting set performing Linkin Park classics such as 'Papercut', 'Points of Authority', and 'Bleed It Out'. Jay Fitzpatrick covers Chester's vocals in L1NKN P4RK, and he gives a brief rundown on starting the tribute band, and his experience of being part of 1000 Lights:

When I was 6, *Hybrid Theory* came out and my dad bought the record, and then he bought *Reanimation*, and *Meteora* a year later, and then *Minutes to Midnight*. Those records were always played around the house, or in the car on long distance trips, getting blasted from cover to cover. Linkin Park is something that's always been there and has been ingrained in me subconsciously from a young age. They are a staple band, and they have been part of my upbringing.

A lot of celebrities pass, and you see with die-hard fans that it really affects them. I never fully understood that until Chester passed. I know you don't know that person but because they've been such a big part of your life, when you find out about it, it does hit a little bit and you're like, 'Damn'. Off the back of that, we decided to do some shows to honour Chester's memory. We planned to do them the following year on the one-year anniversary; free-entry shows and with the idea of raising some mental health awareness and raising some money for charity, and just getting to play the songs that we all grew up listening to. Those shows all packed out, and then that's kind of where we were like, 'Maybe we keep on doing this?' and it's basically our full-time job now, while still donating money to charity and still doing something that feels like it's 'in honour of'.

We've been doing this for six or seven years now, and we've done some shows at The Asylum in Birmingham. They've always been good to us and been really hospitable, and we've always gone there and played killer shows. Those guys then launched the UPRAWR Foundation and we made some donations to their charity, and then they came up with this whole idea and concept and they approached us to be like the house band and to lead it all.

We were absolutely in, it sounded amazing, and it was incredible. We got to play with musicians we all grew up listening to like Bullet for My Valentine and The Blackout, and be surrounded by, and it was awesome. Actually getting to play that show was a dream come true, and it was a big moment for all of us to be doing what we thought was just a little tribute band that's grown into this massive thing that we're doing now, and I got to sing songs that Chester sang on that stage for the last time ever.

We were chatting to the guys leading up to it, and it looked like it wasn't going to happen at one point, but then it all came together and the amount of money they raised was incredible. They made all the money they needed to launch the charity, and it's a really great cause having free mental health counselling for people that need it. Those guys are incredible, and I think what they are doing is great.

Even more incredible was the awe-inspiring sight of a thousand musicians playing along to 'Numb' and 'In the End' in perfect synchronicity, to a spine-tingling backdrop of phone lights and audience singalongs as everyone in the Utilita Arena paid an emotional tribute to Chester, and to Linkin Park. 1000 Lights raised £130,000 for the UPRAWR Mental Health Foundation, which enables qualified counsellors to run one-to-one sessions, group therapies, and seminars for people aged 18–35 who are in some way related to the alt rock scene in the Birmingham area. Offering both online and face-to-face sessions, which take place in custom-built suites inside UPRAWR Studios and make for a more friendly and relaxed environment, the foundation is at last thriving in acting on its original intentions. Jack continues:

1000 Lights was born out of the same mission- to honour Chester's memory in a powerful, unifying way, and raise funds to help those who need it. Seeing one thousand musicians come together in his name was emotional and electric. It wasn't just a tribute, it was a promise- that we would keep showing up for one another. Chester inspired millions in life, and through the work of this charity, his legacy is still saving lives today.

Sean Smith from The Blackout, who acted as the honorary host of the 1000 Lights event, agrees:

It was absolutely magic. The feeling in that room was just love. I got to walk down on the floor and meet a lot of the musicians, and everyone was just grateful for the opportunity. Everyone was there because of their love for Chester Bennington and Linkin Park. It was an unbelievably brilliant and loving day. The tribute band who played the songs was brilliant and they were all good guys, and it was just amazing to look around onstage and see everybody smiling. We were all there for the same purpose, and it helped the UPRAWR Mental Health Foundation because after that event, they now have the ability to pay for therapy for people who need it and who can get to them in Birmingham. It was a special thing to be a part of, and I'm very grateful I was asked to take part.

Another of the performers who joined L1NKN P4RK onstage that night was Jessie Powell, who fronts the rising post-hardcore band Dream State, and in her own right has become one of the most popular female singers in the British rock scene. Jessie is a big fan of Linkin Park, and she has had her own mental health struggles in the past. As an ambassador for the UPRAWR Mental Health Foundation, being asked to take part in 1000 Lights in any way, no matter how big or small, was a no-brainer for her:

Mental health is really important to me, and especially looking after it, and even more so in the alt community. I was asked by UPRAWR to take part in the charity, and now I am an ambassador for them. I was very honoured to be asked to do so.

Linkin Park was one of the first bands I heard growing up that had screaming, and they were also one of the bands where I realised I could do that kind of vocal, especially the Chester fury, and even the rap vocals. I'd say they are a massive influence for me. Chester's words were so raw and deep, and when you're in that teenage angst phase, it felt comforting to know you aren't alone in some of your thoughts and feelings. Their music is so powerful and has connected with millions and millions of people all over the world. How special is that?

I can only describe being part of 1000 Lights as pure magic. The event showed that music truly is a powerful thing, and it brought so many people from all walks of life together as one. It was an event I won't ever forget, and one I'm truly grateful to have played a small part in. The success of the event was iconic, to be honest, and all the money raised is so important. It's going to help so many people and that is really special, and something everyone who was involved should be incredibly proud of.

It shouldn't take a celebrity, or anyone for that matter, to succumb to suicide for mental health awareness to be taken more seriously. If Chester's death has taught us anything, it's that no one should be left to hide in the darkness and let depression consume them.

Chester wasn't the first celebrity to commit suicide, and he certainly hasn't been the last, and as important as the UPRAWR Mental Health Foundation is to the rock community of Birmingham, there are numerous charities around the world offering the same essential support and understanding to those in need. According to the private healthcare provider Priority, one in four people experience a mental health issue every year in the UK, while in America, whose population is five times that of the UK, the National Institute of Mental Health (NIMH) estimates that more than one in five live with some kind of mental illness. Most of these charities have been around for years, but like UPRAWR, Talinda's 320 Changes Direction and Linkin Park's One More Light Fund were set up in the aftermath of Chester's tragic passing, and they too are invested in helping tackle the vicious cycle surrounding mental health, and the constant rise in the number of cases which, more than ever, are being seen not just in adults, but also among children and teenagers. Linkin Park's lyrics have long offered a friendly hand on the shoulder to let us know we aren't alone, but the band have only been able to do so much. Mental health charities are there to help navigate us through the gloom, but they too can only do so much, because in taking an important first step in actually asking for help, that is down to us.

*   *   *

Linkin Park brought the clash of rock and hip hop to its commercial peak at the beginning of the Noughties, and like their genre-bending exploits in later years, their influence on others shows no boundaries.

Artists far and wide have openly cited the band as a major inspiration in igniting their own careers, from heavy rock acts like Bring Me the Horizon, Architects, Of Mice & Men and My Chemical Romance, to those who draw more direct comparisons such as Hollywood Undead, and From Ashes to New. Outside of rock, DJ extraordinaire Steve Aoki, the electronic duo Purity Ring, popstar Billie Eilish and rappers Machine Gun Kelly and The

Weeknd have all spoken of how Linkin Park have inspired them over the years, but those names are just the tip of the iceberg. If you search deep enough on Spotify or YouTube, you will unearth no end of artists who in some way identify with the sonic power of Linkin Park's enduring legacy, and the amount of cover songs out there further attest to just how revered their music remains after all these years.

The band's philanthropy also deserves another honourable mention, where since its formation, Music for Relief has raised over $11 million for the various causes the charity has supported. From the staging of benefit concerts and visiting sites of some of nature's most destructive storms, to jumping on other shows and helping spread the word, Linkin Park's belief – and desire to use their name and voices to help others less fortunate than themselves when it would've been so easy to turn a blind eye – is just another reason why the band has always been a cut above the rest.

It hasn't always been easy for them, though. In the early days, record label politics tried to blur the vision of the band. Mike could so easily have been booted out, if Chester and the rest of the guys had not had his back, and even with all the naysaying that has followed their every move and stylistic change, Linkin Park's unity and the results of their creativity always made their refusal to bow down all the more spectacular. The band has sold over 100 million records worldwide (albums and singles combined), and from their record-setting streaming figures, YouTube viewing numbers, and the various chart successes throughout their career, Linkin Park have always done things their way, and never once have they played it safe.

Today, Linkin Park are as big as ever. As this book is being written, 'In the End' is spending its tenth consecutive week at the top of Billboard's Hard Rock Streaming chart. The *Hybrid Theory* cut, like the *Meteora* highlight 'Numb', have both been on the chart for over five years at this point without ever falling off it. 'In the End' is a 25-year-old song and it is still topping charts. Let that sink in for a moment. As of June 2025, Linkin Park has six songs that have surpassed 1 billion streams on Spotify, where the band has approximately 675 million active monthly listeners. According to Kworb.net, 'In the End' and 'Numb' sit either side of 2.5 billion, which is double what 'Numb'/'Encore', 'What I've Done', 'Faint', and the most recent addition of 'One Step Closer' have each amassed at this time. In total, fifty-two of the band's songs have over 100 million streams, and by the time this book hits the shelves, those figures are guaranteed to be much higher across the board. 'There are huge numbers of new fans, in the multiple tens of millions, on streaming platforms,' said Mike in an open-ed for *The Guardian* in January 2024. 'Back then, I would never have guessed the music we were making would continue to connect with people twenty years later.'

The band is playing their biggest non-festival headline shows of their entire career and regularly playing to crowds upwards of 70,000, and with Emily and Colin now onboard, the quality of their music is as strong as ever. In May 2025, the release of the deluxe edition of *From Zero* came with three new songs written during or just after the original album sessions. The explosive post-hardcore thud of 'Let You Fade', the intrinsically catchy 'Unshatter', and the enormously hooky 'Up from the Bottom', which gave Linkin Park their latest number 1 on the Mainstream Rock chart, display the same attentive songwriting and effortless execution the band has been delivering since the late-'90s, and while it might be a different Linkin Park today, it is one that Chester would be extremely proud of. He would be proud of Brad, Dave, Joe and Mike for firing up the Linkin Park engine once again and getting back to doing what they have always been destined to do: to create, perform and inspire. Chester's imperious talent and personality will always hover over the band, but it's with a remembrance of the past, and a guiding light towards the future. Chester is still a part of Linkin Park, and he is with them wherever they go.

As a fan, it has been emotional but also inspiring to witness the band's return, and it's exciting to be part of everything that comes next. It's great to see them performing with beaming smiles on their faces, and that they are having so much fun makes it all the more special. In the end, it's all that matters.

Acknowledgements

Writing this book has been a labour of love, and the hardest of any I have written thus far. While I was preparing to begin work on it, I was also building up to my wedding, and then my grandmother passed away less than six months before she was due to celebrate her 100th birthday. It was a strange time that mixed happiness and sadness, and in the aftermath, I was a little lost and void of creation.

It wasn't until January 2025 that I went full throttle into paying tribute to a band who has meant so much to me for the last twenty-five years. Upon the release of Linkin Park's 'Crawling' single in the UK, I was immediately drawn to its heaviness, its melodies, and the deeply personal subject matter. And of course, the voice of Chester Bennington. Korn was the first metal band I fell in love with, but Linkin Park wasn't too far behind, and *Hybrid Theory* became a staple album for me. It also became a staple album for my mother, who was going through her own trials and tribulations at the time, and in Mike and Chester's words and emotive vocal deliveries, she too, like myself and millions of others, found solace in them seemingly speaking directly to her, and letting her know she wasn't alone no matter how much she felt that way.

I have already written a book on Korn, which provided a full circle kind of moment for me, and with the release of *Lost in the Echo: the Story of Linkin Park*, I feel that same sense of emotional satisfaction all over again. Because of the dedicated fanbase that Linkin Park has amassed over the years, the incredible amount of archive footage, interviews and features that can be found on the internet have been extremely helpful in my research efforts. The Linkinpedia.com and Lplive.net websites have particularly offered a treasure trove of information, and they do a fantastic job in making sure everything that goes up on their sites is authenticated and comprehensively documented. One of the most enjoyable parts of writing a book is the research phase, in which I love to dig as deep as possible to find the tiniest nuggets of information that may not be so easily accessible, and I hope this shows during parts the book.

This is not the official, authorised biography of Linkin Park, but the importance of their music is the reason behind me wanting to tell the story of how they came to be, and how they fought tooth and nail to get into a position where they could show the whole world what they were truly capable of. It's the story of humble beginnings, and even after their many successes, the story of a set of humble human beings who never forgot where they came from. This is the story of Linkin Park, written as honestly, accurately, emotionally and respectfully as I could tell it. After all, Linkin Park is just as important a band to me as they are to all of you.

Thank you to the following people for their support, belief, and assistance in helping bring this book to life: my wife, Carly. I love you more! My mother, Sally. My father, David. Everyone at White Owl for putting their trust in me, and especially Jon Wright, who gave me the opportunity to offer up ideas after I originally reached out with a different concept for a book. To Olivia Camozzi-Jones for her guidance throughout the publishing process, and enduring my endless questions. Karyn Burnham for her editing expertise. Thank you to those who have contributed their time and voices for interviews: Barton Applewhite, Ciaran O'Shea, Sean Smith, Jay Fitzpatrick, Jessie Powell, Jack Davis (and for his fantastic work in founding and building the UPRAWR Mental Health Foundation), and Tye Zamora.

And last but not least, thank you LINKIN PARK. Thank you Brad, Chester, Dave, Joe, Mike and Rob for all the incredible music over the years. Like millions of others, your songs shaped my teenage years like you could never imagine. And thank you Colin, Emily and Alex, who are all doing an incredible job in helping continue the band's legacy in both the studio, and on stages around the world.

References

Interviews undertaken with Barton Applewhite, Ciaran O'Shea, Sean Smith, Jay Fitzpatrick, Jessie Powell and Tye Zamora have been condensed for clarity. Quotes from Jack Davis are as received through email.

Fig. 1: Beginning at Xero

Baltin, Steve. 'Linkin Park Looks Back on Its Pre-'Hybrid Theory' Early Days.' *Variety*, 9 Oct. 2020, https://variety.com/2020/music/news/linkin-park-hybrid-theory-early-days-1234799442/.

'History.' *Whisky a Go Go*, https://whiskyagogo.com/calendar/history/.

'Hybrid Origins: A Look Back At The Early Days.' *Linkin Park Live*, https://lplive.net/interviews/hybridorigins/.

Karma – Linkinpedia. https://linkinpedia.com/wiki/Karma.

MTV.Com: Linkin Park: In The Beginning. 30 Sept. 2008, https://web.archive.org/web/20080930135447/http://www.mtv.com/bands/l/linkin_park/news_feature_mar_02/index.jhtml.

Price, Simon. 'Walk This Way: How Run-DMC and Aerosmith Changed Pop.' *The Guardian*, 4 July 2016. *The Guardian*, https://www.theguardian.com/music/musicblog/2016/jul/04/walk-this-way-run-dmc-aerosmith.

Relative Degree – Linkinpedia. https://linkinpedia.com/wiki/Relative_Degree.

Staff (no name). *The Story behind Anthrax and Public Enemy's Bring The Noise – RapReviews*. 16 June 2025, https://www.rapreviews.com/2021/01/the-story-behind-anthrax-and-public-enemys-bring-the-noise/.

The Pricks – Linkinpedia. https://linkinpedia.com/wiki/The_Pricks.

The Snax – Linkinpedia. https://linkinpedia.com/wiki/The_Snax.

Xero (Demo Cassette Tape 2) – Linkinpedia. https://linkinpedia.com/wiki/Xero_(Demo_Cassette_Tape_2).

Fig. 2: Who Can Rock a Rhyme Like This?

'Chester Bennington: Substance and Mental Health Struggles.' *FHE Health*, 10 Aug. 2019, https://fherehab.com/learning/chester-bennington-substance-abuse-mental-health/.

Schaffner, Lauryn SchaffnerLauryn. 'Linkin Park's 'Hybrid Theory': 10 Facts Only Superfans Would Know.' *Loudwire*, 24 Oct. 2023, https://loudwire.com/linkin-park-hybrid-theory-facts/.

Team, News. 'Linkin Park Has Settled The Lawsuit Filed Against the Band by Former Bassist Kyle Christner.' *Ghost Cult Magazine*, 30 Mar. 2024, https://ghostcultmag.com/linkin-park-has-settled-the-lawsuit-filed-against-the-band-by-former-bassist-kyle-christner/.

'Through Stormy Weather – The Story of Grey Daze.' *Moths and Giraffes*, https://www.mothsandgiraffes.com/theactualcontent/greydaze.

Wolch, By Ryan. 'Legend's Never Die: The Life of Chester Bennington.' *The Tartan*, https://mcctartan.com/900/arts-and-entertainment/legends-never-die-the-life-of-chester-bennington/.

Fig. 3: Unleashing a Monster

Baltin, Steve. 'Q&A: Linkin Park's Mike Shinoda And Joe Hahn Revisit The Life-Changing 'Hybrid Theory' 20 Years Later.' *Forbes*, https://www.forbes.com/sites/stevebaltin/2020/10/09/qa-linkin-parks-mike-shinoda-and-joe-hahn-revisit-the-life-changing-hybrid-theory-20-years-later/.

Carter, Emily. *Linkin Park's In The End Is the First Nu-Metal Song to Pass One Billion Spotify Streams | Kerrang!* https://www.kerrang.com/amp/linkin-parks-in-the-end-is-the-first-nu-metal-song-to-pass-one-billion-spotify-streams.

Dailey, Hannah. 'Linkin Park's 'In the End' Music Video Surpasses 2 Billion Views on YouTube.' *Billboard*, 16 Apr. 2025, https://www.billboard.com/music/music-news/linkin-park-in-the-end-music-video-2-billion-youtube-views-1235948412/.

Grogan, Siobhan. "We Wouldn't Sign You for a Million Dollars." *The Guardian*, 21 Mar. 2003. *The Guardian*, https://www.theguardian.com/music/2003/mar/21/artsfeatures.

Hammer, Metal. 'How the Family Values Tour Started the Nu Metal Revolution.' *Louder*, 2 Mar. 2018, https://www.loudersound.com/features/how-the-family-values-tour-started-the-nu-metal-revolution.

Hickie, James. 'The Story of Linkin Park's Hybrid Theory: 'Something Told Me That….'' *Kerrang!*, 24 Oct. 2019, https://www.kerrang.com/linkin-park-the-inside-story-of-hybrid-theory.

Kennelty, Greg. 'LINKIN PARK's Mike Shinoda Recalls Winning 2001 Ozzfest Crowds Over With SLAYER's 'Raining Blood." *Metal Injection*, 30 Nov. 2018, https://metalinjection.net/news/linkin-parks-mike-shinoda-recalls-winning-2001-ozzfest-crowds-over-with-slayers-raining-blood.

Lamothe, Dan. 'Family Values Rocked.' *Massachusetts Daily Collegian*, https://dailycollegian.com/2001/10/family-values-rocked/.

Leivers, Dannii. 'The Story Behind The Song: In The End by Linkin Park.' *Louder*, 23 Oct. 2020, https://www.loudersound.com/features/linkin-park-in-the-end-story-behind-the-song.

———. 'Linkin Park's Mike Shinoda: 'We Never Wanted to Be Part of Nu Metal." *Louder*, 23 Oct. 2020, https://www.loudersound.com/features/linkin-park-mike-shinoda-interview-we-never-wanted-to-be-part-of-nu-metal.

Morton, Luke. 'The Secret History of Linkin Park's Hybrid Theory: In Their Own Words.' *Kerrang!*, 7 Oct. 2020, https://www.kerrang.com/the-secret-history-of-linkin-parks-hybrid-theory-in-their-own-words.

Mythical Kitchen. 'Linkin Park's Mike Shinoda Eats His Last Meal.' 7 Jan. 2025, – *YouTube*. https://www.youtube.com/watch?v=1I8LiVAyYVg&t=894s.

Saraceno, Christina. 'Linkin Park Have Year's Top Album.' *Rolling Stone*, 4 Jan. 2002, https://www.rollingstone.com/music/music-news/linkin-park-have-years-top-album-188442/.

Sheffield, Rob. 'Linkin Park's Compassionate Thrash.' *Rolling Stone*, 29 Mar. 2001, https://www.rollingstone.com/music/music-features/linkin-parks-compassionate-thrash-191959/.

Stutz, Colin. 'Linkin Park's 'Hybrid Theory' Producer Calls Working With Chester Bennington a 'Dream Come True." *Billboard*, 24 July 2017, https://www.billboard.com/music/rock/linkin-park-hybrid-theory-producer-don-gilmore-chester-bennington-7874220/.

Unterberger, Andrew. 'Forever No. 1: Crazy Town's 'Butterfly.'" *Billboard*, 26 June 2024, https://www.billboard.com/music/chart-beat/crazy-town-butterfly-forever-number-one-hot-100-1235717449/.

Fig. 4: Reinterpretations
Carter, Emily. 'Linkin Park To Stream Previously Unseen 2002 Projekt Revolution Show.' *Kerrang!*, 5 Oct. 2020, https://www.kerrang.com/linkin-park-to-stream-previously-unseen-2002-projekt-revolution-show.
Fiasco, Lance. 'Linkin Park Guests On X-Ecutioners Track.' *Idobi*, 16 Jan. 2002, https://idobi.com/news/linkin-park-guests-on-xecutioners-track/.
——. 'Linkin Park Singer Guests On Cyclefly's Next Album.' *Idobi*, 28 Mar. 2001, https://idobi.com/news/linkin-park-singer-guests-on-cycleflys-next-album/.
Florino, Rick. *A Look Back: Linkin Park — 'Reanimation' @ARTISTdirect*. 21 Dec. 2014, https://web.archive.org/web/20141221232430/http://www.artistdirect.com/entertainment-news/article/a-look-back-linkin-park-reanimation/9517899.
Hammer, Metal. 'How Jonathan Davis Became 'a 400-Year-Old Vampire' to Write Songs for Queen Of The Damned.' *Louder*, 7 Mar. 2022, https://www.loudersound.com/features/jonathan-davis-queen-of-the-damned-unreleased-songs.
Hosken, Patrick. 'Rap, Rock, And Remixes: Linkin Park's 'Reanimation,' 15 Years Later.' *Billboard*, 31 July 2017, https://www.billboard.com/music/rock/linkin-park-reanimation-remix-album-anniversary-7882124/.
'Interview with Christian of Cyclefly.' *Linkin Park Live*, https://lplive.net/interviews/christiancyclefly/.
Jersey, Jay Lustig. 'Linkin Park Revives Projekt Revolution.' *Nj*, 24 Aug. 2007, https://www.nj.com/entertainment/music/2007/08/linkin_park_revives_projekt_re.html.
Linkin Park Words From The Studio: 22nd April 2002 – Writing. 5 June 2007, https://web.archive.org/web/20070605084527/http://www.forfeitthegame.com/wfts-20020422.html.
Linkinpedia. '*Projekt Revolution 2002*.' Linkinpedia.com, last edited 20 June 2025, https://linkinpedia.com/wiki/Projekt_Revolution_2002.
NME. 'LINKIN PARK REANIMATE DEBUT.' *NME*, 21 June 2002, https://www.nme.com/news/music/linkin-park-109-1373387.
Phoenician, The. '9 Non-Linkin Park Songs That Show a Different Side of Chester Bennington.' https://www.ultimate-guitar.com/articles/features/9_non-linkin_park_songs_that_show_a_different_side_of_chester_bennington-133795.
Scott, Dana. 'How Linkin Park Shredded Rap-Rock Stigmas For Hip Hop Purists.' *HipHopDX*, 22 July 2017, https://hiphopdx.com/editorials/id.3833/title.how-linkin-park-shredded-rap-rock-stigmas-for-hip-hop-purists.
Stone, Rolling. 'Linkin Park Explain What Goes Into a Projekt Revolution Tour: Audio.' *Rolling Stone*, 29 Aug. 2007, https://www.rollingstone.com/music/music-news/linkin-park-explain-what-goes-into-a-projekt-revolution-tour-audio-86894/.
Zollo, Paul. 'Behind The Song: 'My December' by Linkin Park.' *American Songwriter*, 15 Dec. 2020, https://americansongwriter.com/todays-song-december-15-2020-linkin-park-my-december/.

Fig. 5: Close to Something Real
Baker, Jenny. 'Breaking the Habit – Linkin Park.' *Recovery from Shame*, https://www.recoveryfromshame.com/music/breaking-the-habit-linkin-park.

Böhmer, Dominik. 'A SCENE IN RETROSPECT: Linkin Park – 'Meteora." *Everything Is Noise*, 16 Sept. 2017, https://everythingisnoise.net/features/a-scene-in-retrospect-linkin-park-meteora/.

'Chester Bennington's Battle with Depression: The Story Behind Linkin Park's 'Numb." *Our Mental Health*, https://www.ourmental.health/stars-struggles/chester-benningtons-fight-with-depression-the-story-behind-numb.

Childers, Chad ChildersChad. '22 Years Ago: Linkin Park Release Their Second Album 'Meteora." *Loudwire*, 25 Mar. 2024, https://loudwire.com/linkin-park-meteora-album-anniversary1234/.

Edwards, Luke. "Meteora': The Story Behind Linkin Park's Impactful Second Album.' *Dig!*, https://www.thisisdig.com/feature/meteora-linkin-park-album-story-2/.

Krovatin, Chris. 'How Linkin Park's Meteora Fought the Odds and Won.' *Kerrang!*, 1 Feb. 2023, https://www.kerrang.com/how-linkin-parks-meteora-fought-the-odds-and-won.

Leivers, Dannii. 'How Linkin Park's Numb Became Nu Metal's Last Blockbuster Hit and Racked up a Billion Streams on the Back of It.' *Louder*, 6 Feb. 2023, https://www.loudersound.com/features/linkin-park-numb-story-behind-the-song.

——. 'How Meteora Showed Linkin Park Were No One-Hit Wonder: 'It Proved Hybrid Theory Wasn't an Accident." *Louder*, 4 May 2023, https://www.loudersound.com/features/linkin-park-meteora-proved-hybrid-theory-wasnt-an-accident.

Linkinpedia. *Summer Sanitarium 2003 – Linkinpedia*. https://linkinpedia.com/wiki/Summer_Sanitarium_2003.

Maddocks, Frank. 'LINKIN PARK | METEORA.' *Frank Maddocks Design*, http://frankmaddocks.com/linkin-park-meteora.

——. 'METEORA 15 Years.' *Instagram*, 25 Mar. 2018, https://www.instagram.com/p/BgwRTUID0v4/.

McIntyre, Hugh. 'Linkin Park's 'Numb' Is Back In A Major Way.' *Forbes*, https://www.forbes.com/sites/hughmcintyre/2024/09/18/linkin-parks-numb-is-back-in-a-major-way/.

Music, I. G. N. 'Metallica Summer Sanitarium Tour 2003 Announced.' *IGN*, 5 Feb. 2003, https://www.ign.com/articles/2003/02/05/metallica-summer-sanitarium-tour-2003-announced.

Songfacts. *Breaking The Habit by Linkin Park – Songfacts*. https://www.songfacts.com/facts/linkin-park/breaking-the-habit.

Niass. '8 Things You Didn't Know About Chester Bennington.' https://www.ultimate-guitar.com/articles/features/8_things_you_didnt_know_about_chester_bennington-64713.

——. *Numb by Linkin Park – Songfacts*. https://www.songfacts.com/facts/linkin-park/numb.

STAFF. 'LINKIN PARK's BENNINGTON: Still In Hospital, But Improving.' *BLABBERMOUTH.NET*, 6 Jun. 2003, https://www.blabbermouth.net/news/linkin-park-s-bennington-still-in-hospital-but-improving/.

STAFF, (no name). 'The 11 Greatest Reading & Leeds Headline Sets.' *Kerrang!*, 27 Aug. 2020, https://www.kerrang.com/the-11-greatest-reading-festival-headline-sets.

Yerger, Jeff. 'Linkin Park's 'Meteora' Turns 20.' *Stereogum*, 23 Mar. 2023, https://www.stereogum.com/2216792/linkin-park-meteora-turns-20/reviews/the-anniversary/.

Fig. 6: World's Collide

STAFF, (no name). 'Beatles Remix Was 'Art Project.' 26 Feb. 2004. *news.bbc.co.uk*, http://news.bbc.co.uk/2/hi/entertainment/3488670.stm.

Cromelin, Richard. 'Danger Mouse\'s Mix of the Beatles and Jay-Z Raises Questions.' *The Herald-Times*, https://www.heraldtimesonline.com/story/news/2004/02/26/danger-mouses-mix-of-the-beatles-and-jay-z-raises-questions/48502155/.

Linkin Park On Winning A GRAMMY & Performing With Jay-Z | GRAMMY Red Carpet Flashback | GRAMMY.Com. https://grammy.com/videos/linkin-park-2006-grammys-interview.

MTV Ultimate Mash-Ups. Linkin Park & Jay-Z Live at the Roxy Theatre. 'Live:20040718.' *Linkinpedia*, 3 Oct. 2025, https://linkinpedia.com/wiki/Live:20040718.

Ollack, Phyllis. 'The Battle Over the Double Black CD.' *CounterPunch.Org*, 23 Mar. 2004, https://www.counterpunch.org/2004/03/23/the-battle-over-the-double-black-cd/.

Staff, Billboard. 'Jay-Z, Linkin Park 'Mash-Up' Tops Album Chart.' *Billboard*, 8 Dec. 2004, https://www.billboard.com/music/music-news/jay-z-linkin-park-mash-up-tops-album-chart-65357/.

STAFF, (no name). 'When Copyright Law Meets the 'Mash-Up.'' *Los Angeles Times*, 21 Mar. 2004, https://www.latimes.com/archives/la-xpm-2004-mar-21-ca-healey21-story.html.

Swingle, Emily. "We Were All Saying, 'We'Re Gonna Make This Something They Can Never Follow up.' How Linkin Park and Jay-Z United for the Ultimate Metal and Hip Hop Crossover, Collision Course.' *Louder*, 24 Jan. 2024, https://www.loudersound.com/features/linkin-park-jay-z-story-of-collision-course.

Unterberger, Andrew. 'Yes, We're Going to Talk About How Awesome Linkin Park & JAY-Z's 'Collision Course' Was.' *Billboard*, 21 July 2017, https://www.billboard.com/music/rock/linkin-park-jay-z-collision-course-mashup-flashback-7873912/.

Watkins (@GrouchyGreg), Grouchy Greg. 'Linkin Park: Walk This Way.' *AllHipHop*, 10 Nov. 2004, https://allhiphop.com/features/linkin-park-walk-this-way/.

Fig. 7: Turn My Mic Up Louder, I Got to Say Somethin'

Alderslade, Merlin. 'Loads of People Have Started Adding Linkin Park's What I've Done to Classic Movie Endings and It's Hilarious.' *Louder*, 24 Aug. 2022, https://www.loudersound.com/news/what-ive-done-movie-endings.

Beckner, Justin. *'Produced By Rick Rubin, This Album Put a Nail in Nu Metal's Coffin. But It's an Underrated Gem and Band's Leap Forward.'* https://www.ultimate-guitar.com/articles/features/produced-by-rick-rubin-this-album-put-a-nail-in-nu-metals-coffin-but-its-an-underrated-gem-and-bands-leap-forward-178109.

Carter, Emily. 'Linkin Park Release Deluxe Minutes To Midnight with Four Bonus Songs.' *Kerrang!*, 16 May 2022, https://www.kerrang.com/linkin-park-release-deluxe-minutes-to-midnight-with-four-bonus-songs.

Childers, Chad. 'Linkin Park Earn New 'Minutes to Midnight' Platinum Album + Song Certifications.' *Loudwire*, 13 May 2022, https://loudwire.com/linkin-park-minutes-to-midnight-platinum-album-song-certifications/.

Doherty, Niall. 'How Rick Rubin Helped Linkin Park Break Free from Nu Metal.' *Louder*, 19 May 2023, https://www.loudersound.com/features/linkin-park-rick-rubin.

Doroc, Karlo. 'In Defense Of: Minutes to Midnight.' *Heavy Blog Is Heavy*, 7 Jul. 2016, https://www.heavyblogisheavy.com/2016/07/07/in-defence-of-minutes-to-midnight/.

Fricke, David. 'Minutes To Midnight.' *Rolling Stone*, 30 May 2007, https://www.rollingstone.com/music/music-album-reviews/minutes-to-midnight-250696/.

Gensler, Andy. 'How Linkin Park Battled Warner Music Group At The Height Of Their Success And Came Out Ahead.' *Billboard*, 20 Jul. 2017, https://www.billboard.com/

music/music-news/how-linkin-park-battled-warner-music-group-at-the-height-of-their-success-7873845/.

Hickie, James. "You Can Shove Nu-Metal up Your Ass!': The inside Story of Linkin….' *Kerrang!*, 17 May 2019, https://www.kerrang.com/linkin-park-the-inside-story-of-minutes-to-midnight.

Johnson, Neil. *The Evolution of Linkin Park's Minutes to Midnight – Riffology: Iconic Rock Albums*. 28 Sep. 2024, https://riffology.co/2024/09/28/the-making-of-minutes-to-midnight-by-linkin-park/.

Moss, Corey. *MTV News | Linkin Park Say Nu-Metal Sound Is 'Completely Gone' On Next LP*. 8 May 2007, https://web.archive.org/web/20070508115318/http://www.mtv.com/news/articles/1541846/09272006/linkin_park.jhtml?headlines=true.

STAFF, (no name). 'LINKIN PARK Guitarist: 'There Is No Negotiation' With WARNER MUSIC GROUP.' *BLABBERMOUTH.NET*, 9 May 2005, https://www.blabbermouth.net/news/linkin-park-guitarist-there-is-no-negotiation-with-warner-music-group/.

——. 'It's Weird': Mike Shinoda Reveals What Rick Rubin Is Really Like to Work With, Names One Important Lesson Linkin Park Learned From Him.) https://www.ultimate-guitar.com/news/general_music_news/its-weird-mike-shinoda-reveals-what-rick-rubin-is-really-like-to-work-with-names-one-important-lesson-linkin-park-learned-from-him.

——. *The Star Online eCentral: Defining a New Era*. 1 Oct. 2007, https://web.archive.org/web/20071001233910/http://www.star-ecentral.com/news/story.asp?file=/2007/4/13/music/17401016&sec=music.

TeamRock. 'Thinking Out Loud: Chester Bennington on Drugs, Success and Going to the Shops.' *Louder*, 6 Dec. 2016, https://www.loudersound.com/features/chester-bennington-interview-linkin-park.

Teather, David. 'Share Float Cash or We Quit, Linkin Park Tells Warner.' *The Guardian*, 4 May 2005. *The Guardian*, https://www.theguardian.com/business/2005/may/04/media.citynews.

Yadav, Dylan. 'How Linkin Park's Urgent Message In 'Minutes To Midnight' Is Still Relevant Today.' *Immortal Reviews*, 11 May 2017, http://www.immortalreviews.com/home/2017/5/11/how-linkin-parks-urgent-message-in-minutes-to-midnight-is-still-relevant-today.

Fig. 8: Across This New Divide

Baltin, Steve. 'Chester Bennington Opens Up About His Past Addictions.' *Noisecreep*, 16 Jul. 2009, https://noisecreep.com/chester-bennington-opens-up-about-his-past-addictions/.

Blabbermouth. 'LINKIN PARK's SHINODA Talks 'New Divide' Track.' *BLABBERMOUTH.NET*, 12 Jun. 2009, https://www.blabbermouth.net/news/linkin-park-s-shinoda-talks-new-divide-track/.

Bosso, Joe. 'Linkin Park's Chester Bennington Talks Dead By Sunrise.' *MusicRadar*, 20 Nov. 2009, https://www.musicradar.com/news/guitars/linkin-parks-chester-bennington-talks-dead-by-sunrise-227226.

Fiasco, Lance. 'Linkin Park Crosses 'New Divide' for 'Transformers." *Idobi*, 23 May 2009, https://idobi.com/news/linkin-park-crosses-new-divide-for-transformers/.

Graff, Gary. 'Linkin Park Crosses 'New Divide' for 'Transformers." *Reuters*, 23 May 2009. *www.reuters.com*, https://www.reuters.com/article/lifestyle/linkin-park-crosses-new-divide-for-transformers-idUSTRE54M023/.

Kelly, Amy. 'Chester Bennington: 'Now I Can Write About Anything I Want.' *Ultimate Guitar*, 3 Oct. 2009, https://www.ultimate-guitar.com/news/interviews/chester_bennington_now_i_can_write_about_anything_i_want.html.

Linkin Park Live – 2009.06.22 – Westwood, CA, United States – Linkinpedia. https://linkinpedia.com/wiki/Live:20090622.

'Linkin Park Myspace Interview + DBS Interview with Chester.' *Linkin Park Live*, 14 Sep. 2008, https://lplive.net/forums/topic/149-linkin-park-myspace-interview-dbs-interview-with-chester/.

Out Of Ashes – Linkinpedia. https://linkinpedia.com/wiki/Out_Of_Ashes.

Reporter, News. 'Linkin Park Return to 'Transformers' Film Soundtrack.' *NME*, 13 May 2009, https://www.nme.com/news/music/linkin-park-61-1320589.

'Revenge of the Fallen – 'New Divide' Theme Song by Linkin Park.' *The SuperHeroHype Forums*, 18 May 2009, https://forums.superherohype.com/threads/new-divide-theme-song-by-linkin-park.324546/.

Transformers: Revenge of the Fallen (2009) – Quotes – IMDb. www.imdb.com, https://www.imdb.com/title/tt1055369/quotes/. Accessed 27 Oct. 2025.

Fig. 9: Try to Catch Up Motherfucker

Blum, Jordan. '10 Reasons Why Linkin Park's 'A Thousand Suns' Is Better Than You Remember.' *Loudwire*, 10 Mar. 2022, https://loudwire.com/linkin-park-thousand-suns-album-anniversary-better-remember/.

Chauhan, Ayush. 'Resonating Echoes: Linkin Park's Lyrics and Oppenheimer's Words.' *Medium*, 22 Jul. 2023, https://medium.com/@by_ayush/resonating-echoes-linkin-parks-lyrics-and-oppenheimer-s-words-77e6669644b1.

Hickie, James. 'Linkin Park's A Thousand Suns Changed the Way We Think about Concept….' *Kerrang!*, 10 Sep. 2021, https://www.kerrang.com/linkin-parks-a-thousand-suns-changed-the-way-we-think-about-concept-albums.

Johnson, Neil. *The Making of A Thousand Suns: Linkin Park's Bold Evolution – Riffology: Iconic Rock Albums*. 28 Sep. 2024, https://riffology.co/2024/09/28/the-making-of-a-thousand-suns-by-linkin-park/.

Kasko, Jordy. *Linkin Park – A Thousand Suns | Review Rinse Repeat*. 12 Sep. 2010, https://web.archive.org/web/20100912001511/http://www.reviewrinserepeat.com/artist/linkin-park/album/a-thousand-suns/review.

Montgomery, James. *Linkin Park's A Thousand Suns: Kid A, All Grown Up? – News Story | Music, Celebrity, Artist News | MTV News*. 3 Sep. 2010, https://web.archive.org/web/20100903171649/http://www.mtv.com/news/articles/1646930/20100831/linkin_park.jhtml.

Press, Associated. 'Linkin Park Says 'A Thousand Suns' Is Like 'A Musical Drug.'' *Billboard*, 30 Sep. 2010, https://www.billboard.com/music/music-news/linkin-park-says-a-thousand-suns-is-like-a-musical-drug-955999/.

Pusey, Andre. 'Linkin Park Modestly Reinvent Music with A Thousand Suns.' *The Edge*, 2 Dec. 2010, https://theedgesusu.co.uk/records/albums/2010/12/02/linkin-park-modestly-reinvent-music-with-a-thousand-suns/.

Yadav, Dylan. 'The End Of Humanity Is Foretold In Linkin Park's 'A Thousand Suns.'' *Immortal Reviews*, 18 May 2017, http://www.immortalreviews.com/home/2017/5/18/the-end-of-humanity-is-foretold-in-linkin-parks-a-thousand-suns.

Fig. 10: Building It Up to Break It Back Down

(Audio), Chester Bennington. 'Linkin Park Tells Us About Their New Music. LIVE 105 To World Premiere The New Single On Monday, April 16th' *LIVE 105 Radio*, 12 April. 2012, [Audio] Linkin Park Tells Us About Their New Music. LIVE 105 To World Premiere The New Single On Monday, April 16th.

Baltin, Steve. 'Linkin Park Planning Album for Early Next Year.' *Rolling Stone*, 26 Jul. 2011, https://www.rollingstone.com/music/music-news/linkin-park-planning-album-for-early-next-year-181873/.

Foran, Tyler. '2012: A Year of Ellipses: Linkin Park'LIVING THINGS' Album First Listen and Review.' *Medium*, 15 Sep. 2023, https://medium.com/@theforaner/2012-a-year-of-ellipses-linkin-park-living-things-album-first-listen-and-review-6d6b25d8f918.

Goodwyn, Tom. 'Linkin Park: 'We Finally Feel Comfortable in Our Own Skin." *NME*, 19 Apr. 2012, https://www.nme.com/news/music/linkin-park-35-1277746.

Johnson, Neil. *The Evolution of Living Things: Linkin Park's 2012 Triumph – Riffology: Iconic Rock Albums.* 28 Sep. 2024, https://riffology.co/2024/09/28/the-making-of-living-things-by-linkin-park/.

Law, Sam. 'Linkin Park: Every Album Ranked from Worst to Best.' *Kerrang!*, 31 Oct. 2021, https://www.kerrang.com/every-linkin-park-album-ranked-from-worst-to-best.

McBain, Hamish. 'Linkin Park – 'Living Things." *NME*, 22 Jun. 2012, https://www.nme.com/reviews/reviews-linkin-park-13330-308732.

Montgomery, James. *Linkin Park Talk Next Album From Moscow's Red Square – Music, Celebrity, Artist News | MTV.* 26 Jun. 2011, https://web.archive.org/web/20110626031316/http://www.mtv.com/news/articles/1666401/linkin-park-a-thousand-suns-album.jhtml.

Yadav, Dylan. 'How Linkin Park's 'Living Things' Proved They Are The Most Versatile Band Ever.' *Immortal Reviews*, 16 Feb. 2017, http://www.immortalreviews.com/home/2017/2/16/how-linkin-parks-living-things-proved-they-are-the-most-versatile-band-ever.

Fig. 11: Even If It Sucks

Bosso, Joe. Brad Delson Talks Linkin Park's Upcoming, Guitar-Heavy New Album | Brad Delson Talks Linkin Park's Upcoming, Guitar-Heavy New Album | Guitar News | MusicRadar. 4 Jul. 2015, https://web.archive.org/web/20150704225451/http://www.musicradar.com/news/guitars/brad-delson-talks-linkin-parks-upcoming-guitar-heavy-new-album-596469/2.

Brandle, Lars. 'Stone Temple Pilots, Chester Bennington Split.' *Billboard*, 9 Nov. 2015, https://www.billboard.com/music/music-news/stone-temple-pilots-chester-bennington-split-6754094/.

Cooper, Leonie. 'Linkin Park Close Second Night of Download Festival Playing 'Hybrid Theory' in Full.' *NME*, 15 Jun. 2014, https://www.nme.com/news/music/linkin-park-11-1228269.

Daly, Joe. "Don't like It? Go ****king Listen to Something Else!' How Linkin Park Rediscovered Rock and Came out Swinging with The Hunting Party.' *Louder*, 11 May 2024, https://www.loudersound.com/features/linkin-park-hunting-party-interview-2014.

Grow, Kory. 'Linkin Park Talk New Album: 'We Need to Weed Out the Emo." *Rolling Stone*, 10 Apr. 2014, https://www.rollingstone.com/music/music-news/inside-linkin-parks-heavy-new-album-we-need-to-weed-out-the-emo-247025/.

Hickie, James. "We Got so Sick of Bands Playing It Safe the Whole Time': The Story....' *Kerrang!*, 11 Jun. 2021, https://www.kerrang.com/the-story-of-linkin-parks-the-hunting-party.

Iandoli, Kathy. Mike Shinoda of Linkin Park – Talks Rakim Collaboration, Says He's On The 'Kendrick Got Robbed' Team From The Grammy's | Watch Hip Hop Music Videos & New Rap Videos | HipHop DX. 13 Aug. 2014, https://web.archive.org/web/20140813205352/http://www.hiphopdx.com/index/videos/id.15811/title.mike-shinoda-of-linkin-park-talks-rakim-collaboration-says-he-s-on-the-kendrick-got-robbed-team-from-the-grammy-s.

JorgeM93. *10 Years Ago, We Got a Glimpse of Old-School Linkin Park… But Was It Actually Good?* https://www.ultimate-guitar.com/articles/features/10_years_ago_we_got_a_glimpse_of_old-school_linkin_park_but_was_it_actually_good-166533.

Leatherman, Benjamin. 'Chester Bennington on Joining Stone Temple Pilots: 'We Definitely Need to Prove Ourselves." *Phoenix New Times*, https://www.phoenixnewtimes.com/music/chester-bennington-on-joining-stone-temple-pilots-we-definitely-need-to-prove-ourselves-6585151.

Millard, Drew. 'Linkin Park: Hunting for the Perfect Beat.' *VICE*, 9 Apr. 2014, https://www.vice.com/en/article/mike-shinoda-linkin-park-interview-the-hunting-party-cover-reveal/.

Montgomery, James. *Linkin Park's RECHARGED: Hear The Entire Album Right Now! – Music, Celebrity, Artist News | MTV.Com.* 24 Oct. 2013, https://web.archive.org/web/20131024214418/http://www.mtv.com/news/articles/1716081/linkin-park-recharged-album-stream.jhtml.

Oswald, Derek. *Chester Bennington Interview: Stone Temple Pilots – AltWire.* 12 Mar. 2015, https://altwire.net/interview-chester-bennington/.

Pearl, Max. 'Rap/Rock/Rave: The Unholy Alliance of Steve Aoki and Linkin Park.' *VICE*, 22 Oct. 2013, https://www.vice.com/en/article/raprockrave-the-unholy-alliance-of-steve-aoki-and-linkin-park/.

Renshaw, David. 'Linkin Park to Play 'Hybrid Theory' in Full at Download Festival 2014.' *NME*, 5 Nov. 2013, https://www.nme.com/news/music/linkin-park-23-1234015.

Weiderhorn, Jon. "I Lived with This False Hope That Weiland Was One Day Gonna Get It Together. I Kick Myself Because We Let It Go on for so Long': How Chester Bennington Helped Rebuild Grunge Icons Stone Temple Pilots.' *Louder*, 6 Apr. 2024, https://www.loudersound.com/features/stone-temple-pilots-chester-bennington-interview.

Fig. 12: Tell Us Again What You Think We Should Be

Baltin, Steve. 'Linkin Park Shine A Different 'Light' On Band For New Album.' *Forbes*, https://www.forbes.com/sites/stevebaltin/2017/05/26/linkin-park-shine-a-new-light-on-band-for-new-album/.

Caulfield, Keith. 'Linkin Park Scores Sixth No. 1 Album on Billboard 200 Chart With 'One More Light.'' *Billboard*, 28 May 2017, https://www.billboard.com/pro/linkin-park-billboard-200-chart-one-more-light/.

Fiasco, Lance. 'Linkin Park's Bennington Suffering From Bite.' *Idobi*, 14 Aug. 2001, https://idobi.com/news/linkin-parks-bennington-suffering-from-bite/.

Hickie, James. 'The Story of Linkin Park's One More Light: 'The Most Important Thing….' *Kerrang!*, 14 Jan. 2021, https://www.kerrang.com/linkin-park-the-story-behind-their-final-album-one-more-light.

Jomatami. *Linkin Park: 'One More Light' Is About Losing a Friend, Chester Could Barely Perform It Without Choking Up.* https://www.ultimate-guitar.com/news/general_music_news/linkin_park_one_more_light_is_about_losing_a_friend_chester_could_barely_perform_it_without_choking_up.html.

——. *Linkin Park: Why We Decided to Work With Pop Songwriters on Our New Album.* https://www.ultimate-guitar.com/news/upcoming_releases/linkin_park_why_we_decided_to_work_with_pop_songwriters_on_our_new_album.html.

Lipshutz, Jason. 'Julia Michaels on Co-Writing 'Heavy' With Linkin Park: 'I Have a Hard Time Listening To It." *Billboard*, 7 Aug. 2017, https://www.billboard.com/music/pop/julia-michaels-chester-bennington-heavy-linkin-park-interview-7890155/.

Manders, Hayden. 'Linkin Park Goes Pop With 'One More Light." *Nylon*, 19 May 2017, https://www.nylon.com/articles/linkin-park-one-more-light-interview-review.

Milekic, Miljan. 'Is the New Linkin Park Record Really That Bad, or Are They Just the New Band 'Everyone Loves to Hate'? [REVIEW].' *EDM.Com – The Latest Electronic Dance Music News, Reviews & Artists*, 18 Feb. 2018, https://edm.com/features/linkin-park-one-more-light-review.

Niass. *8 Things You Didn't Know About Chester Bennington.* https://www.ultimate-guitar.com/articles/features/8_things_you_didnt_know_about_chester_bennington-64713.

Reed, Ryan. 'Linkin Park Cancel 'Hunting Party' Tour.' *Rolling Stone*, 21 Jan. 2015, https://www.rollingstone.com/music/music-news/linkin-park-cancel-hunting-party-tour-following-injury-164425/.

'Sean Dowdell: 'Chester Was so Bummed out' about 'One More Light' Criticism.' *Linkin Park Live*, 28 Jul. 2020, https://lplive.net/forums/topic/14294-sean-dowdell-chester-was-so-bummed-out-about-one-more-light-criticism/.

Sievers, Alex. 'One Year On: Linkin Park's Last Album With Chester Bennington – 'One More Light." *The Music*, https://themusic.com.au/features/one-year-on-linkin-parks-last-album-with-chester-bennington-one-more-light/B3cTGxodHB8/25-07-18.

Fig. 13: One More Light Goes Out

'320 Changes Direction.' *Give an Hour*, https://giveanhour.org/wellnessambassador/initiatives/320-changes-direction/.

Appleford, Steve. 'Watch Linkin Park's Powerful Concert Honoring Life of Chester Bennington.' *Rolling Stone*, 28 Oct. 2017, https://www.rollingstone.com/music/music-news/watch-linkin-parks-powerful-star-studded-concert-honoring-chester-bennington-127806/.

Banas, Erica. 'Chris Cornell, Chester Bennington Perform 'Hunger Strike." *93.3 WMMR*, 20 Jul. 2024, https://wmmr.com/2024/07/20/chris-cornell-chester-bennington-hunger-strike-2008-2/.

Almasy, Steve. 'Chester Bennington Dies on His Good Friend Chris Cornell's Birthday.' *CNN*, 21 Jul. 2017, https://www.cnn.com/2017/07/20/celebrities/chris-cornell-chester-bennington-friendship.

Bartleet, Larry. 'Mike Shinoda Discusses Chester Bennington's Reaction to Chris Cornell's Suicide.' *NME*, 21 Jul. 2017, https://www.nme.com/news/music/chester-bennington-chris-cornells-grief-2113797.

Beech, Mark. 'Linkin Park Music Floods Chart, Sales Surge 5,300 per cent After Chester Bennington's Death.' *Forbes*, https://www.forbes.com/sites/markbeech/2017/07/24/linkin-park-music-floods-chart-sales-surge-5300-after-chester-benningtons-death/.

Bennington, Chester (@ChesterBe). 'With all my love @chriscornell.' X, 18 May. 2017, 9:28a.m. https://twitter.com/ChesterBe/status/865227703091208192.

CNN to Air a Special Town Hall on Suicide Prevention. https://cnnpressroom.blogs.cnn.com/2018/06/21/cnn-to-air-a-special-town-hall-on-suicide-prevention/.

Copsey, Rob. 'Linkin Park Records Dominate This Week's Official Charts after Death of Frontman Chester Bennington.' *Official Charts*, 28 Jul. 2017, https://www.officialcharts.com/chart-news/linkin-park-records-dominate-this-week-s-official-charts-after-death-of-frontman-chester-bennington__19804/.

DeWald, Mike. 'Chester Bennington's Widow Turns Adversity into Mental Health Advocacy | Interview.' *RIFF Magazine*, 6 May 2020, https://riffmagazine.com/podcast/talinda-bennington-320-changes-direction-chester-bennington/.

DiVita, Joe. 'Linkin Park Dedicate 'Kimmel' Performance to Chris Cornell.' *Loudwire*, 19 May 2017, https://loudwire.com/linkin-park-one-more-light-jimmy-kimmel-live-chris-cornell/.

'Donate to One More Light Fund: Music for Relief, Organized by Christopher Albano.' *Gofundme.Com*, https://www.gofundme.com/f/one-more-light-fund-music-for-relief?lang=en_US.

Farrell, David Phoenix (phoenixlp). 'Heartbroken.' X, 20 July. 2017, 2:09p.m. https://twitter.com/phoenixlp/status/888128773492678657.

Graff, Gary. 'Talinda Bennington on 320 Changes Direction, Strange 80s Benefit Concert & Suicide Prevention.' *Billboard*, 11 Oct. 2018, https://www.billboard.com/music/rock/strange-80s-concert-benefit-8479491/.

Koerber, Brian. "F*ck Depression': Linkin Park Tribute Concert Celebrates Chester Bennington's Life.' *Mashable*, 28 Oct. 2017, https://mashable.com/article/linkin-park-and-friends-chester-bennington-concert-hollywood-bowl.

Kreps, Daniel. 'Chris Cornell: Police Report Details Singer's Final Hours.' *Rolling Stone*, 19 May 2017, https://www.rollingstone.com/music/music-news/chris-cornell-police-report-details-singers-final-hours-123420/.

'Linkin Park's Chester Bennington Dies, Stars of Music Pay Tribute.' *BBC News*, 20 Jul. 2017. *www.bbc.co.uk*, https://www.bbc.com/news/newsbeat-40677204.

Linkin Park (@linkinpark). 'In my opinion, the best fans on the planet really did put us where we are.'- Chester Bennington. X, 9 Oct. 2020, 6:11p.m.

LINKIN PARK on X: "In my opinion, the best fans on the planet really did put us where we are.' -Chester Bennington Hybrid Theory 20th Anniversary Edition is out now. #HybridTheory20' / X

Loughrey, Clarisse. 'Why Chris Cornell Should Be Remembered for His Incredible Voice.' *The Independent*, 18 May 2017, https://www.the-independent.com/arts-entertainment/music/news/chris-cornell-dead-soundgarden-audioslave-casino-royale-best-voice-vocal-performances-a7742401.html.

Lynch, Joe. 'Chris Cornell, Singer of Soundgarden and Audioslave, Dies at 52.' *Billboard*, 18 May 2017, https://www.billboard.com/music/music-news/chris-cornell-obit-7800264/.

PA. 'Chester Bennington Said Linkin Park Was 'Best Relationship' Months before Death.' *Jersey Evening Post*, 31 Mar. 2022, https://jerseyeveningpost.com/morenews/entertainment/2022/03/31/chester-bennington-said-linkin-park-was-best-relationship-months-before-death/.

Press, Associated. 'Chris Cornell's Funeral Includes Chester Bennington Singing 'Hallelujah,' Tom Morello & Josh Brolin Eulogies.' *Billboard*, 26 May 2017, https://www.billboard.com/music/rock/chris-cornell-funeral-chester-bennington-tom-morello-josh-brolin-7809573/.

Quan, Denise. 'Top 5 Moments at Linkin Park & Friends Concert Celebrating Chester Bennington's Life & Legacy.' *Billboard*, 28 Oct. 2017, https://www.billboard.com/music/

rock/top-5-moments-at-linkin-park-friends-concert-celebrating-chester-bennington-mike-shinoda-8015037/.

Reilly, Nick. 'Linkin Park Lead Tributes to Chester Bennington on the First Anniversary of His Death.' *NME*, 20 Jul. 2018, https://www.nme.com/news/linkin-park-lead-tributes-chester-bennington-first-anniversary-death-2356921.

Sacks, Brianna. 'Artists Remember Linkin Park's Chester Bennington On Social Media.' *BuzzFeed News*, 20 Jul. 2017, https://www.buzzfeednews.com/article/briannasacks/tributes-to-chester-bennington.

Shinoda, Mike (@Mikeshinoda). 'Shocked and heartbroken, but it's true. An official statement will come out as soon as we have one.' *X*, 20 July. 2017, 8:03pm. https://x.com/mikeshinoda/status/888112045190561793?lang=en

STAFF. 'ALICE COOPER To Present Stevie Ray Vaughan Award To CHRIS CORNELL.' *BLABBERMOUTH.NET*, 2 May 2007, https://www.blabbermouth.net/news/alice-cooper-to-present-stevie-ray-vaughan-award-to-chris-cornell/.

Weiderhorn, John. *Chris Cornell: A Changed Man | Guitar.Com.* 16 Jun. 2017, https://web.archive.org/web/20170616173119/https://www.guitar.com/articles/chris-cornell-changed-man.

Wilkinson, James. 'Rock Royalty Attend Funeral for Soundgarden's Chris Cornell.' *Mail Online*, 26 May 2017, http://www.dailymail.co.uk/~/article-4546408/index.html.

Fig. 14: One More Light Goes Out

Ali, Inqiad Bin. 'Chester's Memory Lives on with Linkin Park's 'Lost.'' *The Daily Star*, 11 Feb. 2023, https://www.thedailystar.net/shout/news/chesters-memory-lives-linkin-parks-lost-3245151.

Atkinson Katie, Renner Brown, Eric, Glicksman, Josh, Lynch, Joe, Unterberger, Andrew. 'Five Burning Questions: Linkin Park's 'Lost' Debuts in the Hot 100's Top 40.' *Billboard*, 22 Feb. 2023, https://www.billboard.com/music/chart-beat/linkin-park-lost-chart-debut-five-burning-questions-1235258092/.

Blistein, Jon. 'Linkin Park Drop Demo 'She Couldn't,' Off of 'Hybrid Theory' 20th-Anniversary Edition.' *Rolling Stone*, 13 Aug. 2020, https://www.rollingstone.com/music/music-news/linkin-park-demo-she-couldnt-hybrid-theory-reissue-1043842/.

Garro, Adrian. 'Linkin Park Celebrates Key Era – and Chester Bennington' with 'Meteora|20.'' *Rock Cellar Magazine*, 6 Apr. 2023, https://rockcellarmagazine.com/linkin-park-meteora-20-reissue-review-listen-chester-bennington/.

Goodman, Eleanor. 'First Reaction: Linkin Park's Pictureboard, the Song Fans Waited 20 Years to Hear.' *Louder*, 8 Oct. 2020, https://www.loudersound.com/features/first-reaction-linkin-parks-pictureboard-the-song-fans-waited-20-years-to-hear.

Howell, Maddy. 'Linkin Park Unveil Greatest Hits Album 'Papercuts (Singles Collection 2000-2023).'' *Rock Sound*, 12 Apr. 2024, https://rocksound.tv/news/linkin-park-unveil-greatest-hits-album-papercuts-singles-collection.

Lipshutz, Jason. 'Linkin Park Announces 'Papercuts' Greatest Hits Album, Unveils Never-Before-Released Song 'Friendly Fire': Listen.' *Billboard*, 23 Feb. 2024, https://www.billboard.com/music/rock/linkin-park-papercuts-greatest-hits-album-friendly-fire-1235613062/.

LPAssociation. 'Linkin Park Association Podcast with Mike Shinoda.' YouTube video, 1:18:37, 8 Dec, 2015. https://www.youtube.com/watch?v=kXVEzC6PiBY

Munro, Scott. 'Linkin Park to Celebrate Hybrid Theory's 20th Anniversary.' *Louder*, 9 Mar. 2020, https://www.loudersound.com/news/linkin-park-to-celebrate-hybrid-theorys-20th-anniversary.

Ouellette, Mary. 'Linkin Park's Chester Bennington To Be Honored at 9th Annual MusiCares MAP Fund Benefit.' *Loudwire*, 3 Apr. 2013, https://loudwire.com/linkin-park-chester-bennington-to-be-honored-9th-annual-musicares-map-fund-benefit/.

Szatan, Gabriel. 'Linkin Park: Hybrid Theory (20th Anniversary Edition).' *Pitchfork*, https://pitchfork.com/reviews/albums/linkin-park-hybrid-theory-20th-anniversary-edition/.

Trapp, Philip. 'Linkin Park Release the Unheard 'Friendly Fire,' Announce New Singles Compilation.' *Loudwire*, 23 Feb. 2024, https://loudwire.com/linkin-park-friendly-fire-video-papercuts-album/.

Wilson-Taylor, James. 'Linkin Park's Mike Shinoda On How 'Lost' Got Lost.' *Rock Sound*, 4 Apr. 2023, https://rocksound.tv/news/linkin-park-lost-meteora-why-not-released.

Fig. 16: Beginning (Again) at Zero

Alderslade, Merlin. 'Amy Lee Says Having a Rap Forced into Bring Me To Life Was 'a Difficult Pill to Swallow', Doesn't Agree with Genre 'Boxes."' *Louder*, 31 Mar. 2023, https://www.loudersound.com/news/amy-lee-bring-me-to-life-rap.

——. 'Evanescence's Amy Lee on Rumours She Could Replace Chester Bennington in Linkin Park: 'It's Not True…but They Should Ask Me about That, I Might Do It Part Time."' *Louder*, 24 Apr. 2024, https://www.loudersound.com/news/amy-lee-linkin-park-singer-rumours.

Aroesti, Rachel. "People Lashed out Because She Wasn't a Guy': Linkin Park on Nu-Metal, Nostalgia and Their New Frontwoman.' *The Guardian*, 18 Jul. 2025. *The Guardian*, https://www.theguardian.com/music/2025/jul/18/linkin-park-interview-mike-shinoda-emily-armstrong-from-zero.

Baltin, Steve. 'Q&A: Dead Sara's Emily Armstrong On The L.A. Band's Creative Rebirth And New Music.' *Forbes*, https://www.forbes.com/sites/stevebaltin/2020/12/16/qa-dead-saras-emily-armstrong-on-the-la-bands-creative-rebirth-and-new-music/.

Brannigan, Paul. "It's Good to See You Again.' Linkin Park Introduce New Vocalist Emily Armstrong at Livestream Concert, Announce New Album From Zero, New Single The Emptiness Machine, World Tour Dates.' *Louder*, 5 Sep. 2024, https://www.loudersound.com/news/linkin-park-introduce-new-vocalist-emily-armstrong-at-livestream-concert-announce-new-album-from-zero.

Brooks, Dave. 'Linkin Park Considering 2025 Reunion Tour With New Vocalist.' *Billboard*, 30 Apr. 2024, https://www.billboard.com/music/rock/linkin-park-reunion-tour-new-vocalist-considered-2025-1235670184/.

Carter, Emily. 'Linkin Park Announce over 50 Dates for Their From Zero World Tour 2025.' *Kerrang!*, 14 Nov. 2024, https://www.kerrang.com/linkin-park-announce-more-than-50-dates-for-their-from-zero-world-tour-2025-mike-shinoda-emily-armstrong-wembley-stadium-queens-of-the-stone-age-architects-spiritbox-afi.

——. 'Why Founding Drummer Rob Bourdon Isn't a Part of Linkin Park's….' *Kerrang!*, 6 Sep. 2024, https://www.kerrang.com/why-founding-drummer-rob-bourdon-isnt-a-part-of-linkin-parks-comeback.

Childers, Chad. 'Vibrant Photos From Linkin Park's 2024 Global Livestream Concert.' *Loudwire*, 6 Sep. 2024, https://loudwire.com/linkin-park-2024-global-livestream-concert-photos/.

——. 'Who Is Colin Brittain, Linkin Park's New Drummer? What You Need to Know.' *Loudwire*, 6 Sep. 2024, https://loudwire.com/linkin-park-drummer-colin-brittain-facts/.

DiVita, Joe. 'Lzzy Hale Shares New Linkin Park Cover One Week Before Mystery Event.' *Loudwire*, 30 Aug. 2024, https://loudwire.com/halestorm-lzzy-hale-linkin-park-crawling/.

——. 'Setlist + Video – Linkin Park Play First Show With New Singer.' *Loudwire*, 5 Sep. 2024, https://loudwire.com/linkin-park-setlist-first-show-emily-armstrong/.

Garcia, Thania. 'Linkin Park Selects Emily Armstrong From Rock Band Dead Sara as New Singer, Reveals Tour and Album 'From Zero.'' *Variety*, 5 Sep. 2024, https://variety.com/2024/music/news/linkin-park-emily-armstrong-new-singer-from-zero-album-tour-1236120238/.

Garner, Emily. 'Linkin Park Announce New Single, Heavy Is The Crown.' *Kerrang!*, 23 Sep. 2024, https://www.kerrang.com/linkin-parks-new-single-heavy-is-the-crown-is-the-league-of-legends-world-championship-anthem.

——. 'Listen to Linkin Park's Anthemic New Single, Let You Fade.' *Kerrang!*, 16 May 2025, https://www.kerrang.com/linkin-park-from-zero-deluxe-edition-new-single-let-you-fade-mike-shinoda-emily-armstrong.

Garro, Adrian. 'Linkin Park 'From Zero' Deluxe, Ft. Three New Songs, Out Now.' *Rock Cellar Magazine*, 16 May 2025, https://rockcellarmagazine.com/linkin-park-from-zero-deluxe-edition-listen-stream-2025/.

——. 'Linkin Park: Global Live Stream Event/Announcement 3 p.m PT 9/5.' *Rock Cellar Magazine*, 5 Sep. 2024, https://rockcellarmagazine.com/linkin-park-live-stream-announcement-watch-details-2024/.

Hé, Kristen S. ''This Is Not the End, This Is Not the Beginning': Linkin Park Look to the Future with New Faces.' *NME*, 6 Sep. 2024, https://www.nme.com/features/music-features/linkin-park-new-singer-emily-armstrong-chester-bennington-from-zero-3791172.

Irvin, Jack. 'Amy Lee Jokes '50 Cent Hates My Guts' Since Losing Best New Artist Grammy to Evanescence in 2004.' *People.Com*, https://people.com/amy-lee-50-cent-2004-best-new-artist-grammy-evanescence-8406970.

Kalu15051. *Emily Armstrong Opens Up on What It Was Really Like to Join Linkin Park: 'It Was Like I Stepped Into Disney World.'* https://www.ultimate-guitar.com/news/general_music_news/emily-armstrong-opens-up-on-what-it-was-really-like-to-join-linkin-park-it-was-like-i-stepped-into-disney-world.

Kaufman, Gil. 'Linkin Park Drop Epic League of Legends World Championship Anthem 'Heavy Is the Crown': Listen.' *Billboard*, 24 Sep. 2024, https://www.billboard.com/music/rock/linkin-park-league-of-legends-world-championship-anthem-heavy-is-the-crown-new-tour-dates-1235782692/.

Ledek, Christian. *Linkin Park's 'The Emptiness Machine' Is Far From Empty – SLUG Magazine.* 19 Sep. 2024, https://www.slugmag.com/music/national-music-reviews/linkin-parks-the-emptiness-machine-is-far-from-empty/.

Lewry, Fraser. 'Linkin Park Launch 'the Best Song We've Ever Made' Up From The Bottom.' *Louder*, 28 Mar. 2025, https://www.loudersound.com/news/linkin-park-up-from-the-bottom.

Mills, Matt. 'Linkin Park Go Full Nu Metal on New Single Two Faced, Which Lands Ahead of Tomorrow's Comeback Album From Zero.' *Louder*, 14 Nov. 2024, https://www.loudersound.com/news/linkin-park-release-two-faced-single-2024.

———. "Over the Years I've Realized I Thrive Most When I'm Actively Working with My Bandmates behind the Scenes': Linkin Park's Brad Delson Steps Back from Live Lineup.' *Louder*, 8 Sep. 2024, https://www.loudersound.com/news/linkin-park-brad-delson-steps-back-live-shows-2024.

Molloy, Laura. 'Emily Armstrong Talks Fitting into Linkin Park and Chester Bennington's Legacy: 'I Would Love to Do Him Proud.'" *NME*, 8 Sep. 2024, https://www.nme.com/news/music/emily-armstrong-talks-fitting-into-linkin-park-and-chester-benningtons-legacy-i-would-love-to-do-him-proud-3791684.

Padilla, Sebastian. 'Let's Talk about: Evanescence 'Bring Me to Life." *Steemit*, 29 Jul. 2018, https://steemit.com/rock/@sebastianpadilla/let-s-talk-about-evanescence-bring-me-to-life.

Pilley, Max. 'Are Linkin Park Returning with a New Singer? Orgy's Jay Gordon Issues Statement after Sparking Rumours.' *NME*, 3 Apr. 2024, https://www.nme.com/news/music/are-linkin-park-returning-with-a-new-singer-orgys-jay-gordon-issues-statement-after-sparking-rumours-3612877.

Russell, Shania. 'Linkin Park Address Backlash to New Lead Singer after Chester Bennington's Death.' *EW.Com*, https://ew.com/linkin-park-address-backlash-to-new-lead-singer-emily-armstrong-11775607.

Simpson, Will. "Hybrid Theory Came out and Nu Metal Was Everything. I Bought the Album and Showed It to Everybody at School': New Linkin Park Singer Emily Armstrong Says She Was a Fan of the Band in High School.' *MusicRadar*, 21 Mar. 2025, https://www.musicradar.com/artists/hybrid-theory-came-out-and-nu-metal-was-everything-i-bought-the-album-and-showed-it-to-everybody-at-school-new-linkin-park-singer-emily-armstrong-says-she-was-a-fan-of-the-band-in-high-school.

Waite, Thom. 'Amy Lee Tells the Real Story behind Evanescence's 'Bring Me to Life." *Dazed*, 1 Sep. 2022, https://www.dazeddigital.com/music/article/56815/1/amy-lee-tells-the-real-story-behind-evanescences-bring-me-to-life.

'(WATCH) Orgy Singer Jay Gordon Talks to Mike Z-Wired In The Empire.' *KCAL-FM*, 8 Aug. 2025, https://www.kcalfm.com/watch-orgy-singer-jay-gordon-talks-to-mike-z-wired-in-the-empire/.

Fig. 17: Legacy

Benetti, Achi. *The Legacy of Linkin Park: How They Defined a Generation – FM Famemagazine. Co.Uk*. https://www.famemagazine.co.uk/the-legacy-of-linkin-park-how-they-defined-a-generation/.

Disorderly, Punk N. 'Linkin Park's Enduring Legacy: Exploring Their Impact on Music and Mental Health.' *Medium*, 11 Oct. 2023, https://punkndisorderly.medium.com/linkin-parks-enduring-legacy-exploring-their-impact-on-music-and-mental-health-326c957a05a1.

Gibsone, Harriet. 'Mike Shinoda Looks Back: 'Would I Have Wanted Linkin Park to Be Successful without Being Recognisable? Probably." *The Guardian*, 13 Jan. 2024. *The Guardian*, https://www.theguardian.com/lifeandstyle/2024/jan/13/mike-shinoda-linkin-park-looks-back.

Griffiths, Kadeen. 'Chester Bennington's Legacy Is In What Linkin Park's Music Did For Teens Like Me.' *Bustle*, 20 Jul. 2017, https://www.bustle.com/p/chester-benningtons-legacy-is-in-what-linkin-parks-music-did-for-teens-like-me-71587.

'Homepage.' *Uprawr Mental Health Foundation*, https://uprawrfoundation.org/.

Linkin Park – Spotify Top Songs. https://kworb.net/spotify/artist/6XyY86QOPPrYVGvF9ch6wz_songs.html#google_vignette.

'Mental Health Statistics UK 2025.' *Priory*, https://www.priorygroup.com/. Accessed 24 Jul. 2025.

Mental Illness – National Institute of Mental Health (NIMH). https://www.nimh.nih.gov/health/statistics/mental-illness.

'Music For Relief.' *Entertainment Industry Foundation*, https://www.eifoundation.org/fiscally-sponsored-funds/music-for-relief-linkin-park/.

Roberts, Rachel. "Their Songs Helped Me Not Only Understand Those Feelings, but Get….' *Kerrang!*, 27 Aug. 2024, https://www.kerrang.com/1000-lights-linkin-park-uprawr-mental-health-foundation-birmingham-the-blackout-dream-state-as-december-falls.

Shaw, Andy. *1000 Lights Shines Bright For Mental Health At Utilita Arena*. 22 Aug. 2024, https://www.metaltalk.net/1000-lights-shines-bright-for-mental-health-at-utilita-arena.php.

'UPRAWR Mental Health Foundation – About.' *UPRAWR Mental Health Foundation*, https://www.musicglue.com/uprawrmhf/.